MW00396043

GIORGIO AGAMBEN

GIORGIO AGAMBEN

Sovereignty and Life

Edited by Matthew Calarco
and Steven DeCaroli

STANFORD UNIVERSITY PRESS

STANFORD, CALIFORNIA

Stanford University Press
Stanford, California

©2007 by the Board of Trustees of the Leland Stanford Junior University.
All rights reserved.

No part of this book may be reproduced or transmitted in any form or by any means, electronic or mechanical, including photocopying and recording, or in any information storage or retrieval system without the prior written permission of Stanford University Press.

Printed in the United States of America on acid-free, archival-quality paper

Library of Congress Cataloging-in-Publication Data

Giorgio Agamben : sovereignty and life / edited by Matthew Calarco and Steven DeCaroli.

    p. cm.

 Includes bibliographical references (p.   ) and index.

 ISBN 978-0-8047-5049-3 (cloth : alk. paper) -- ISBN 978-0-8047-5050-9 (pbk. : alk. paper)

  1. Sovereignty--Philosophy. 2. Sovereignty. 3. Agamben, Giorgio, 1942- I. Calarco, Matthew, 1972- II. DeCaroli, Steven.

JA71.G56 2007

320.1'501--dc22   2007000014

Typeset at Stanford University Press in 11/13.5 Adobe Garamond

Contents

LIFE

Preface

The first of Giorgio Agamben's books to appear in English was *Language and Death*, in 1991, but it was the publication of the English translation of *The Coming Community*, two years later, that accelerated scholarly interest in Agamben's writings within the United States. Over the next decade, as more of Agamben's works found their way into the English-speaking context, it became increasingly evident that Agamben's influence on the current generation of scholarship would be a lasting one. Given the growing enthusiasm for both Agamben's writing and the questions his writings raise, the time has come for a broader dialogue about his work. The current volume was conceived to be part of this dialogue. Contributors were selected not merely for the respect they have for Agamben and his work, but for the incisiveness of their interpretation and for their honest engagement with the work's virtues as well as its limitations. We have not set topical restrictions, nor have we avoided including those who are unsympathetic to Agamben's ideas. In doing so we hope that this volume will contribute to the deepening dialogue about Giorgio Agamben's scholarship and, more importantly, foster a discussion about the larger issues his work addresses.

The editors wish to thank the publishers for permission to reprint the following essays:

William E. Connolly, "The Complexities of Sovereignty," in *Sovereign Lives: Power in Global Politics*, edited by Jenny Edkins, Véronique Pin-Fat, and Michael J. Shapiro (New York: Routledge, 2004), 23–40.

Dominick LaCapra, "Approaching Limit Events: Siting Agamben," in *Witnessing the Disaster: Essays on Representation and the Holocaust*, edited by Michael Bernard-Donals and Richard Glejzer (Madison: University of Wisconsin Press, 2003), 263–304.

Abbreviations

CC *The Coming Community.* Translated by Michael Hardt. Minne-apolis: University of Minnesota Press, 1993.

HS *Homo Sacer: Sovereign Power and Bare Life.* Translated by Daniel Heller-Roazen. Stanford, CA: Stanford University Press, 1998.

LD *Language and Death: The Place of Negativity.* Translated by Karen E. Pinkus, with Michael Hardt. Minneapolis: University of Min-nesota Press, 1991.

MWC *The Man Without Content.* Translated by Georgia Albert. Stan-ford, CA: Stanford University Press, 1999.

MWE *Means Without End: Notes on Politics.* Translated by Vincenzo Binetti and Cesare Casarino. Minneapolis: University of Minne-sota Press, 2000.

O *The Open: Man and Animal.* Translated by Kevin Attell. Stanford, CA: Stanford University Press, 2004.

P *Potentialities: Collected Essays in Philosophy.* Edited and translated, with an introduction, by Daniel Heller-Roazen. Stanford, CA: Stanford University Press, 1999.

RA *Remnants of Auschwitz: The Witness and the Archive.* Translated by Daniel Heller-Roazen. New York: Zone Books, 1999.

SdE *Stato di eccezione.* Turin: Bollati Boringhieri, 2003.

SE *State of Exception.* Translated by Kevin Attell. Chicago: University of Chicago Press, 2005.

TcR *Il tempo che resta: Un commento alla Lettera ai Romani.* Turin: Bollati Boringhieri 2000.

Contributors

Giorgio Agamben teaches philosophy at the University of Verona, and has also taught at the University of Haute-Bretagne, Rennes (1970 to 1973); the University of Siena (1982); Ecole des hautes études en sciences sociales (1983, 1987); Collège international de philosophie (1986–92); and the University of Macerata (1988–93). He holds visiting positions at the University of California, at Berkeley, Los Angeles, Irvine, and Santa Cruz. Among his several books are *Language and Death* (1991); *Infancy and History* (1993); *The Coming Community* (1993); *Categorie italiane* (1996); *Homo Sacer: Sovereign Power and Bare Life* (1998); *Man Without Content* (1999); *Potentialities* (1999); *Remnants of Auschwitz* (1999); *Means Without End* (2000); and *L'aperto* (2002).

Matthew Calarco is Assistant Professor of Philosophy at Sweet Briar College in Virginia. He has published widely on leading figures in contemporary Continental thought, including Agamben, Derrida, Levinas, and Nancy. With Peter Atterton, he is author of *On Levinas* (2003), and editor of *The Continental Ethics Reader* (2003); *Animal Philosophy* (2004); and *Radicalizing Levinas* (2004). His forthcoming monograph is entitled *Derrida and the Question of the Animal.*

William E. Connolly is Professor and Chair of the Department of Political Science at the Johns Hopkins University. His most recent books are *The Ethos of Pluralization* (1995); *Identity/Difference* (2002); and *Neuropolitics* (2002). Other volumes include *Why I Am Not a Secularist* (1999) and *Political Theory and Modernity* (1988, 1993). His work *The Terms of Political Discourse* won the 1999 Benjamin Lippincott Award.

Steven DeCaroli is Assistant Professor of Philosophy at Goucher College in Baltimore. His recently published articles include "Visibility and History: Giorgio Agamben and the Exemplary," "Assuming Identities: Technology and the Ethics of Privacy," and "The Greek Profile: Hegel's *Aesthetics* and the Implications of a Pseudo-Science." He is a founding member of the Society for Social and Political Philosophy and is the coeditor of the book series Out Sources. His current work includes a forthcoming monograph, *Exemplarity: Aesthetics, Politics, and the End of Sovereignty.*

Jenny Edkins is Professor of International Politics at the University of Wales. She is author and editor of several volumes, including *Poststructuralism and International Relations: Bringing the Political Back* (1999); *Sovereignty and Subjectivity* (1999; with Nalini Persram and Véronique Pin-Fat); *Whose Hunger? Concepts of Famine, Practices of Aid* (2000); *Trauma and the Memory of Politics* (2003); and *Sovereign Lives: Power in Global Politics* (2004; with Véronique Pin-Fat and Michael J. Shapiro).

Bruno Gullì teaches philosophy at LaGuardia Community College. His recent publications include "Beyond Good and Evil: A Contribution to the Analysis of the War Against Terrorism" and "Praxis and the Danger: The Insurgent Ontology of Antonio Gramsci." He has also published two books of poetry: *Lines of Another Re-search* and *Figures of a Foreign Land.*

Dominick LaCapra is Bryce and Edith M. Bowmar Professor in Humanistic Studies at Cornell University. He is author of numerous articles and has recently published the following books: *History and Reading: Tocqueville, Foucault, French Studies* (2000); *Writing History, Writing Trauma* (2001); and *History in Transit: Experience, Identity, Critical Theory* (2004).

Ernesto Laclau is Chair in Political Theory at the University of Essex, where he is also Director of the doctoral program in Ideology and Discourse Analysis at the Centre for Theoretical Studies in the Humanities and Social Sciences. He has been Visiting Professor at the universities of Toronto, Chicago, California (Irvine), Paris (Nouvelle Sorbonne), and the New School for Social Research, as well as at various Latin American universities; and has lectured extensively in many universities in North America, Latin America, western Europe, Australia, and South Africa. He is author of *Politics and Ideology in Marxist Theory* (1977); *New Reflections on the Revolution of Our Time* (1990); and *Emancipation(s)* (1996); coauthor (with Chantal Mouffe) of *Hegemony and Socialist Strategy* (1985); and editor and contributor to *The Making of Political Identities* (1994).

Catherine Mills is Lecturer in Philosophy at the University of New South Wales, where she specializes in ethics, feminist theory, and contemporary European political philosophy. Her current research projects include a book on biopolitics, as well as research on the ethical implications of new biotechnologies. She has written articles on a wide range of figures in recent political philosophy, including Agamben, Foucault, and Judith Butler.

Antonio Negri has taught political science at the Universities of Padua and Paris VIII and is currently an independent researcher. Among his numerous publications are *Marx Beyond Marx* (1979); *The Savage Anomaly* (1981); *The Politics of Subversion* (1986); *Revolution Retrieved* (1988); *The Labor of Dionysos* (1994); *Communists Like Us* (written in collaboration with Félix Guattari) (1990). He is coauthor (with Michael Hardt) of the widely acclaimed book *Empire* (2000).

Paul Patton is currently Professor of Philosophy and Head of the School of Philosophy at the University of New South Wales. He has published widely on aspects of twentieth-century French philosophy, political philosophy, and social and cultural theory, and is currently a coeditor of the journal *Theory & Event*. Among the several volumes he has edited and coauthored are *Michel Foucault: Power, Truth, Strategy* (1979); *Nietzsche, Feminism, and Political Theory* (1993); *Deleuze: A Critical Reader* (1996); *Deleuze and the Political* (2000); *Jacques Derrida: Deconstruction Engaged* (2001); and *Political Theory and the Rights of Indigenous Peoples* (2001).

William Rasch is Assistant Professor of Germanic Studies at Indiana University. His research and teaching interests encompass the German intellectual and literary traditions of the eighteenth through twentieth centuries, concentrating heavily on social and political theory. He is also Assistant Professor in Comparative Literature, Philosophy, and the Cultural Studies Program. Rasch has published widely in contemporary political thought, and his recent books include *Niklas Luhmann's Modernity* (2000) and *Observing Complexity* (2000).

The Work of Man

Giorgio Agamben

Translated by Kevin Attell

In the first book of the *Nicomachean Ethics* (1097b, 22 ff.), Aristotle poses the problem of defining the "work [*opera*] of man" (*to ergon tou anthrōpou*). The context of this definition is the determination of the highest good as the object of *epistēmē politikē*, political science, to which the treatise on ethics represents a sort of introduction. This highest good is happiness. And it is precisely in order to define happiness that Aristotle begins his inquiry into the work of man.

Just as for a flute player, a sculptor, or any artisan (*tekhnitē*), and, in general, for all those who have a certain kind of work (*ergon*) and an activity (*praxis*), the good (*tagathon*) and the "well" (*to eu*) seem [to consist] in this work, so it should also be for man, if indeed there is for him something like a certain work (*ti ergon*). Or [must we say] that there is a certain work and an activity for the carpenter and the shoemaker, and for man there is none, that he is born with no work (*argos*)?[1]

Ergon in Greek means "labor," "work." Yet, in the passage in question, the meaning of the term is complicated because of the close relation that links it to one of the fundamental concepts of Aristotle's thought: *energeia* (lit. "being at work"). The term was, in all probability, created by Aristotle, who uses it in functional opposition to *dunamis* ("potentiality").

The adjective *energos* ("working," "active"), from which Aristotle takes it, is already found in Herodotus. The opposite term *argos* (from *aergos*, "not working," "lacking *ergon*"; cf. *argia*, "inactivity") already occurs in Homer. That the work of man, therefore, does not, in this context, simply mean "work," but rather that which defines the *energeia*, the activity, the being-in-act that is proper to man, is proved by the fact that a few lines later Aristotle will define happiness as *psukhēs energeia . . . kat' aretēn*, the being-at-work of the soul in accordance with excellence (1098a, 16). The question concerning the work or absence of work of man therefore has a decisive strategic importance, for on it depends the possibility not only of assigning him a proper nature and essence, but also, as we have seen, of defining his happiness and his politics.

The question is not simply a rhetorical one. In opposing four types of artisans—the flute player, the maker of *agalmata*, the carpenter, and the shoemaker—to man in general, Aristotle intentionally employs figures in which the work (and the being-at-work) can be identified without difficulty. But the choice of such, so to speak, "menial" examples does not mean that the list could not be continued upward (a few lines earlier, he had mentioned the doctor, the architect, and the strategist). That is to say, the problem has a broader meaning, and involves the very possibility of identifying the *energeia*, the being-at-work of man as man, independently of and beyond the concrete social figures that he can assume. Even if in the form of a paradoxical question, the idea of an *argia*, of an essential inactivity [*inoperosità*] of man with respect to his concrete occupations and functions [*operazioni*] is unequivocally put forward. The modern (or, rather, postmodern) problem of a fulfilled realization of human work and thus of a possible *désoeuvrement* (*désoeuvré* corresponds perfectly to *argos*) of man at the end of history here has its logical-metaphysical foundation. The *voyou désoeuvré* in Queneau, the *shabbat* of man in Kojève, and the "inoperative community" in Nancy would then be the posthistorical figure corresponding to the absence of a truly human work. More generally, however, what is at issue in this question is the very nature of man, who appears as the living being that has no work, that is, the living being that has no specific nature and vocation. If he were to lack an *ergon* of his own, man would not even have an *energeia*, a being in act that could define his essence: he would be, that is, a being of pure potentiality, which no identity and no work could exhaust.

That this hypothesis must not have appeared as out of the question to Aristotle is shown by the fact that, in *De anima*, at the moment when he is defining *nous*, human intellect, he asserts that, "it has no other nature than being in potentiality" (429a, 21). For this reason even when it passes into act, thought "remains in some way still in potentiality . . . and is thus able to think of itself" (429b, 9). Moreover, in Greek the vocabulary of inactivity, to which *argos* as well as *skholē* belong, has no negative connotations at all. From the perspective of Aristotle's Christian commentators, however, the hypothesis of an essential inactivity of man could not have appeared as anything but scandalous. For this reason, in his commentary on the passage in question from the *Nicomachean Ethics*, Thomas is careful to specify that "it is impossible that man be by nature idle, as if he had no proper function [impossibile est, quod sit naturaliter otiosus, quasi non habens propriam operationem]" (*Sententia libri ethicorum*, 1.10.4).

Nevertheless, in the subsequent passage, Aristotle seems to back away from the hypothesis that there is no work of man as man, and, with a sudden turn, he seeks man's *ergon* in the sphere of life.

Or as the eye, the hand, the foot, and each of the parts of the body seem to have their work, must we then suppose that alongside (*para*) all of these man similarly has a certain work? And what then might this be? The simple fact of living (*to zēn*) seems to be common even to plants, but we are seeking something that is proper to man. We must therefore set aside (*aphoristeon*) nutritive life and the life of growth (*tēn threptikēn kai auxētikēn zōēn*). Next would be a form of sensitive life (*aisthētikē tis*). But even this seems to be common to the horse, the ox, and every living thing. There remains (*leipetai*) the form of practical life (*praktikē tis*) of a being who has *logos*. But since this has two meanings, we must consider life in accordance with being-at-work (*kat' energeian*), which is the more proper sense of the term.

This analogy between the relation of individual *erga* to the work of man and that of the individual parts of the body to the body in its totality strategically serves to prepare for the passage to the sphere of life. Indeed, this passage is not obvious. If individual human activities (playing the lyre, making shoes, sculpting images) cannot exhaust the work proper to man as such, this does not mean that it must necessarily be sought in the sphere of life. That the work of man (on the individuation of which depends the individuation of the end of "political science") is defined as a certain form of life bears witness to the fact that the nexus between politics and life belongs, from the beginning, to the way the Greeks think of the *polis*.

In a typically Aristotelian gesture, the individuation of the *ergon* of man comes about by working a series of caesurae in the *continuum* of life. This *continuum* is divided into nutritive, sensitive, and practical-rational life. The articulation of the concept of life in a series of functions had already been carried out in *De anima*. Here Aristotle had isolated, from among the various senses of the term "to live," the most general and separable one:

It is through life that what has soul in it differs from what has not. Now this term "to live" has more than one sense, and provided any one alone of these is found in a thing, we say that the thing is living—viz. thinking, sensation, local movement and rest, or movement in the sense of nutrition, decay, and growth. Hence we think of all species of plants also as living, for they are observed to possess in themselves a principle and potentiality through which they grow and decay. . . . This principle can be separated from the others, but not they from it—in mortal beings at least. The fact is obvious in plants; for it is the only psychic potentiality they possess. Thus, it is through this principle that life belongs to living things. . . . By nutritive power we mean that part of the soul which is common also to plants. (413a, 20 ff.)

It is important to observe that Aristotle in no way defines what life is: he limits himself to breaking it down, by isolating the nutritive function, in order then to rearticulate it in a series of distinct and correlated faculties (nutrition, sensation, thought). In *De anima*, as well as in the *Nicomachean Ethics* and the *Politics*, nutritive life (or vegetative life, as it will be called as early as the ancient commentators, on the basis of that peculiar, obscure status as absolutely separated from *logos* that plants constantly have in Aristotle's thought) is that on the exclusion of which the definition of man, that is, of the living being that has *logos*, is founded.

The determination of the work of man is achieved, then, by means of the segregation of vegetative and sensitive life, which leaves life in accordance with *logos* as the only possible "remainder." And, since this life in accordance with *logos* can also be seen as in accordance with its pure potentiality, Aristotle is careful to specify that the work of man cannot be a mere potentiality or faculty, but only the *energeia* and the exercise of this faculty.

If, therefore, the work of man is the being at work of the soul in accordance with *logos*, or not without *logos*, and if we say that the work of this particular individual and this particular good individual is the same in kind (e.g., a lyre player and a good lyre player, and similarly in all cases), eminence in respect of excellence being added to the work (for the work of a lyre player is to play the lyre, and that of a good lyre player is to do so well); if this is the case, we must suppose that the work of man is a certain kind of life (*zōēn tina*) and that this is the being-at-work of the soul and a praxis in accordance with *logos*, and that the work of the good man is these same things, performed well and in a beautiful way, each act in accordance with its own excellence; if this is the case, human good turns out to be the being-at-work of the soul in accordance with excellence, and if there are more than one excellence, in accordance with the best and most perfect.

At this point, Aristotle can proceed to the definition of the "work of man." As was implicit in the immediately preceding passage, this is a form of living, a "certain kind of life" (*zoē tis*), life that is in act in accordance with *logos*. This means that Aristotle determines the highest good—which the entire treatise was aimed at identifying and which also constitutes the end of politics—through the relation to a certain kind of *ergon*, a certain kind of activity or being-at-work. This activity consists, as we have seen, in the actualization of the vital rational potentiality (and not, therefore, of the nutritive or sensitive potentiality). Consequently, human ethics and politics will be defined by the participation in this function, in general and in accordance with excellence (playing the lyre and playing it well, living and living well, in accordance with *logos*). We should not be surprised if, consistently with these premises, Aristotle's definition of the *polis*, that is, of the perfect political community, is articulated through the difference between living (*zēn*) and living well (*eu zēn*): "originating for the sake of life, but existing for living well" (*Politics* 1252b, 30).

Aristotle's determination of the work of man entails, therefore, two theses on politics:

1. Insofar as it is defined in relation to an *ergon*, politics is a politics of activity [*operosità*] and not of inactivity [*inoperosità*], of the act and not of potentiality.
2. This *ergon*, however, is ultimately a "certain kind of life," which is defined above all through the exclusion of the simple fact of living, of bare life.

This is the legacy that Aristotle's thought has left to Western politics. An aporetic legacy, (1) because it binds the destiny of politics to a kind of work, which remains unassignable with respect to individual human activities (playing the lyre, making statues, producing shoes), and

(2) because its single determination is ultimately biopolitical, insofar as it rests on a division and articulation of *zoē*. The political, as the work of man as man, is drawn out of the living being through the exclusion—as unpolitical—of a part of its vital activity.

In the modern era, Western politics has consequently been conceived as the collective assumption of a historical task (of a "work") on the part of a people or a nation. This political task coincided with a metaphysical task, that is, the realization of man as rational living being. The problematicity inherent in the determination of this "political" task with respect to the concrete figures of labor, action, and, ultimately, human life has gradually grown. From this perspective, the thought of Marx, which seeks the realization of man as a generic being (*Gattungswesen*), represents a renewal and a radicalization of the Aristotelian project. Hence the two aporias implicit in this renewal: (1) the subject of the work of man must necessarily be an unassignable class, which destroys itself insofar as it represents a particular activity (for example, the working class); (2) the activity of man in the classless society is impossible or, in any case, extremely difficult to define (hence the hesitations of Marx concerning the destiny of labor in the classless society and the right to laziness claimed by Lafargue and Malevich).

And when, beginning with the end of World War I, the paradigm of the work enters into crisis and it becomes clear for the nation-states that there no longer are historical tasks that can be assigned, a reformulation of the biopolitical legacy of classical political philosophy becomes the extreme outcome of Western politics. In the impossibility of defining a new "work of man," it is now a question of taking on biological life itself as the last and decisive historical task. The "work" of the living being in accordance with *logos* is the assumption and the care of that nutritive and sensitive life on whose exclusion Aristotelian politics had defined the *ergon tou anthrōpou*.

.   .   .

However, a different reading of this passage from Aristotle is possible. This reading is contained in two heterogeneous, though not unrelated, texts. The first is Averroes' commentary on Plato's *Republic*, which has been preserved for us only in a Hebrew translation. The second is Dante's *Monarchy*. Both begin with the Aristotelian determination of human perfection as the actualization of the rational potentiality; both take up the Aristotelian opposition between man on the one hand and plants and animals on the other. However, both, as we will see, emphasize the moment of potentiality as the specific characteristic of man. Indeed, for both Averroes and Dante, animals in some way participate in rational activity ("many animals," writes Averroes, "have this part in common with men"); what specifically characterizes human *logos*, however, is that it is not always already in act, but exists, first and foremost, only in potentiality ("since the rational part," writes Averroes, "does not exist in us from the beginning in its ultimate perfection and in act, its existence in us is only potential"). But let us read Dante's text (*Monarchy* I.3), which is articulated as an undeclared commentary on Aristotle's determination of the work of man in the *Nicomachean Ethics*, the lexicon and argumentation of which it takes up:

> We must therefore now see what is the end of human society as a whole. . . . And to throw light on the matter we are inquiring into, it should be borne in mind that, just as there is an end for which nature produces the thumb, and a different one for which she produces the whole hand, and again an end different from both of these for which she produces the arm, and an end different from all these for which she produces the whole person; in the same way there is an end for which the individual person is designed, another for the household, another for the village, yet another for the city, and another for the kingdom; and finally the best end of all is the one for which God Everlasting with his art, which is nature, brings into being the whole of humankind (*universaliter genus humanum*).[2]

Here Dante takes up Aristotle's example of the relation between the individual parts of the body and the whole person (*totus homo*); but the accent is shifted from the plurality of human activities to the multiplicity of the forms of community (added to the family, the village, and the city, which are already in Aristotle's *Politics*, are the kingdom and the end, for the moment unnamed, which corresponds to the universality of humankind). It is at this point that Dante reformulates the Aristotelian question concerning the work of man.

> Consequently the first thing to bear in mind is that God and nature make nothing that is idle (*nil otiosum facit*); on the contrary, all things come into being to perform some function (*ad aliquam operationem*). For in the intention of its creator *qua* creator no created essence is an ultimate end in itself; the end is rather the function which is proper to that essence; and so it is that the function does not exist for the sake of the essence, but the essence for the sake of the function. There

is therefore some function proper to humankind as a whole (*humane universitatis*), for which it is designed in such a great multitude (*in tanta multitudine ordinatur*), and no single man, or individual household, or village, or city, or individual kingdom can fully realize it.

Operatio is the Latin term that corresponds to *ergon* in the Latin translation of the *Ethics* that both Thomas and Dante had before them. Thus in Thomas's commentary we read: "Si igitur hominis est aliqua operatio propria, necesse est quod in eius operatione propria consistat finale bonum ipsius [If then man has some proper function, his final good must consist in this function]" (1.10.2). Like Thomas, Dante takes up (and, as we will see, modifies) the Aristotelian motif of the act's superiority over the essence (or potentiality); but for him the determination of this "work" of humankind as such immediately entails the introduction of the figure of the multitude. And just as in Aristotle no single concrete activity of man could exhaust the *ergon* of man as such, in Dante the actualization of the *operatio humane universitatis* transcends the limits of individual men and individual communities.

What this function is will become clear once we clarify what is the highest potentiality of the whole of humanity. . . . The highest potentiality in man is not simply to be, because the elements too share in this; nor is it to be in compound form, for that is found in minerals; nor is it to be an animate thing, for plants too share in that; nor is it to be a creature who apprehends, for that is also shared by the animals; but it is to be a creature who apprehends by means of the possible intellect (*esse apprehensivum per intellectum possibilem*), which belongs to no creature (whether higher or lower) other than man. For while there are indeed other essences who are endowed with intellect, nonetheless their intellect is not "possible" in the way that man's is, since such essences exist only as intelligences and nothing else, and their very being is simply the act of understanding that which they are; and this occurs without interruption (*sine interpolatione*), otherwise they would not be eternal. It is thus clear that the highest potentiality of humankind is its intellectual potentiality or faculty. And since that potentiality cannot be fully and all at once reduced in act through any one individual or any one of the particular communities enumerated above, there must needs be a multitude in humankind, through whom the whole of this potentiality can be actualized, just as there must be a multitude of things which can be generated so that the whole potentiality of prime matter lies under the act (*sub actu*); otherwise there would be a separate potentiality, which is impossible.

At this point Dante defines the work proper to humankind as such. And he does it by broadening, with respect to Aristotle, the context of the definition of human specificity: not only plants and animals but also inanimate beings (the elements and minerals) and supernatural creatures (the angels). From this perspective, rational activity is no longer enough to identify the proper characteristic of man, since he shares it with the *bruta* and the angels. In keeping with the fundamental motif of Averroes' interpretation of Aristotle's *De anima*, what defines human rationality is now its potential—that is, its contingent and discontinuous—character. While the intelligence of the angels is perpetually in act without interruption (*sine interpolatione*) and that of the animals is inscribed naturally in each individual, human thought is constitutively exposed to the possibility of its own lack and inactivity: that is to say, it is, in the terms of the Aristotelian tradition, *nous dunatos, intellectus possibilis*. This is why, insofar as it is essentially potentiality and can be in act only beginning from an "interpolation" (which, in the Averroist tradition, coincides with the imagination), the work of man requires a multitude, and indeed makes the multitude (and not a people, a city, or a particular community) the true subject of politics.

The motif of the *multitudo* in Dante takes up Averroes' theory of the eternity of humankind as a correlative to the oneness of the possible intellect. Since, according to Averroes, the perfection of man's potential to think is bound essentially to the species and accidentally to single individuals, there will always be at least one individual—a philosopher—who realizes in act the potentiality of thought. According to the formulation in one of the theses condemned by Etienne Tempier in 1277, the numerically singular possible intellect, though separate from this or that individual body, is never separate from any body.

Dante develops and radicalizes this theory, making the *multitudo* the subject of both thought and political life. The *multitudo* is not simply idle, because it is not, like the individual, essentially separated from the one intellect; on the other hand, it is not solely active [*operosa*], because the passage to the act always depends contingently on this or that individual. *The multitude, then, is the generic form of existence of potentiality*, which in this way always maintains itself in an essential proximity to the act (*sub actu* not *in actu*). The expression *sub actu* is not an invention of Dante's. We find it used in contemporary texts (for example, in Dietrich of Freiberg, whose treatise *De intellectu et intellegibili* Dante could have read) to express the mode of being of prime matter, which can never be completely separate from some form and therefore stands *sub actu*. But while Dietrich explicitly opposes the possible intellect, which is wholly separate from the act, to prime matter, Dante sets up an analogy between the mode of being of the intellect in potentiality and that of matter. Though it can suffer "interpolations" with respect to thought in act, the potentiality of thought is not entirely separate from it, and the multitude is this existence of potentiality *sub actu*, that is, in proximity to the act.

Dante conceives a politics that corresponds to the inactivity of man, one which is determined, that is, not simply and absolutely beginning from the being-at-work of human rationality, but from a working that exposes and contains in itself the possibility of its own not existing, of its own inactivity. From this inactivity, Dante deduces the necessity of the multitude as the subject of politics that exceeds every particular community, and of the Monarchy or the Empire as the regulating principle corresponding to this excess. What other consequences thought can draw from the awareness of its own essential inactivity, and whether, in general, there is a politics possible today that is equal to the absence of a work of man, and will not simply fall back into the assumption of a biopolitical task— this must for now remain in suspense. What is certain, however, is that it will be necessary to put aside the emphasis on labor and production and to attempt to think of the multitude as a figure, if not of inaction, at least of a working that in every act realizes its own *shabbat* and in every work is capable of exposing its own inactivity and its own potentiality.

Bare Life or Social Indeterminacy?

Ernesto Laclau

I have great admiration for the work of Giorgio Agamben. I particularly appreciate his dazzling classical erudition, his skill—both intuitive and analytical—in dealing with theoretical categories, and his ability to relate systems of thought whose connections are not immediately obvious. This appreciation does not go, however, without some deep reservations concerning his theoretical conclusions, and these reservations are what I want to elaborate upon here. If I had to put them in a nutshell, I would assert that Agamben has—inverting the usual saying—the vices of his virtues. Reading his texts, one often has the feeling that he jumps too quickly from having established the *genealogy* of a term, a concept or an institution, to determine its actual working in a contemporary context, that in some sense the *origin* has a secret determining priority over what follows from it. I am not, of course, claiming that Agamben makes the naïve mistake of assuming that ethimology provides the cipher or clue to what follows from it, but, I would argue, many times his discourse remains uneasily undecided between genealogical and structural explanation. Let us take an example from Saussurean linguistics: the Latin term *necare* (to kill) has become in modern French *noyer* (to drown), and we can examine as much as we want this diachronic change in the relation between signifier and signified and we will still not find in it any explanation of the meaning resulting from their last articulation—signification depends entirely on a *value* context which is strictly singular and which no diachronic genealogy is able to capture. This is the perspective from which we want to question Agamben's theoretical approach: his genealogy is not sensitive enough to structural diversity and, in the end, it risks ending in sheer teleology.

Let us start by considering the three theses in which Agamben summarises his argument towards the end of *Homo Sacer*:

1. The original political relation is the ban (the state of exception as zone of indistinction between outside and inside, exclusion and inclusion).
2. The fundamental activity of sovereign power is the production of bare life as originary political element and as threshold of articulation between nature and culture, between *zoē* and *bios*.
3. Today it is not the city but rather the camp that is the fundamental biopolitical paradigm of the West. (*HS*, 181)

Let me start with the first thesis. According to Agamben—who is quoting Cavalca—"'to ban' someone is to say that anybody may harm him" (*HS*, 104–5). That is why the "sacred man" can be killed but not sacrificed—the sacrifice is still a figure representable within the legal order of the city. The life of the bandit clearly shows the kind of exteriority belonging to the sacred man: "The life of the bandit, like that of the sacred man, is not a piece of animal nature without any relation to law and the city. It is, rather, a threshold of indistinction and of passage between animal and man, *physis* and *nomos*, exclusion and inclusion: the life of the bandit is the life of the *loup garou*, the werewolf, who is precisely *neither man nor beast*, and who dwells paradoxically within both while belonging to neither" (*HS*, 105). Sovereignty is at the source of the ban, but it requires an extension of the territory within which the ban applies, for if we were only to deal with the exteriority to law of the *loup garou* we would still be able to establish a clear line of partage between the "inside" and the "outside" of the community. Agamben is very much aware of the complexity of the relation between outside and inside. For that reason, speaking about Hobbes's "state of nature," he indicates that it is not a primitive condition which has been eradicated once the covenant has transferred sovereignty to the Leviathan, but a constant possibility within the communitarian order, which arises whenever the city is seen as *tamquam dissoluta*. In that sense, we are not dealing with a pure, pre-social nature, but with a "naturalization" which keeps its reference to the social order as far as the latter ceases to work. This explains how the state of exception emerges. Carl Schmitt had asserted that there is no rule applicable to chaos, and that the state of exception is required whenever the agreement between the legal order and the wider communitarian order has been broken.

> Far from being a prejuridical condition that is indifferent to the law of the city, the Hobbesian state of nature is the exception and the threshold that constitutes and dwells within it. It is not so much a war of all against all as, more precisely, a condition in which everyone is thus *wargus, gerit caput lupinum*. And this lupization of man and humanization of the wolf is at every moment possible in the *dissolutio civitatis* inaugurated by the state of exception. This threshold alone, which is neither simple natural life nor social life but rather bare life or sacred life, is the always present and always operative presupposition of sovereignty. (*HS*, 106)

This explains why sovereign power cannot have a contractual origin: "This is why in Hobbes, the foundation of sovereign power is to be thought not in the subjects' free renunciation of their natural right but in the sovereign's preservation of his natural right to do anything to any one, which now appears as the right to punish" (*HS*, 106). Thus, the ban holds together bare life and sovereignty. And it is important for Agamben to point out that the ban is not simply a sanction—which as such would still be representable within the order of the city—but that it involves *abandonment*: the *homo sacer* and the other figures that Agamben associates to him are simply left outside any communitarian order. That is why he can be killed but not sacrificed. In that sense the ban is non-relational: their victims are left to their own separatedness. This is for Agamben the originary political relation, linked to sovereignty. It is a more originary extraneousness than that of the foreigner, who still has an assigned place within the legal order. "We must learn to recognise this structure of the ban in the political relations and public spaces in which we will live. *In the city the banishment of sacred life is more internal than every interiority and more external than every extraneousness*" (*HS*, 111). The ban has, thus, been at the source of sovereign power. The state of exception, which reduces the citizens to bare life (he has in mind Foucault's biopolitics), has determined modernity from its very beginning.

Agamben has, no doubt, touched with the category of the ban something crucially important concerning the political. There is certainly, within the political, a moment of negativity that requires the construction of an inside/outside relation and requires that sovereignty is in an ambiguous position vis-à-vis the juridical order. The problem, however, is the following: does the articulation of dimensions through which Agamben thinks the structure of the ban exhaust the system of possibilities that such a structure opens? In other words: has not Agamben chosen just one of those possibilities and hypostatized it so that it assumes a unique character? Let us consider the matter carefully. The essence of a ban is given by its effects—that is, to put somebody outside the system of differences constituting the legal order. But in order to assimilate *all* situations of being outside the law to that of *homo sacer*, as described by Agamben, some extra presuppositions have to be added. In the first place, the sheer separatedness—absence of relation—of the outside involves that he/she is a naked individuality, dispossessed of any kind of collective identity. But, secondly, it also involves that the situation of the outsider is one of radical indefension, wholly exposed to the violence of those inside the city. Only at that price can sovereign power be absolute. Are, however, these two extra presuppositions justified? Do they logically emerge from the mere category of "being outside the law"? Obviously not. The outsider does not need to be outside *any* law. What is inherent to the category is only the fact of being outside the law *of the city*. Abandonment comes only from the latter. Let us consider the following passage from Franz Fanon, which I have discussed in another context:

> The *lumpenproletariat*, once it is constituted, brings all its forces to endanger the "security" of the town, and is the sign of the irrevocable decay, the gangrene ever present at the heart of colonial domination. So the pimps, the hooligans, the unemployed, and the petty criminals . . . throw themselves into the struggle like stout working men. These classless idlers will by militant and decisive action discover the path that leads to nationhood. . . . The prostitutes too, and the maids who are paid two pounds a month, all who turn in circles between suicide and madness, will recover their balance, once more go forward and march proudly in the great procession of the awakened nation.[1]

Here we have actors who are entirely outside the law of the city, who cannot be inscribed in any of the categories of the latter, but such an exteriority is the starting point for a new collective identification *opposed* to the law of the city. We do not have lawlessness as against law, but two laws that do not recognise each other. In another work (*SE*), Agamben discusses the notion of "necessity" as elaborated by the Italian jurist Santi Romano and points out that, for Romano, revolutionary forces—strictly speaking, according to the State juridical order, outside the law—create their own new law. The passage from Romano quoted by Agamben is most revealing:

After having recognised the antijuridical nature of the revolutionary forces, he adds that this is only the case with respect to the positive law of the state against which it is directed, but that does not mean that, from the very different point of view from which it defines itself, it is not a movement ordered and regulated by its own law. This also means that it is an order that must be classified in the category of originary juridical orders, in the now well-known sense given to this expression. In this sense, and within the limits of the sphere we have indicated, we can thus speak of a law of revolution. (*SE*, 28–29)

So we have two incompatible laws. What remains as valid from the notion of ban as defined by Agamben is the idea of an uninscribable exteriority, but the range of situations to which it applies is much wider than those subsumable under the category of *homo sacer*. I think that Agamben has not seen the problem of the inscribable/uninscribable, of inside/outside, in its true universality. In actual fact, what the mutual ban between opposed laws describes is the constitutive nature of any radical antagonism—radical in the sense that its two poles cannot be reduced to any super-game which would be recognised by them as an objective meaning to which both would be submitted.

Now, I would argue that only when the ban is mutual do we have, *sensu stricto*, a *political* relation, for it is only in that case that we have a radical opposition between social forces and, as a result, a constant re-negotiation and re-grounding of the social bond. This can be seen most clearly if we go back for a moment to Agamben's analysis of Hobbes. As we have seen, he asserts that contrary to the contractarian view, the sovereign is the only one that preserves his natural right to do anything to anybody—that is, the subjects become bare life. The opposition between these two dimensions, however, does not stand; in order for the sovereign to preserve his natural right, he needs such a right to be recognised by the rest of the subjects, and such a recognition, as Agamben himself points out, finds some limits.

Corresponding to this particular state of the "right of Punishing" which takes the form of a survival of the state of nature at the very heart of the state, is the subjects' capacity not to disobey but to resist violence exercised on their own person, "for . . . no man is supposed bound by Covenant, not to resist violence; and consequently it cannot be intended, that he gave any right to another to lay violent hands upon his person." Sovereign violence is in truth founded not on a pact but on the exclusive inclusion of bare life in the state. (*HS*, 106–7)

Agamben draws from the minimal nature of the notion of a right to resist violence against one's person a further proof of his argument concerning the interconnections between bare life, sovereignty, and the modern State. It is true that the Hobbesian view invites such a reading, but only if a conclusion is derived from it: that it amounts to a radical elimination of the political. When a supreme will within the community is not confronted by anything, politics necessarily disappears. From this viewpoint the Hobbesian project can be compared with another which is its opposite but, at the same time, identical in its anti-political effects: the Marxian notion of the withering away of the State. For Hobbes, society is incapable of giving itself its own law and, as a result, the total concentration of power in the hands of the sovereign is the prerequisite of any communitarian order. For Marx, a classless society has realised full universality and that makes politics superfluous. But it is enough that we introduce some *souplesse* within the Hobbesian scheme, that we accept that society is capable of *some partial* self-regulation, to immediately see that its demands are going to be more than those deriving from bare life, that they are going to have a variety and specificity that no "sovereign" power can simply ignore. When we arrive at that point, however, the notion of "sovereignty" starts shading into that of "hegemony." This means that, in my view, Agamben has clouded the issue, for he has presented as a political moment what actually amounts to a radical elimination of the political: a sovereign power which reduces the social bond to bare life.

I have spoken of social self-regulation as being partial. By this I mean that social and political demands emerge from a variety of quarters, not all of which move in the same direction. This means that society requires constant efforts at re-grounding. Schmitt, as we have seen, asserted that the function of the sovereign—in the state of exception—is to establish the coherence between law and the wider communitarian order (one cannot apply law to chaos). If this is so, however, and if the plurality of demands requires a constant process of legal transformation and revision, the state of emergency ceases to be exceptional and becomes an integral part of the political construction of the social bond. According to Wittgenstein, to apply a rule requires a second rule specifying how the first one should be applied, a third one explaining how the second will be applied, and so on. From there he draws the conclusion that the instance of application is part of the rule itself. In Kantian terms—as Agamben points out—this means that in the construction of the social bond we are dealing with reflective rather than determinative judgements. Vico's remarks—also quoted by Agamben—about the superiority of the exception over the rule is also highly pertinent in this context. This explains why I see the history of the state of exception with different lenses than Agamben. While he draws a picture by which the becoming rule of the exception represents the unavoidable advance towards a totalitarian society, I try to determine, with the generalization of the "exceptional," also countertendencies that make it possible to think about the future in more optimistic terms. We discussed earlier what Santi Romano said concerning revolutionary laws. Now, that does not only apply to periods of radical revolutionary breaks— what Gramsci called "organic crises"—but also to a variety of situations in which social movements constitute particularistic political spaces and give themselves their own "law" (which is partially internal and partially external to the legal system of the State). There is a molecular process of partial transformations which is absolutely vital as an accumulation of forces whose potential becomes visible when a more radical transformation of a whole hegemonic formation becomes possible.

What we have so far, already pre-announced that in our view, the second thesis of Agamben concerning bare life as resulting from the activity of sovereign power, does not fare any better. To start with, the distinction between *zoē* and *bios* cannot play the central role in historical explanation to which Agamben assigns it. As he himself asserts at the beginning of *Homo Sacer*, the Greeks used two terms to refer to life: "*zoē*, which expressed the simple fact of living common to all living beings (animals, men or gods), and *bios*, which indicated the form or way of living proper to an individual or a group" (*HS*, 1). This means that living beings are not distributed between two categories—those who have exclusively *bios* and those who have exclusively *zoē*—for those who have *bios* obviously have *zoē* as well. So *zoē* is primarily an abstraction. Even the *oikos*, whose aim was merely concerned with reproductive life, has its own internal structure, based on a hierarchical distribution of functions, so that although its aims are not political, it is far from being bare life, for it has its own configuration and system of rules. Ergo, if Agamben's thesis is going to hold, he would have to prove that, in some circumstances, bare life ceases to be an abstraction and becomes a concrete referent.

It is at this point that Agamben brings into the picture Foucault's biopolitics. "According to Foucault, a society's 'threshold of biological modernity' is situated at the point at which the species and the individual as a simple living body become what is at stake in a society's political strategies'" (*HS*, 3). It is most revealing that Agamben links Foucault's biopolitical hypothesis to the earlier work of Hannah Arendt: "Hannah Arendt had already analyzed the process that brings *homo laborans*—and, with it, biological life as such—gradually to occupy the very centre of the political scene of modernity. In *The Human Condition*, Arendt attributes the transformation and decadence of the political realm in modern societies to this primacy of natural life over political action" (*HS*, 4). Of course, to present the argument in these terms is grotesquely biased. One could more plausibly make the opposite argument, namely that in modernity there is no primacy of natural life over political action, but rather a politicization of a terrain previously occupied by "natural" life (and it is already to concede too much to assume that that life was merely "natural"). What is, anyway, wrong in the argument about a rigid opposition between political sovereignty and bare life is the assumption that it necessarily involves an increasing control by an over-powerful state. All that is involved in the notion of a politicization of "natural" life is that increasing areas of social life are submitted to processes of human control and regulation, but it is a non sequitur to assume that such a control has to crystallize around a tendentially totalitarian instance.

Given Agamben's assertion of a strict correlation between ban and sovereignty, the postulation of an *ad quem* totalitarian trend was, of course, to be expected. The result is that he equates human situations whose nature is entirely dissimilar. In order to have a "bare life," as we have seen, the receiving end of the ban has to be entirely without defense and fully submitted to the "abandonment" dictated by the sovereign power. Some of the situations that Agamben describes approach, actually, the state of a bare life which is the mere object of a political intervention. Thus he refers to the figure of the *Muselmann*, an inhabitant of the concentration camps, "a being from whom humiliation, horror and fear had so taken away all consciousness and all personality as to make him absolutely apathetic" (*HS*, 185). Or to a biochemist suffering leukemia who decides to transform his body in a laboratory: "His body is no longer private, since it has been transformed into a laboratory; but neither is it public, since only insofar as it is his own body can he transgress the limits that morality and law put into experimentation. . . . It is a *bios* that has, in every particular sense, so concentrated itself in its own *zoē* as to become indistinguishable from it" (*HS*, 186). Or to the body of Karen Quinlan, an over-comatose person whose organs are going to be transplanted: "Here biological life—which the machines are keeping functional by artificial respiration, pumping blood into the arteries, and regulating the blood temperature—has been entirely separated from the form of life that bore the name Karen Quinlan: here life becomes (or at least seems to become) pure *zoē*" (*HS*, 186).

Up to this point, Agamben's argument concerning "bare life" would be just plausible, although one could wonder about its political relevance. But later on he tries to extend it to entirely different situations. From the comatose we move to the bandit:

His entire existence is reduced to a bare life stripped of every right by virtue of the fact that anyone can kill him without committing homicide; he can save himself only in perpetual flight or a foreign land. . . . He is pure *zoē*, but his *zoē* is as such caught in the sovereign ban and must reckon with it at every moment, finding the best way to elude or deceive it. In this sense, no life, as exiles and bandits know well, is more "political" than his. (*HS*, 183–84)

The life of the bandit or the exile can be entirely political, but they are so in an entirely other sense than that of Karen Quinlan, because they, on the difference with Quinlan, are capable of engaging in antagonistic social practices. They have, in that sense, their own law, and their conflict with the law of the city is a conflict between laws, not between law and bare life. Agamben is aware of a potential criticism to the extreme and marginal character of his examples of bare life, and he tries to answer in anticipation with examples that he calls "no less extreme and still more familiar": "the Bosnian woman at Omarska, a perfect threshold of indistinction between biology and politics, or—in an apparently opposite, yet analogous, sense—military interventions on humanitarian grounds, in which war efforts are carried out for the sake of biological ends such as nutrition or the care of epidemics" (*HS*, 187). At this point, however, we no longer know what is the issue under discussion: the care for the biological survival of populations or the reduction of people to *zoē*, entirely stripped of any *bios*? Agamben, in his argument, constantly mixes both levels.

If the example of the bandit shows already a displacement of the logic of exclusion to something which clearly exceeds the notion of "bare life," this excess is only more visible when Agamben tries to expand the logic of sovereignty / bare life into a general theory of modernity. He starts by pointing out an undeniable fact: in most languages the notion of "the people" is ambiguous: on the one side it refers to the community as a whole (*populus*); on the other to the underdog (*plebs*). His reading of this ambiguity, however, is that the community is sharply divided and that the totalitarian logic of modernity is an attempt to overcome that division.

> In this sense, our age is nothing but the implacable and methodical attempt to overcome the division dividing the people, to eliminate radically the people that is excluded. This attempt brings together, according to different modalities and horizons, Right and Left, capitalist countries and socialist countries, which are united in the project—which is in the last analysis futile but which has been partially realized in all industrialized countries—of producing a single and undivided people. (*HS*, 179)

There is something basically wrong with this analysis. In the first place, division is perfectly compatible with the status quo, as far as the differences resulting from social diversity are not constructed in an antagonistic way. Hierarchy means, precisely, social differentiation, so that the elimination of division, conceived as multiplicity, is not something that the dominant groups are systematically aiming at. But, in the second place, if we are speaking about an antagonistic division, one which constructs "the people" as an underdog, the *plebs* that this division creates does not perpetuate but attempts to supersede the original division. We are dealing with a part that attempts to incarnate the whole, with a heterogeneity aspiring to be re-absorbed into a new homogeneity. So the dialectic between part and whole, between homogeneity and heterogeneity, is far more complex than Agamben's simplistic alternative of either "division" or "undivided people" allows us to think. The Gramscian distinction between "corporative" and "hegemonic" class allows for more complex strategic moves than Agamben's mechanical teleology. Differences can be partialities within a whole—as the *plebs* was for patrician eyes—or the names of alternative totalities (requiring the investment of the whole within the part, as in Lacan's object *a*). Homogenizing logics can be, reductio ad absurdum, thoroughly totalitarian, but they can equally be emancipatory, as when they link, in an equivalential chain, a plurality of unsatisfied demands. Sovereignty, finally, can also be totalitarian in the extreme case in which it involves a *total* concentration of power; but it can also be profoundly democratic, if it involves an articulating rather than a determining power—that is, when it "empowers" the underdog. In that case, as we have already pointed out, sovereignty should be conceived as hegemony.

Needless to say, we fully reject Agamben's third thesis, according to which the concentration camp is the *nomos* or fundamental biopolitical paradigm of the West. He asserts:

The birth of the camp in our time appears as an event that decisively signals the political space of modernity itself. It is produced at the point at which the political system of the modern nation-state, which was founded on the functional nexus between a determinate localization (land) and a determinate order (the State) and mediated by automatic rules for the inscription of life (birth or the nation), enters into a lasting crisis, and the State decides to assume directly the care of the nation's biological life as one of its proper tasks. . . . Something can no longer function within the traditional mechanisms that regulated this inscription, and the camp is the new, hidden regulator of the inscription of life in the order—or, rather, the sign of the system's inability to function without being transformed into a lethal machine. (*HS*, 174–75)

This series of wild statements would only hold if the following set of rather dubious premises were accepted:

1. That the crisis of the functional nexus between land, State, and the automatic rules for the inscription of life has freed an entity called "biological—or bare—life"
2. That the regulation of that freed entity has been assumed by a single and unified entity called the State
3. That the inner logic of that entity necessarily leads it to treat the freed entities as entirely malleable objects whose archetypical form would be the ban

Needless to say, none of these presuppositions can be accepted as they stand. Agamben, who has presented a rather compelling analysis of the way in which an ontology of potentiality should be structured, closes his argument, however, with a naïve teleologism, in which potentiality appears as entirely subordinated to a pre-given actuality. This teleologism is, as a matter of fact, the symmetrical *pendant* of the "ethymologism" we have referred to at the beginning of this essay. Their combined effect is to divert Agamben's attention from the really relevant question, which is the system of structural possibilities that each *new* situation opens. The most summary examination of that system would have revealed that: (1) the crisis of the "automatic rules for the inscription of life" has freed many more entities than "bare life," and that the reduction of the latter to the former takes place only in some extreme circumstances that cannot in the least be considered as a hidden pattern of modernity; (2) that the process of social regulation to which the dissolution of the "automatic rules of inscription" opens the way involved a plurality of instances that were far from unified in a single unity called "the State"; (3) that the process of State building in modernity has involved a far more complex dialectic between homogeneity and heterogeneity than the one that Agamben's "camp-based" paradigm reflects. By unifying the whole process of modern political construction around the extreme and absurd paradigm of the concentration camp, Agamben does more than present a distorted history: he blocks any possible exploration of the emancipatory possibilities opened by our modern heritage.

.   .   .

Let me conclude with a reference to the question of the future as it can be thought from Agamben's perspective. He asserts: "Only if it is possible to think the Being of abandonment beyond every idea of law (even that of the empty form of laws being in force without significance) will we have moved out of the paradox of sovereignty towards a politics freed from every ban. A pure form of law is only the empty form of relation. Yet the empty form of relation is no longer a law but a zone of indistinguishability between law and life, which is to say, a state of exception" (*HS*, 59). We are not told anything about what a movement out of the paradox of sovereignty and "towards a politics freed from every ban" would imply. But we do not need to be told: the formulation of the problem already involves its own answer. To be beyond any ban and any sovereignty means, simply, to be beyond politics. The myth of a fully reconciled society is what governs the (non-)political discourse of Agamben. And it is also what allows him to dismiss all political options in our societies and to unify them in the concentration camp as their secret destiny. Instead of deconstructing the logic of political institutions, showing areas in which forms of struggle and resistance are possible, he closes them beforehand through an essentialist unification. Political nihilism is his ultimate message.

The Complexities of Sovereignty

William E. Connolly

The Persistence of Sovereignty

The fall of the Soviet Union; the breakup of Yugoslavia; the extension and intensification of global capital; the consolidation of the European Union; the NATO intervention in Kosovo to overturn ethnic cleansing of the region by Slobodan Milosevic; the trial of Milosevic by an international tribunal; lectures to George W. Bush by European and Japanese leaders about the importance of global action to reverse global warming; the attacks of 9/11 linked to a virtual network of terrorists definitively linked to no single state; the low-grade civil war between Israel and Palestinians—these are just a few events that pose the question: What is happening to state sovereignty today? Is it being overtaken by global capital, international humanism, a global ecological crisis? Or does it persist, while its terms and sites are changing? My sense is not only that sovereignty persists, but that it does so amid an intensification of ambiguities and uncertainties that have inhabited it all along. Perhaps the first thing is to explore ambiguities and uncertainties that have haunted sovereignty since its inception.

The Paradox of Sovereignty

According to theorists from a variety of intellectual traditions, there is a fundamental paradox located at the center of the rule of law in democratic states. Jean-Jacques Rousseau, Carl Schmitt, Franz Kafka, Paul Ricoeur, Hannah Arendt, Jacques Derrida, Gilles Deleuze, and Giorgio Agamben, while disagreeing on numerous other issues, concur in asserting that a democratic state seeking to honor the rule of law is also one with a sovereign power uncertainly situated within and above the law. The rule of law in a state is enabled by a practice of sovereignty that rises above the law. Often the paradox of sovereignty is asserted with respect to the founding of a state, but those who locate a paradox in the founding act typically discern its echoes and reverberations in the state that results as well.[1] Jean-Jacques Rousseau, a founder of modern democratic theory, puts the paradox this way:

In order for an emerging people to appreciate the healthy maxims of politics and follow the fundamental rules of statecraft, the effect would have to become the cause; the social spirit which should be the result of the institution, would have to preside over the founding of the institution itself; and men would have to be prior to the laws what they ought to become by means of laws.[2]

For a polity of self-rule through law to emerge out of a nondemocratic condition, "effect would have to become cause." This is so because the spirit needed to nourish democratic self-rule can only grow out of a prior ethos of community already infused into the populace. The complication revolves around, first, whether these infusions exceed or express the self-rule of the people itself and, second, how to wheel either condition, each of which depends upon the other, into place without first installing the other that depends upon it. Rousseau "resolved" the paradox of sovereignty through recourse to the fiction of a wise legislator who imbues people with the spirit of self-rule before they begin to rule themselves. But he knew this fiction was insufficient to the actuality of any people already set in history. Moreover, well before Wittgenstein's account of how every rule and law encounters uncertainty and indeterminacy as it bumps into new and unforeseen circumstances, Rousseau understood that issue too. He knew that the paradox of founding returns as a recurring paradox of democratic sovereignty: if the populace is not infused by the right spirit of community, even a written constitution would be insufficient to guide it when new and unforeseen circumstances arise.

His response to the paradox is to reduce the arrival of new and unforeseen things to a minimum. Hence his portrayal of the kind of place where self-rule through law is possible: a small, isolated polity; a highly unified educational system; general festivals and rituals that instill common sentiments in all citizens; a national mode of dress that discourages amorous relations with people from other countries; tight rules of chastity for men and women to regulate and discipline the passions; the minimization of commerce through the regularity of self-subsistent family farms; the close regulation of commerce with foreigners; the regulation of theater; severe limits on economic inequality; a citizen militia; a nuclear family in which the male is supreme; and so forth. The objective of these institutions, disciplines, prohibitions, and injunctions is to instill the same sentiments, habits, and restraints in the citizenry. Self-rule, Rousseau thought, is circular when it works: its preconditions of possibility require citizen habitualization to common sentiments that they then express as their collective will. To be a sovereign, territorial people, it is necessary to become a highly unified nation.

Rousseau seems to have thought that if democratic sovereignty was to maintain itself, the element of arbitrariness in its formation and maintenance had to be obscure to those who were its objects. Why? Because to consent to being the object of sovereignty, it is best to see yourself as the subject or agent of sovereignty. So he invested a ruse in the Wise Legislator at the very founding of sovereignty: "It is this sublime reason, which rises above the grasp of common men, whose decisions the legislator places in the mouths of the immortals in order to convince by divine authority those who cannot be moved by human prudence."[3] The Legislator, by instilling the right sentiments into the populace and linking them to divine authority, forges them into a sovereign people. But this means that they are crafted by a sublime reason above their grasp into a form through which they rule, making that rule oscillate uncertainly between obedience to something prior to the people and the decisions of the people.

Perhaps no democrat has plumbed the paradox of sovereignty as deeply as Rousseau. He is wise in trying to negotiate its terms rather than simply transcend them. For the people to rule, it must be infused with an ethos that precedes and exceeds its rule; to make that rule legitimate to the people, it must interpret what it has already become as expressive of what divine authority calls upon it to be. Sometimes, a written constitution or the traditions of Western civilization stand in for divine authority.

But Rousseau's basic understanding of the paradox has withstood the test of numerous attempts to dissolve it into proceduralism, or narrow, prudential renderings of a social contract, or representation by a high court of the simple dictates of a written constitution. To negotiate the paradox is to somehow come to terms with the indispensability of a positive ethos to politics, sovereignty, and the democratic state.

But, for all that, the particular ethos of sovereignty that Rousseau embraces is so inconsonant with the defining features of the contemporary condition that the worst kind of nightmare would result were it to emerge as an active agenda today. The Serbian drive to create a state of ethnic purity approximates the sort of action that would have to be taken to try to forge a sovereign people today with the characteristics that Rousseau seeks. Thus, Rousseau helps us to appreciate the complexity of sovereignty, but not to negotiate a response through which democracy, law, state, and sovereignty speak affirmatively to each other.

Sovereignty and Biopolitics

Giorgio Agamben also finds a paradox within sovereignty. He thinks it has become stark in late modernity, as the state inserts itself more deeply into biological life, that is, as issues of biology become prominent in decisions regarding abortion, artificial insemination, the line between life and death, organ transplant, strategies of citizen induction, and standards of "racial" inclusion and exclusion. In a way that is reminiscent of Rousseau's myth of the Legislator, he also contends that the practice of sovereignty is tied to the sacred. The aura of sovereign authority is sustained through the mystique of the sacred.

For Agamben, the paradox of sovereignty resides in the fact that the state requires a final authority to resolve questions of law, while the final authority is insufficiently informed by any law that precedes it. Modern sovereignty carries forward, if implicitly, the pagan logic of *homo sacer*, or the sacred man. *Homo sacer* is "the life that cannot be sacrificed and yet may be killed" (*HS*, 8). It is connected to sovereignty because the "sovereign sphere is the sphere in which it is permitted to kill without committing homicide and without celebrating a sacrifice" (*HS*, 83). This logic sinks more deeply into the world as the state increasingly participates in "biopolitics," penetrating more deeply into the biological depths of human life.

Agamben contends that the "logic" that binds sovereignty, the sacred, and biopolitics together leads (inexorably?) to a state in which a supreme power can annihilate a whole minority in the name of national unity. It is the nexus between the paradox of sovereignty, the sacred, and biopolitics that makes the concentration camp the paradigm of modern politics, with the German Nazi regime expressing its outer limit. If Agamben is right, the emergence of biopolitics plunges the paradox of sovereignty beyond constitutional disputes over democratic rule into the very logic of the Nazi Holocaust.

It is because he finds this logic so compelling and disastrous that Agamben insists that it must be overcome entirely. Here are two formulations in which he announces this necessity:

And only if it is possible to think the relation between potentiality and actuality differently—and even to think beyond this relation—will it be possible to think a constituting power wholly released from the sovereign ban. Until [this happens] a political theory freed from the aporias of sovereignty remains unthinkable. (*HS*, 44)

Only if it is possible to think the Being of abandonment beyond every idea of law will we have moved out of the paradox of sovereignty toward a politics of freedom from every ban. (*HS*, 59)

Nowhere in *Homo Sacer*, however, is a way out of the logic actually disclosed. The response of Hannah Arendt—to pull the state out of biopolitics—is considered and appropriately rejected as unviable. But nothing else is offered to replace it. Agamben thus carries us through the conjunction of sovereignty, the sacred, and biopolitics to a historical impasse. This combination is almost enough to make one return to Rousseau. Indeed, Agamben helps us to see the persistent attraction to the Rousseauian idea of the nation, in a world where its preconditions of attainment are even less propitious than in Rousseau's day. For Rousseau tried to conceal from many the paradox he encountered, while Agamben's analysis exacerbates a paradox that he cannot imagine how to transcend.

Perhaps it is possible both to resist the fantasy to return to a past that never was and to slip past Agamben's insistence that the paradox must be overcome in a new way. At any rate, I want to suggest that while Agamben's analysis is insightful in identifying three critical elements in the paradox and in pointing to dangers that flow from it, the formalism of his analysis disarms the most promising ways to negotiate it. To show this, I reconsider three key elements in his account: the meaning and role of the sacred, the relation between biopolitics and sovereignty, and the "logic" of sovereignty.

The Sacred

Agamben's account of the sacred, drawing its credibility from one statement written in the early days of the Roman empire, needs to be revised. I concur that sovereignty and the sacred touch one another historically. Rousseau's invocation of the Legislator expresses this connection. Sovereignty and the sacred are connected historically, partly because kings have linked their rule to divinity and partly because the persistence of a political regime sometimes imparts the ability to locate a single body powerful enough to resolve key issues of governance. But the sacred is not well defined as that which is both the highest and the most susceptible to annihilation. Rather, the sacred is said to deserve awe because it is thought to be closest to the divine, or at least to touch the highest concerns of human existence.

Something might be sacred because it represents or symbolizes a divine law, because it is a book that is divinely inspired, because it is a ruler divinely authorized, or because it is a set of rituals expressive of the highest human relation to the divine. Those who defile these things are said to be worthy of punishment, or even death, not because they touch the sacred, but because they do so in a blasphemous manner. They translate a divine being into an idol; or ridicule a sacred text; or disrespect an authoritative priesthood; or question the connection between sovereignty and the sacred. When Spinoza challenged the faith of the Elders in the beleaguered Hebrew community of Amsterdam in the seventeenth century, the Elders accused him of defiling their faith. He was officially cursed and banned. This action fits Agamben's model of one who is "included while being excluded": but it does fit that of one who is to be killed without being sacrificed because he participates *in* the sacred. Spinoza was banned (*included* as a pariah through enforced exclusion) because he defiled the sacred. When the Khomeini of Iran offered a reward for the execution of Salman Rushdie, the latter became a target of annihilation. Again, not because he was part of the sacred, but because he defiled it. When I call the majority of the American Supreme Court that decided the 2000 election in favor of a candidate from the political party they already supported, "The Gang of Five," some take that to show lack of awe for a body that stands at that point where sovereignty and the sacred touch.

Agamben's attempt to fold a double sense into the logic of the sacred should be rejected in favor of the conventional rendering he seeks to overturn. The sacred is that which is to be approached with awe. There might well be ambivalence in people's orientation to the sacred, one they do not themselves acknowledge because of the fear of divine or human retribution. Those most punitive toward others who criticize or "defile" what they consider to be sacred often enough harbor such ambivalence. The intensity of their drive to punish is a displacement of that ambivalence. That is familiar enough. Spinoza, Nietzsche, and Freud, among others, read narrow definitions and harsh punishments of blasphemy this way.

To construe the sacred in the more conventional way is to pave the way to relax the demands of those who seek to impose their understandings of the sacred upon others in a culture with a plurality of renderings of the divine and the sacred. It sets the stage for a more public and active pluralization of the sacred. Thereby, it identifies one (among several others to be pursued) precondition for renegotiating the ethos of sovereignty to mesh more smoothly with a culture of deep pluralism. At this point, I merely suggest that a return to the conventional idea of the sacred can help to loosen the nexus between sovereignty and the sacred without eliminating presumptive respect for sovereign decisions.

Biopolitics and Sovereignty

Agamben contends that biopolitics has become intensified today. This intensification translates the paradox of sovereignty into a potential disaster. The analysis that he offers at this point seems not so much wrong to me as overly formal. It reflects a classical liberal and Arendtian assumption that there was a time when politics was restricted to public life and biocultural life was kept in the private realm. What a joke. Every way of life involves the infusion of norms, judgments, and standards into the affective life of participants at both private and public levels. Every way of life is biocultural and biopolitical. Aristotle, Epicurus, Lucretius, Augustine, Spinoza, Rousseau, and Hegel, writing during different periods, all appreciate the layering of culture into different layers of biological life and the concomitant mixing of biology into culture. They treat the biological not as merely the genetic or fixed, but as zones of corporeality infused with cultural habits, dispositions, sentiments, and norms.

Biocultural life has been intensified today with the emergence of new technologies of infusion. But the shift is not as radical as Agamben makes it out to be. In late-modern life, new technologies enable physicians, biologists, geneticists, prison systems, advertisers, media talking heads, and psychiatrists to sink deeply into human biology. They help to shape the cultural being of biology, although not always as they intend to do. Agamben's review of new medical technologies to keep people breathing after their brains have stopped functioning captures something of this change, showing why a sovereign authority now has to *decide* when death has arrived rather than letting that outcome *express* the slow play of biocultural tradition. Numerous such judgments, previously left to religious tradition in predominantly Christian cultures, have now become explicit issues of technology and sovereignty in religiously diverse states.

Agamben tends to describe the state as the "nation-state." He does not ask whether disturbing developments in the logic of sovereignty are bound, not merely to a conjunction between biopolitics and sovereignty, *but to a conjunction between them and renewed attempts to consolidate the spirituality of the nation during a time when it is ever more difficult to do so.* As the reactive drive to restore the fictive unity of a nation is relaxed, it becomes more possible to negotiate a generous ethos of pluralism that copes in more inclusive ways with the nexus between biology, politics, and sovereignty. More than anything else, the dubious drive to translate deep plurality into nationhood translates sovereignty into a punitive, corrective, exclusionary, and marginalizing practice.[4] The shape of the ethos infusing the practice of sovereignty is therefore critical, and not a mere conjugation of sovereignty and biopolitics.

The "Logic" of Sovereignty

Agamben retains one habit of several theorists whom he criticizes: he acts as if an account of the "logic of sovereignty" reveals ironclad paradoxes, paradoxes that could be resolved only by transcending that logic altogether. His mode of analysis engenders the eschatological gesture through which it closes. I doubt, however, that politics or culture possesses as tight a logic as Agamben delineates. If I am right, biocultural life displays neither the close coherence that many theorists seek nor the tight paradox that Agamben and others discern. Biocultural life exceeds any textbook logic because of the nonlogical character of its materiality. It is more messy, layered, and complex than any logical analysis can capture. The very illogicalness of its materiality ensures that it corresponds entirely to no design, no simple causal pattern, no simple set of paradoxes. Agamben displays the hubris of academic intellectualism when he encloses political culture within a tightly defined logic.

Some social theorists, again, express this hubris by presenting a tight model of causal explanation, others by displaying a closed model of historical realization, and others by dissolving the first two images into tightly defined paradoxes. All three stances overstate the extent to which the complexity of biopolitical culture is resolvable into a consummate logic. The attraction of these perspectives of coherence, realization, and tight paradox is that, if accepted, they allow social and cultural theorists to assume the role that ecclesiastical authorities once played in Christian states: that of definitive public visionaries who articulate the larger picture of the actual, the possible, and the desirable in which sovereignty, law, and politics are encased. Kant, for example, participated in such a political drive. He sought to replace ecclesiological authority with the public authority of academic (Kantian) philosophers who continued the Christian tradition by other means. The continuing attraction of the Kantian problematic in academic philosophy is bound to the authoritative standing that it bestows upon academic philosophers in biocultural life. Agamben, of course, translates Kantian antinomies into paradoxes. But just below that facelift beats the heart of another scholar who reduces cultural life to a logic.

If you loosen the logic that Agamben articulates, you may both express more appreciation for the materialization of culture and locate more space for maneuver within the paradoxes that he delineates. There is a paradox of sovereignty, but it is a social or cultural paradox, one with more room for negotiation, adjustment, and honing than Agamben suggests. The best way to pursue this issue is to delineate two ambiguities residing in sovereignty that escape Agamben's attention.

The first ambiguity, almost detected by Agamben, is an equivocation in the idea of sovereignty between acting with final authority and acting with irresistible power. This finds expression in the *Oxford English Dictionary*, in the definition of sovereignty as "supremacy in respect of power, domination, or rank; supreme dominion, authority or rule." The idea of finality flows through these terms, but in some it expresses final authority and in others an irresistible effect. Both dimensions find presence in the terms *rank* and *rule*. Agamben senses this difference, in his assertion that the sovereign decides the exception. But, within the idea of the exception "decided" by sovereignty, an oscillation flows between a juridically established authority that authoritatively decides the exception and social powers that assert themselves irresistibly in and around the decision.

This ambivalence within sovereign finality finds expression in Christian theology as well as human law. The point of the nominalist critique of those scholastics who had projected an immanent purpose into the world is that this traditional projection implicitly undermines the very idea of God's omnipotence. A sovereign God, they contended, is One governed by no prior purpose implicitly limiting His power. So they attacked the doctrine of an expressive or enchanted world through which traditional theology had bestowed meaning and direction upon human life. They expanded the human experience of contingency in nature by subtracting purpose, belonging, and intrinsic meaning from it, in the interests of honoring a God of absolute sovereign power over being. They increased God's sovereign power by depleting the sovereign purpose to which He conformed. Their opponents, of course, said that in doing so they subtracted meaning and purpose from the world over which God presided. Today, they would be called theological nihilists.

The theological oscillation and debate subsists within the contemporary language of state sovereignty, as the finality of sovereignty circulates uncertainly between authoritativeness and irresistibility. The practice of sovereignty thrives on this instability.

The significance of the dissonant conjunction between effective and expressive sovereignty becomes apparent when linked to a second oscillation. Alexis de Tocqueville captures much of it in his exploration of nineteenth-century American democracy. "The principle of sovereignty of the people," he says, "which is always to be found, more or less, at the bottom of almost all human institutions, usually remains buried there."[5] In European societies, divine right invested sovereign authority in the king, but below that authority, enabling and confining it, were specific traditions already infused into the multitude. This underground interplay between the multitude, tradition, and official sovereignty supported some initiatives by the official or positional sovereign, resisted others, and rendered others barely thinkable. Think of a monarch who commanded the people to convert from Christianity to Buddhism in one generation. He might face the fate that met Pharaoh Akhenaton when he converted Egyptians to a new, austere faith: they barely conformed to its external dictates for a generation and then reverted aggressively to the old rituals upon his death.

The multitude, already infused with tradition, comes even more into the fore in a democratic, constitutional regime. It helps to set the ethos in which official sovereignty is set. Better put, in democratic constitutionalism, sovereignty circulates uncertainly between the multitude, the traditions it embodies, constitutionally sanctioned authorities, and, where operative, the written constitution that the authorities interpret. The relative weight of each element can be specified more closely, although never completely, according to need and context. The police in American cities thus both express and help to shape the ethos of sovereignty. They can find evidence or plant it, follow the spirit of Miranda or render it ineffective, intimidate a section of the populace or act evenhandedly, depending upon the unstable confluence of legal rulings given to them, the larger ethos in which they participate, and the professional police ethos carved out of dangers, ethnic loyalties, and hostilities in the city. What would happen to a court that "decides" that cops must walk without guns? Or that they are free to shoot at any citizen? An unconscious context of the thinkable and the unthinkable, the habitually expected and the impermissible, would enter into readings of constitutional texts and sovereign decisions.

According to Tocqueville, the tradition that infused the ethos of sovereignty in nineteenth-century America was, above all, Christianity. This was the main reason why Amerindians could not be included in the polity: they lacked Christianity. So when a Supreme Court decision supported the autonomy of the Cherokee in southeastern United States, the sovereign ethos of a superior Christian civilization overturned that mere legality, even though a minority of Christians protested such a rendering of the Christian spirit. Tocqueville saw how this slippery circulation of sovereign power/authority operated. Here is what he says about how the "American government" and "the white population" enter into asymmetrical relations each time a new area is reserved by treaty for the "Indians":

Who can guarantee that they will be able to remain in peace in their new asylum? The United States pledges itself to maintain them there, but the territory they now occupy was formerly secured to them by the most solemn oaths. Now, the American government does not, it is true, take their land from them, but it allows encroachments on it. No doubt within a few years the same white population which is now pressing around them will again be on their tracks in the solitudes of Arkansas; then they will suffer again from the same ills without the same remedies; and because sooner or later there will be no land left for them, their only refuge will be the grave.[6]

A sovereign majority of the white population, infused with a generic sense of Christian superiority, defined and decided the exception in this case. Was any court going to decide with effective finality against the population that it recognized to be legitimate citizens? Would it, for instance, order all Christian whites in and around Georgia to march north and west instead of allowing *them* to drive the Cherokee west to Oklahoma in the march of tears? Tocqueville himself had regrets about this result. But he did not dissent from it because of his view that sovereignty circulates between the people, the highest court, and a Christendom that forms the first "political institution" of American civilization. Lacking Christianity, Amerindians became the sovereign exception, the (non)people to be excluded from the territory that they occupied first. In every territorial civilization, Tocqueville says, "there are certain great social principles which a people either introduces everywhere or tolerates nowhere."[7] Strict constructionists in the United States understand this equation at a visceral level, concurring with Tocqueville that Christianity, which exercises no explicit power over the state, functions as the first political institution in imparting specific meaning and weight to the porous words of the Constitution.

The process that Tocqueville describes is already invested in the fateful conjunction between biopolitics and sovereignty. The living space available to Amerindians was squeezed by the effective sovereignty of Euro-American Christians. But the circulation that Tocqueville charts does not conform to the airtight logic of sovereignty that Agamben characterizes. *If* a political movement had successfully changed the cultural ethos in which presidents governed, courts decided, and the Christian populace set the context and reception of decisions, the paradox of sovereignty would still remain, biopolitics would still operate, and the relevant constitutional language would still be insufficient to determine judicial decisions. *But a modified ethos of constitutional action would nonetheless incline the effective range of court decisions and popular responses in a different direction.* A change in ethos, which forms a critical component in the complexity of sovereignty, alters the course of sovereignty.

The contemporary relevance of this point is underlined by saying that the conjunction of biopolitics and article 48 of the Weimar Republic did not alone generate the Nazi Holocaust against Jews, the Romana, and homosexuals. A series of intense relays between these forces and a political culture infused with anti-Semitism and resentment against defeat in World War I generated the devastating result. Without the last element—the element I call an ethos of sovereignty—the conjunction between biopolitics and article 48 might have proceeded in a different direction. The point is to see that, given the paradox that helps to constitute it, an ethos of sovereignty is both external to sovereignty and internal to it, both part of it and one of its cultural conditions of possibility.

Gilles Deleuze and Felix Guattari concur with the perspective adopted here. Agreeing that there is a paradox at the center of sovereignty, they nonetheless find the most powerful sources of fascism to flow from a series of "resonances" between state sovereignty, fascist gangs, and a larger populace ripe for the micropolitics of fascism.

But fascism is inseparable from the proliferation of molecular focuses in interaction, which skip from point to point to point, *before* beginning to resonate together in the National Socialist State. Rural fascism and city or neighborhood fascism, youth fascism and war veteran's fascism, fascism of the Left and fascism of the Right, fascism of the couple, family, school, and office: every fascism is defined by a micro-black hole that stands on its own and communicates with the others, before resonating in a great, generalized, central black hole. . . . Even after the National Socialist State had been established, microfascisms persisted that gave it unequaled ability to act upon the "masses."[8]

Sovereignty and Empire

While attending to the modern intensification of biopolitics, Agamben pays little heed to the changed global context in which sovereignty is set. Once you acknowledge that an ethos is internal as well as external

to sovereignty, you appreciate that territorial sovereignty has always operated within a global as well as an internal context. Hegel saw this, saying
that in the modern world there is always only one real sovereign state. The
World Historical State exercises sovereignty by maintaining the international order as it governs its internal populace. Such a state is contained
and restrained, when the world is lucky, within the world historical pull
of Geist. Other states, ranged around it as satellites, are contained and
restrained by it, making theirs a subordinate sovereignty.

In *Empire* Michael Hardt and Antonio Negri attend to the changing
global context of sovereignty.[9] They claim that, with the acceleration and
expansion of capital into something approaching a global system, the context of sovereignty has changed dramatically. They describe the nineteenth
century idealized by Hegel as the era of imperialism, presided over by a
dominant state. But imperialism today gives way to Empire.

Empire is a worldwide assemblage, an assemblage in which some
states have much more priority than others, but one marked above all
by the migration of sovereignty toward global structures that exceed the
power or control of any single state. Here are some of their descriptions of
the emerging condition:

Empire can only be conceived as a universal republic, a network of powers and
counterpowers structured in a boundless and inclusive architecture. (166)

The recognition of the rise of transnational corporations above . . . the constitutional command of the nation-states should not . . . lead us to think constitutional mechanisms and controls as such have declined. . . . Instead, the constitutional
functions have been displaced to another level. (308–9)

The fundamental principle of Empire . . . is that its power has no actual and local-
izable terrain or center. Imperial power is distributed . . . through mobile and
articulated mechanisms of control. (384)

So not only is the global context of state sovereignty shifting, but
also sovereignty is migrating from states—where it was never entirely an-
chored—to a loosely assembled global system. Let me say a couple of
words on behalf of the Hardt-Negri analysis before proposing some modi-
fications in it.

The idea of Empire—as a loose assemblage of differentiated powers
not entirely under the thumb of a dominant state or a set of supranational
corporations—is both timely and in need of further development. Here,

the elements of sovereignty are distributed in a complex assemblage with multiple sites, not concentrated in the single will of a people, a king, or a dictator. Familiar debates in International Relations theory between imperialistic and anarchistic readings of a world order either place too much control over events in a dominant power or reduce the world to a quasi-autonomous system exerting restraints on sovereign states. The contemporary world assemblage is marked by two tendencies: (a) neither state authorities, corporate elites, market mechanisms, nor international agencies possess sufficient foresight to govern the world intentionally as a system; (b) every state, corporation, labor movement, and supranational movement is nonetheless enabled, contained, and restrained by the larger world assemblage in which it is set. Ambiguities and uncertainties already discernible within sovereignty become magnified as its sites are extended to encompass the world.

Hardt and Negri see how the migration of sovereignty to new sites encourages some states to try to restore a semblance of autonomy that they project into a mythic past by intensifying drives to integrate the population into a nation. But, even as they support the "multitude" against corporate and state priorities, these authors refuse to support this violent course. They refuse the drive to reinstate the nation as the state's bulwark against the new formation of sovereignty.

But things soon take less compelling turns. In a way that recalls Agamben's quest to break the logic of sovereignty, Hardt and Negri also seek a revolutionary transformation of Empire. They seek a dramatic break, rather than forging strategies within and against the current order of things to render it more democratic and less bound to the blind compulsions of capital. This desire for transformation, in turn, severs their politics from the insightful institutional analyses they have just launched. The new possibility becomes a vague gesture, reminiscent of the way in which one brand of Marxism proceeded over the last century. Hardt and Negri demand overthrow and refuse to identify what terms or direction it might take:

Furthermore, we have not yet been able to give any coherent indication of what type of political subjectivities might contest and overthrow the forces of Empire. (205)

Even when we manage to touch on the productive, ontological dimension and the resistances that arise there, we will still not be in a position—not even at the end of this book—to point to any already existing and concrete elaboration of a political alternative to Empire. . . . It will only arise in practice. (206)

We need a force capable of not only organizing the destructive capacities of the multitude, but also constituting through the desires of the multitude an alternative. (214)

This is the point when the modern republic ceases to exist and the postmodern posse arises. This is the founding moment of an earthly city that is strong and distinct from any divine city. . . . Only the multitude through its practical experimentation will offer the models and determine when and how the possible becomes real. (411)

For them, the multitude is not equivalent to the people. The people is forged upon a populace on a politically organized territory, fitting it into the narrow imperatives of a "nation-state." The multitude is those forces in politics, work, and ethos that exceed both the people and the established forces of economic organization.[10] Good enough. But Hardt and Negri then set the multitude against Empire, rather than locating it ambiguously within and outside Empire and showing how various factions of it do and can act to press this global assemblage in new directions. Must the diversion of investment within capitalism toward ecologically sound companies either be reduced to co-optation of the multitude by capital or an act of resistance against the Empire of capitalism? Perhaps these investments act modestly upon capital to stretch its priorities. What about the cross-state citizen divestment movement that helped to end apartheid in South Africa? Does the formation of new forms of property/territory by indigenous peoples participate in the new global assemblage while modifying some of its terms? Or must it be treated as a co-opted movement within Empire? What about movements that stretch the organization of investment and work life within capitalist firms by creating institutional space for gays and women, or by addressing the issue of poverty? Finally, what about a variety of religious movements surging through and across territorial states? Are they inside or outside Empire? The either/or character of such questions presupposes an architecture of Empire tighter than that presented in the authors' best descriptions of the assemblage.

The authors may be at odds with themselves on these questions. The dominant theme is, first, to show how each new effort of change becomes absorbed and contained by the flexible world assemblage and, second, to point to an abstract multitude outside the most highly organized industrial states as agents of vague, fundamental transformation. A subordinate theme, seldom expressed in the summary statements, is to suggest how this supple assemblage with no single authority rising above it could be shoved and pushed in more promising directions without eliminating it as a capitalist assemblage. Again, the dominant tendency is to graft the idea of the multitude onto overthrow of the Empire of Capital.

But in the absence of an imagined alternative linked to a concrete agent, it is counterproductive to join critique to vague, transformational gestures. Many, otherwise sympathetic, who hear it will fear that the existing formations of production, welfare, safety, accountability, and responsibility might be destroyed with nothing else emerging to replace them at the needed architectural scale. Fear does not decline as a motive to resignation and obedience in the age of Empire. Rather, the new fear lifts Hobbesian fear to a new level of being. It is now that the jerry-rigged, fragile world assemblage, upon which depend production, jobs, finance, and commerce, will decompose under the pressure of stress without anything expansive or supple enough to replace it. To point vaguely to the promise of overthrow is to spawn such a fear. The most unpromising side of Marxism is thus recapitulated under even less favorable conditions. The result is to paralyze creative action. Thus, under such circumstances, it is better to identify energies and possible sites of action on a variety of fronts to make the assemblage function more robustly in the interests of ordinary people.

It is surprising that religion, which has become both a national and a transnational force with which to contend, plays no significant role in this analysis of Empire. It is pretty much ignored until near the end, when a new immanent faith of immanent materialism is projected onto the multitude. But surely Christianity, Judaism, Hinduism, and Buddhism did not subsist as dependent variables until immanent materialism emerged. And, just as surely, that variety of existential faiths is not going to dissolve into this new faith, either. It is better to come to terms with the persistence of religious diversity on the globe during a time when the acceleration of speed and the mobilization of capital draw contending faiths into closer and more persistent contact. Today, the goal should be, not to dissolve diverse experiences of the sacred into a new common faith, but to fold greater appreciation of the profound contestability of every faith into our self-portrayals and presentations to others. The best place to start this process is with one's own. So I begin by announcing clearly: immanent materialism, while it inspires me existentially and ethically, is apt to seem strange to those uninhabited by it. It is both worthy of my embrace and a profoundly contestable faith. It is surely not rendered unavoidable in the age of Empire, nor are the other contestable faiths with which it seeks to enter into relations of agonistic respect.

Hardt and Negri are caught in a struggle between the immanent radicalism of Gilles Deleuze and the eschatological tendencies of Karl Marx. While their most creative institutional analyses express this cross-fertilization admirably, the eschatological drive of the book prevails. Capital and religion are the major vehicles of that eschatology: in the drives to overcome capital and to transform diverse metaphysical and religious faiths into immanent naturalism. As I see it, again, the diversity of religion is not apt to fade into a new materialist ontology of the multitude, although the intra- and extra-territorialization of multiple faiths contains promising possibilities. And capital, while it may well emerge in a world crisis, is also unlikely to give way to a world economic assemblage that eschews private investment, earnings on interest, wage-labor, and the commodity form. The new world assemblage, just because it is flexible and complex in its architecture, is not amenable to replacement. But for the same reason, it may be susceptible to significant stretching and reshaping by a variety of movements situated at multiple sites. The task is to infuse it with more flexibility, inclusivity, and plurality, and to act upon localities, states, supranational capital, religious organizations, and international institutions to redistribute the world assemblage.

Capitalism, Property, and Sovereignty

Consider a process under way that could modify state-capitalist forms of property and governance in the new world assemblage without overturning that assemblage itself. It grows out of the contemporary politics between "settler" states and indigenous populations previously conquered and displaced by them.

Before the advent of modern capitalism, the practice of acquiring mining or oil rights over land occupied by others did not exist. Today, oil and mining companies acquire mining rights to land owned in other respects by others. A new property form is emerging out of capitalism. Indeed, in capitalist states new forces are constantly reshaping the property form. Thus, to take a second example, the privately incorporated, non-profit university provides a legal forum of governance that stretches the typical practices of individual or corporate ownership. So does the apart-ment collective.

People do protest vocally about inalienable property rights when the question of distinctive forms of governance over lands previously wrested from indigenous peoples comes up. But these examples of previous cre-ativity in the property form within capitalism may loosen them up a little, and remind them that, in the past, the most creative embellishments have been reserved for those who already control major economic resources. Recall, for instance, that Tocqueville worried about the future effects of the "new manufacturing aristocracy" on the agricultural form of prop-erty that he considered to be indispensable to American democracy. But he did not follow that concern with a call to dismantle the aristocracy of capital; he reserved *that* conclusion for those Amerindians who lacked Christianity and, at least he thought, agriculture.

To chart plural practices of property and governance within capi-talism is to encourage support for the worldwide movement of indige-nous peoples to govern large stretches of territory previously wrested from them. Such practices are being pursued today in large areas of Canada and Australia. New strategies are being proposed for indigenous peoples to participate in world capitalism in ways that stretch and pluralize the paradigmatic practices of capitalist property, ownership, territory, and sov-ereignty. Indigenous casino capitalism might become a way to generate capital for other productive activities.

These changes neither overturn global capital nor remain within its most familiar forms. Such modes of governance enable indigenous peoples both to reject the coercive demand that they be stationary peoples with unchangeable customs and to fold traditional elements of spirituality into new practices of territory, property, capital, and governance.

Such achievements, however, cannot be secured by indigenous people alone, one country at a time. They must be promoted through cross-state assemblages of indigenous peoples, backed by corresponding networks of religious leaders and critical public philosophers within and across settler states, processed through active negotiations with finance capital and state officials. Such multisite negotiations might help to alter the ethos of sov-ereignty and capital alike, without transforming world capitalism into a new world order.

Indeed, old ideas of "place," "land," and "earth" provide new sites for possible metamorphosis today. For instance, a growing number of people in several areas of the world identify the earth as simultaneously a vibrant source of life, a site of diverse energies exceeding possible human mastery, and a fragile planet to be nurtured as a source of sustenance and creative evolution. The earth may be emerging as an immanent field upon which to relocate visceral experiences of identification traditionally reserved for the territorial nation. The earth becomes a rallying cry through which to refashion and tame capital, while exceeding the closed prerogatives of the sovereign, territorial nation. The territorial state retains prominence as one site of action, but the drive to the territorial *nation* is challenged from within and without the state.

Consider the irony. In 1968, *Apollo 8* sent back pictures of a vivid blue planet suspended in the middle of the solar system, a stunning, bright sphere unlike any other planet observable from the earth itself. This reflected image of the earth, the paradigmatic product of a highly organized capitalist state, underlines for many how unique the earth is by comparison to other planets so far encountered. The others cannot even hold water, while the fine balance that the earth maintains between evaporation and precipitation is sustained to a considerable degree by the behavior of *life* on the planet.[11] That is, without the lush vegetation of the earth, the fragile balance between evaporation and precipitation upon which human life depends would not continue.

Today, states and capital collide and collude to jeopardize balances that are favorable to life. But the image of the planet returned to earth by *Apollo 8* also helps to foment a new ethos within that assemblage: a vast microassemblage in which farmers, professors, scientists, religious leaders, and indigenous peoples from several places on earth coalesce to protect the earth/planet from the ravages of global capital. These are not transformative forces. They may also be turned back as they seek to reshape elements in the global assemblage of capital, states, and religions. But, amid that risk, they do incorporate new energies and possibilities into old practices of sovereignty, territory, property, capital, mastery, nationhood, and faith.

Boundary Stones

Giorgio Agamben and the Field of Sovereignty

Steven DeCaroli

After Sovereignty

Jean Bodin's *Six Books of the Commonwealth,* published in 1576, contains perhaps the most consequential political injunction of the modern era: "We must now formulate a definition of sovereignty because no jurist or political philosopher has defined it, even though it is the chief point, and the one that needs most to be explained."[1] Since the mid-sixteenth century, the problem of sovereignty has been central to political theory. From Bodin to Hobbes to Rousseau, the principal questions of politics have evolved in relation to the singular challenge of providing, both in theoretical formulation and juridical practice, a legitimate foundation for increasingly secular forms of constitutional power. In this regard, Bodin's statement is crucial, not because it announces a new politics based on sovereign rule—sovereign political authority predates the modern era by centuries, and depending on how one ultimately defines it, certainly by millennia—but because, in this passage, sovereignty is presented for the first time as a question, a concept in need of a theory. Bodin compels the modern era to place sovereignty under examination, and it is not long before new theories of political legitimacy appear, collectively producing the rich climate of political experimentation for which the modern era is well known. Instead of treating sovereignty as a foregone socio-political fact, the moderns would come to see sovereignty as a problem, so much so that the question of politics becomes largely indistinguishable from the question of sovereign authority. It is, after all, less than a century after Bodin that Hobbes, stirred by a political optimism we no longer share, inaugurates the long project of grounding sovereign political authority in secular institutions. As a result of this broad shift in Western political discourse, political philosophy since Bodin has been burdened with the immense task, not only of formulating the mechanics of political order, but of justifying them—of giving legitimacy to both the right to rule and the duty to obey.

Today, however, even among the most sanguine liberals, optimism for the modern project has all but vanished. The secular faith that once energized modern thinkers to embrace Bodin's injunction has been replaced by a deeply instrumental and increasingly obscurantist politics. Unconvinced of the possibility of grounding the sovereign right to rule on rational principles alone, and more broadly desensitized by the increasingly cultural manifestations of capitalist production, post-industrial democracies, and most conspicuously the United States, have largely returned to the fundamentalisms of faith and nation in the implicit hope that Bodin's challenge can be placed neatly back into its bottle and we can all quietly return to the orderly naiveté of a politics before theory. For those of us who lament these tendencies, however, the question will not dissipate. Instead, it reappears in a much stronger iteration: if not sovereignty, then what? The challenge posed by this question lingers at the edge of our era's most radical confrontations with politics—both practical and theoretical—and invites us, not unlike Bodin four and a half centuries ago, to re-examine the ground of political authority. In this case, however, the task is not to justify sovereign power, but to conceive of a political community that does not presuppose it.

The work of Giorgio Agamben attempts to do just that, placing at its center the project of conceiving a community beyond the tradition of sovereignty. If we are to emerge from the modern era and formulate a theory of politics adequate to the contemporary conditions of life, as Agamben broadly suggests, the modern political project, with its patriotic narratives and exhausted antagonisms, must be altogether abandoned. "All representations of the originary political act as a contract or convention marking the passage from nature to the State in a discrete and definite way must be left wholly behind" (*HS*, 109). In place of the conventional narratives of socio-political genesis, Agamben installs a new political horizon—what he has called the "coming community." It is a project that involves not a reshuffling of terms, but a sustained awareness of the inseparability of politics and subjectivity. By abandoning the traditional juridical question "What legitimates power?"—and by following Michel Foucault in refusing to take sovereignty and the state as the standpoints from which to understand power relations—Agamben roots his analysis of politics in a critique of sovereign power's capacity, which is in fact an operational necessity, to produce (and reproduce) forms of subjectivity that consent to, and even defend, the conditions that make sovereignty, and the subordination it entails, possible. By situating politics squarely within an ontology of the subject and by refusing any absolute separation between political life and life-as-such, Agamben underscores the convergence of power and subjectivity that has, since the earliest appearance of the sovereign command, quietly materialized beneath the political mythologies sanctifying the "right to rule." It is, then, at the intersection of the juridical model of power (What legitimates sovereignty?) with the biopolitical model (What is the subject?) that Agamben's work resides. This project, which extends the work on biopower begun by Foucault, is vast and for this reason remains largely unfulfilled, but the questions it raises, particularly around those liberal forms of political legitimacy that continue to shape our political imaginary—concepts such as democracy, the general will, citizenship, the state, and even the well-meaning essentialism embedded in certain discussions of human rights—are worthy of our attention.

There is plenty of room for pressing Agamben to provide us with a more pragmatic, and thereby more convincing, account of the new politics he outlines. There is clearly a need for this, and eventually for a discussion of the coming community that moves us decidedly beyond analogies to tangible actions, but here I focus on what Agamben does succeed in providing, particularly in his most influential book to date, *Homo Sacer*. In its pages, Agamben assesses the theory and practice of sovereignty, tracing it across the modern era to the earliest days of Roman jurisprudence, revealing in this way the limits of sovereignty as a political first principle. The genealogy he traces opens the door for a critique of Western political discourse, thereby offering us an opportunity to identify areas where a new politics, liberated from the theoretical privilege of sovereignty, might focus its attention. In what follows, I offer a brief appendage to this project.

Much of Agamben's discussion of sovereignty turns on the figure of the banished individual. It is a provocative line of research, revealing not only how sovereignty manifests itself as a positive force, but also how its effects carry over to those who appear to be excluded from it. However, despite the depth of analysis and a careful explanation of the structural parallels between the exile and the sovereign, comparatively few pages are devoted to the actual transgressions of these banished individuals. We hear much about the judicial framework of banishment, its origins in the figure of the Roman *homo sacer*, its "excluded inclusiveness" with respect to the law, its evocative resemblance to the sovereign exception, but little about the specific actions that, for one reason or another, elicit banishment as a punitive response. This is somewhat surprising. Within the context of a project broadly concerned with alternatives to sovereign formations of power (i.e., to arrive at "a politics freed from every ban" [*HS*, 59]), there is potentially much to be gained by pursuing things further. It is true, of course, that Agamben refers us to "the person who goes into exile as a consequence of committing homicide" (*HS*, 110), and to the ancient figure of the *homo sacer*, whose transgressions expel him from both human and divine law, but the specific character of the transgressions made by this figure, while mentioned, are left largely unexamined. Left unaddressed is why these actions, and *these* actions in particular, call forth exceptional measures. Exactly what forms of subjectivity and their associated behaviors elicit non-traditional punitive responses from the state? Why, instead of conventional forms of punishment, do certain forms of political life warrant exile? I believe that in answering these questions, we not only add something to our understanding of what sovereignty is, but also to what it is not—that is to say, we come nearer to knowing what forms of political life constitute an incompatible counterpoint to sovereignty. If it is possible to arrive at a viable politics beyond sovereignty, these forms of political life may help show the way.

Answers to these questions promise not only to elucidate sovereignty by exposing what it fears most, but in doing so, should offer some indication of what the "coming politics" must overcome if, as Agamben maintains, "the concepts of *sovereignty* and of *constituent power*, which are at the core of our political tradition, have to be abandoned or, at least, to be thought all over again" (*HS*, 112). If the future of political community entails conceiving a politics without sovereignty, then perhaps, even more than for Bodin and his generation, our task today is to formulate an understanding of sovereignty precisely so that we can conceive of ways to think beyond it. Ironically then, and certainly for different reasons, Bodin's injunction has never been more urgent.

The Sovereign Field

A necessary condition for the possibility of banishment is a boundary—real or virtual, terrestrial or divine—outside of which one may be abandoned. It is not by coincidence that we see this same conceptual demand also appear in the modern definition of sovereignty, where the twin elements of political authority and a bounded territorial jurisdiction are united. The union of these two elements form a simple, yet entirely apt, definition of what sovereignty came to mean in early modern Europe, and of which most subsequent definitions are merely a variant: "supreme authority within a bounded territory." The connection between authority and territory is fundamental, and it is precisely on the basis of this relation that banishment is a possibility. Given this, instead of approaching the concept of sovereignty from the point of view of the "legitimatization of power" (i.e., the establishment of authority), I will do so from the standpoint of the "*extension* of power," or, more precisely, by examining the necessary, though conventionally underemphasized, bond uniting authority with territory.

While it is obvious that a claim to legal authority must entail reference to the reach of its application, ordinarily this aspect of authority has been treated as a secondary consideration. It is tempting to conclude that it is the obviousness, perhaps even the banality, of jurisdictional matters—that law *must* have a zone over which its power is legitimately exercised—that has drawn attention toward the more abstract considerations of how authority is justified. The preponderance of our modern concern has been with those non-arbitrary reasons—drawn from natural law, divine mandate, heredity, constitutional assemblies, or otherwise—that justify granting to a person or an office not merely coercive power but, as R. P. Wolff has put it, "the right to command and correlatively the right to be obeyed."[2] What we have been most often concerned with is the legitimacy that adheres to the rights vested in political authority, rather than with the necessary correlate of all conceivable definitions of sovereign power, namely, its jurisdiction: the territory, the bodies and the objects over which the right of command holds sway. However, despite the historical bias, the question of jurisdiction is, in fact, the more fundamental problematic for political thought because it directly addresses the mechanisms of inclusion that structure every political community. Consequently, the question most at issue is not "What is authority?" but rather, "What is the field of authority?"

The classic typology of authority, defined as power that is recognized as legitimate not only by those holding positions of privilege but also by subordinates, all too easily envisions authority as a power distinct from those who are affected by it, namely, those individuals whose recognition, support, and obedience constitute the legitimacy authority enjoys. For this reason, it is altogether more helpful to engage the question of authority from the site of this obedience itself, rather than from within the confines of a conceptual debate that seeks to ascertain what constituent authority *is* apart from, or prior to, the social environment in which it is exercised. The point here is that authority, of which sovereignty is the most extreme form, is a context-dependent concept, and to overlook this fact is to treat the authority embodied by sovereignty as a force existing independent of the field in which it is deployed. Instead, the social space in which sovereignty authority is exercised is ultimately the very condition by which power is made sovereign. As Michael Hardt and Antonio Negri have suggested, sovereignty is "two-sided." "Sovereign power is not an autonomous substance and it is never absolute but rather consists of a relationship between the rulers and ruled. . . . Those who obey are no less essential to the concept of the functioning of sovereignty than the one who commands."[3] Consequently, sovereign power ought not to be envisioned as a force from the outside, but rather as an integral part of the political field itself, inseparably linked to the ongoing process of legitimization. Sovereignty is the embeddedness of authority within a field of application—comprised of both a space and a multitude, a territory and a citizenry—and it is this *legitimized connection between authority and territory* that warrants further attention, because if politics is to be placed on a new footing it must do so by reformulating this relation.

With respect to the law, therefore, it is never enough to simply ask how the state extends its laws over a territory, for this presumes too quickly the primacy of the law with respect to jurisdiction and compels us to speak of the law as self-sufficient and entirely independent of the masses on whom it is imposed. Likewise, is it not enough to ask how states secure popular support, that is, how reasonable ideas are sold to a rational public, for here too the scenario assumes that the public arrives to give consent, and thereby legitimacy, to a form of power that precedes it. Instead, we find that territory (sovereign jurisdiction) comes *before* the law; that legality is an epiphenomenon of sovereignty; and that the primary work of sovereignty is not to impose the law, but to maintain a stable, coherent order within a territory such that the logic of a legal system, once created, will be capable of making statements that are juridical true. Here again, it is useful to understand sovereignty as two-sided; however, if one is not careful, even this formulation can easily slip from a co-constitutive relation, in which ruler and ruled arise in tandem, to a far too intentional scenario, in which rulers work outside the modes of social production to manufacture the subjects they desire. Quite the contrary. If sovereignty is truly a relational concept, those who rule participate in maintaining social stability, not by enforcing it from the outside, but by inhabiting it and—just like those over whom they rule—by recognizing themselves within it.

It is therefore essential to maintain a firm terminological distinction between the ruler and sovereignty. These terms must be neither collapsed nor treated as synonymous. They represent two distinct aspects of political life, the first referring to that person, assembly, or constitution invested with the authority to command within a given territory, the second referring to the field of application that comes prior to the rule of law and makes command possible by making obedience normal. Thus, as Maurizio Lazzarato has observed, "The fundamental political problem of modernity is not that of a single source of sovereign power [a ruler], but that of a multitude of forces that act and react amongst each other according to relations of command and obedience."[4] Consequently, every study of sovereignty that begins with an analysis of the ruler will remain inadequate, invariably producing a theory of the subject as a legal being. The conventional image of the sovereign ruler standing outside the law, perched above it, must therefore be dismissed as an inadequate political myth that preserves a misconceived Hobbesian political theology. Only by abandoning this notion of the sovereign set outside the law, only if we categorically refuse to pose the question of power from the vantage of the state, can we begin to grasp the complexities of biopolitics. The study of sovereignty must therefore begin with a study of those seemingly mundane forms of political life that are caught up in relations of power and self-recognition, rather than with the political logic of the state and its rulers. The conditions for obedience are, therefore, not legal, nor are they, temporally speaking, merely pre-legal. Rather, the stabilization of the sovereign field is an ongoing, immanent process that subtends all activity within a jurisdiction, ordering all of its social actors, including he who wears the crown, as well as those who envision themselves as oppositional.

In the early pages of *Homo Sacer*, Agamben quotes a well-known passage from Carl Schmitt's *Political Theology* that embodies this point. In it, Schmitt argues that the law can only exist under pre-given conditions that permit the source of its authority to go unquestioned. This, according to Schmitt, is the primary function of sovereignty. As a constituting power, sovereignty creates the ground upon which both the rule of law and those subject to the law are found to be entirely compatible. Sovereignty creates, or rather *is*, the condition in which something like juridical evidence becomes possible. Schmitt explains,

The exception appears in its absolute form when it is a question of creating a situation in which juridical rules can be valid. Every general rule demands a regular, everyday frame of life to which it can be factually applied. The rule requires a homogeneous medium. This factual regularity is not merely an "external presupposition" that the jurist can ignore; it belongs, rather, to the rule's immanent validity. There is no rule that is applicable to chaos. Order must be established for juridical order to make sense. A regular situation must be created, and sovereign is he who definitely decides if this situation is actually effective. All law is "situational law." The sovereign creates and guarantees the situation as a whole in its totality.[5]

That law cannot be applied to chaos is another way of stating that law is not the essential function of sovereignty. The work of sovereignty precedes the law, creating a regular "frame of life," which the law preserves and codifies but does not instantiate. Thus, the sovereign field precedes and enables the judicial decision. This decision—a legal decision that is readily obeyed—must have a territory to which it is applied. Not a neutral space, but a space that is capable of being obedient. Here, the anarchist maxim "If no one obeys, no one can rule" comes to mind, and its simple truth remains undeniable. Obedience comes before the law; it is the ground of the law and literally makes the law plausible. This is what Schmitt has in mind when he writes that there is no law applicable to chaos, and when in the course of this analysis, I speak of territory, or of jurisdiction, or of field, this fundamental preparedness is what I am referring to. All sovereign authority depends upon this condition of receptiveness in order to function. Among the questions to be asked, then, is how this "field of order" comes to appear as orderly? Why is the refusal to obey so rarely exercised? And how does the connection between administration and territory become so intimate that those bound by a jurisdiction and subject to the law's application find themselves absorbed into the scenarios of sovereignty in ways that are increasingly coherent and naturalized, thereby concealing the mechanisms of legitimatization that make possible the bond between sovereignty authority and its field?

And even in those cases that presumably exceed the law's application and appear to lie well beyond the sovereign field, that is, in various "states of exception" from the law, sovereign power still exerts its force, though perhaps in an impoverished sense. This is the case made by Agamben in *Homo Sacer*, which is worth our consideration because the bond between authority and territory must not be understood as a relation that is merely internal, or to use Agamben's language, *inclusive*. In fact, the political distinction between inside and outside, inclusion and exclusion, structures the basic logic of sovereignty itself, insofar as sovereignty maintains a boundary not between the legal and the illegal, both of which participate fully in the logic of legality, but between the legal and the non-legal, that is, between the lawful and the outlaw, between the citizen and the exile. Consequently, when the legitimacy of this boundary is challenged, when the edges of the sovereign field are made to appear arbitrary, the challenge is directed at the heart of sovereignty itself, and as we shall see, those actions that warrant banishment share the characteristic of having called into question the legitimacy of this boundary.

Ex-capere

Somewhat infamously, Agamben contends in the pages of *Homo Sacer* that the camp—be it refugee or concentration—is the paradigm of the present juridico-political order. Regarding the camp not as an historical anomaly but as the current condition of political life, Agamben argues that the extra-legal circumstances that the camp makes possible have been gradually extended to entire civil populations. In a short essay entitled "What Is a Camp?" Agamben writes, "*The camp is the space that opens up when the state of exception starts to become the rule.* In it, the state of exception, which was essentially a temporal suspension of the state of law, acquires a permanent spatial arrangement that, as such, remains constantly outside the normal state of law" (*MWE*, 38). The camp, it is argued, is the function not of law but of a state of exception in which the law is suspended; and it is because camps constitute this space of the exception that "everything is truly possible in them" (*MWE*, 39). Not unlike Hobbes's "state of nature," the camp represents extreme potentiality, the thoroughly unconditioned. However, unlike the state of nature, the camp is not completely without relation to the law, for it is the law—or more accurately, sovereign authority—that brings the camp into being, and it is in relation to the law that the camp is rendered exceptional. The ability of sovereignty to simultaneously generate both a "state of exception" and juridico-political order provides *Homo Sacer* with its central theme, and it is in reference to this double movement that Agamben concludes that the "exception" (*l'eccezione*) refers to what is "*taken outside* (*ex-capere*), and not simply excluded" (*HS*, 18).

Insofar as the camp's inhabitants have been stripped of every legal right and political status, their ontological condition is reduced to what Agamben refers to as "bare life" (*nuda vita*, in reference to the Greek *zoē*), a term he further refines by referencing the ancient Roman figure of the *homo sacer*. The *homo sacer*, one who can be killed without committing homicide, is not entirely synonymous with bare life, but rather represents bare life insofar as it is included within the political order. In other words, the inhabitants of the camp, those in exile, or those who have otherwise been removed from the proper jurisdiction of the law, are made *homo sacer* precisely because, despite being placed outside of the law and its protection, they retain a (extra-legal) relationship with the law by having been excluded from it. In the final chapter of *Homo Sacer*, Agamben characterizes the relation between bare life and *homo sacer* in reference to those who have been excluded from the law:

his entire existence has been reduced to a bare life stripped of every right by virtue of the fact that anyone can kill him without committing homicide; he can save himself only in perpetual flight or a foreign land. And yet he is in a continuous relationship with power that banished him precisely insofar as he is at every instant exposed to an unconditional threat of death. He is pure *zoē* [bare life], but his *zoē* is as such caught in the sovereign ban and must reckon with it at every moment. (*HS*, 183)

Reduced to this state, the occupants of the camp—unmediated by traditional forms of political belonging, ordinarily expressed in the form of rights—encounter juridico-political power from a condition of comprehensive political abandonment. The camp is, for Agamben, an absolute biopolitical space in which power is exercised not against juridical subjects but against biological bodies. It is, in effect, a space in which sovereignty exists but the law does not, a territory in which actions are neither legal nor illegal.

The life that resides within the state of exception, exemplified here by the camp but perhaps best seen in those who have been sent into exile, is, however, not a new historical formation. In contrast to Foucault, for whom biopower represents a historical shift in paradigm, Agamben maintains that the inclusion of bare life within the political order is absolutely ancient; what makes the current situation noteworthy is the degree to which the realm of bare life has come to coincide with politics proper. Sovereign power has always placed biological life at its center only now the modern state has made this explicit, rendering the distinction between the human and the citizen, between fact and right, all but indistinguishable. What is revealed in this conclusion, and what speaks most directly to the primacy of the sovereign field, is that law, together with the broad array of legal institutions that administer it, forms a secular canopy that both legitimates sovereign authority and obscures the ancient connection between sovereignty and bare life, or between authority and the pre-legal order of its jurisdictional territory. In the early pages of *Homo Sacer*, Agamben observes, "In this sense, biopolitics is at least as old as the sovereign exception. Placing biological life at the center of its calculations, the modern State therefore does nothing other than bring to light the secret tie uniting [sovereign] power and bare life, thereby reaffirming the bond . . . between modern power and the most immemorial of the *arcana imperii* [i.e., the Roman 'mysteries of state']" (*HS*, 6). Bare life, then, has in some sense always been what is at stake for politics and as such is inseparable from the exercise of sovereign power. "*It can even be said,*" Agamben concludes, "*that the production of a biopolitical body is the original activity of sovereign power*"

(*HS*, 6; emphasis in original). Or put somewhat differently, the bare life
that exists within the state, as the state's internal exception, constitutes the
field of obedience that enables the judicial machinery of the state to function. Bare life, then, the object of biopolitics, is precisely that which, within
the state, is made obedient prior to the law. When, on occasion, the contingency of this obedience is brought to light—for instance, in the case of
political anarchy, or in the event of natural, economic, or military crises—
sovereignty responds rapidly. To do otherwise would be to risk "bring[ing]
to light the secret tie uniting power with bare life"; that is, it would be to
risk revealing the concealed (naturalized) bond uniting authority with territory—which as we have seen, is constitutive of sovereignty itself.

Agamben argues correctly that the primary function of sovereign
power is not to establish the law but to determine that which exceeds the
law, arguing that the state of exception is more fundamental to sovereignty
than the law itself, if only because it is precisely within this semi-political
realm, into which the law cannot extend, that the obedience necessary
for sovereignty resides. Referencing Jean-Luc Nancy, Agamben addresses
this point, claiming that sovereignty is the "law beyond the law to which
we are abandoned" (*HS*, 59). Consequently, bare life, that which has been
excluded (banished) from the law, nevertheless "finds itself in the most intimate relation with sovereignty" (*HS*, 67), and it is ultimately this inclusive
relation between bare life and sovereignty, or, as I would add, between territory and authority, that "constitutes the original—if concealed—nucleus
of sovereign power" (*HS*, 6).

The exception marks the site at which the legal enters into relation
with the non-legal. By establishing a threshold between law and non-law
the exception effectively produces them both.[6] The sovereign exception is,
for both Schmitt and Agamben, the condition for the possibility of juridical order, for it is through the state of exception that sovereignty creates and
guarantees the order the law needs for its own validity. Agamben makes
this point in a commentary that refers us back to Schmitt: "The state of
exception is thus not the chaos that precedes order but rather the situation
that results from its suspension" (*HS*, 18)—when chaos ends, what remains
is the order before the law, a sovereignty unmediated by the law. This situation, which is neither chaos nor law, characterizes the state of exception,
and the form of life that corresponds to this state is bare life. The sovereign
decision, then, decides not the licit and the illicit but the originary inclu-

sion of the living within its field of order. And this decision "concerns neither a *quaestio iuris* nor a *quaestio facti*, but rather the very relation between law and fact" (*HS*, 26). This is of particular importance for, as I will argue in what follows, the sentence of banishment, the sanction which speaks most directly to the exclusionary relation (insofar as it is a literal exception, *ex-capere*, a "taking outside"), has been applied, in the most ancient of political settings, not to actions that break the law, the merely illicit, but to those activities that threaten *the relation between the law and its ground.*

But in order to understand the sentence of banishment and its special place in relation to constitutional sovereignty, it is first necessary to highlight a few aspects of Greek and Roman jurisprudence. For it is only after understanding Aristotle's use of banishment in the *Politics*, as well as the concept of *persona* in Roman law, that banishment, and the civil death this implies, becomes clear.

Gods Among Men

The practice of banishment is ancient. Explicit mention of the ban as a means of punishment dates back to at least the Hammurabic Code, where it is prescribed against incest, and the juridical history of classical Greece testifies to a long-standing familiarity with the practice.[7] Despite this, it comes as a surprise to find Aristotle, in book 3 of the *Politics*, speaking of banishment as an acceptable remedy, not for actions that threaten the peace of the state through criminal actions or violence, but for deeds, or rather, ways-of-being, that break no laws whatsoever. Aristotle speaks of banishment within the context of a discussion of a very curious political difficulty, namely, how the *polis* should deal with threats to its stability that are *legal*. The difficulty here is self-evident: how does one guard against something that threatens the state precisely by adhering to the laws and highest ideals of the state and its community? In the course of weighing the obvious difficulty of legislating against that which, on the one hand, is thoroughly obedient to the law, while, on the other, *in virtue of being the way it is*, it disturbs the stability of that law, Aristotle raises the subject of banishment:

If, however, there be some one person, or more than one, although not enough to make up the full complement of a state, whose virtue is so pre-eminent that the virtues or the political capacity of all the rest admit of no comparison with his or theirs, he or they can be no longer regarded as part of a state; for justice will not be done to the superior, if he is reckoned only as the equal of those who are so far inferior to him in virtue and in political capacity. Such a one may truly be deemed a God among men. Hence we see that legislation is necessarily concerned only with those who are equal in birth and in capacity; and that for men of pre-eminent virtue there is no law—they are themselves a law. Any would be ridiculous who attempted to make laws for them. . . . And for this reason democratic states have instituted ostracism; equality is above all things their aim, and therefore they ostracized and banished from the city for a time those who seemed to predominate too much through their wealth, or the number of their friends, or through any other political influence. (1284a, 4–22)[8]

It is a remarkable passage. Aristotle's testimony attests to the fact that the deepest concern of the *polis* is neither law nor justice, but the condition for the possibility of both. In both cases—in the efficient enforcement of law and in the evenhanded rendering of justice—a comparison among equals it required. Where this comparison is not possible, law and justice are also impossible, for "legislation is necessarily concerned only with those who are equal." Upon the appearance of a person whose virtues are so elevated that they "admit of no comparison," the state literally withdraws from them and they are no longer regarded as belonging to it. Equating the *polis* to a ship at sea, Aristotle adds that "mythology tells us that the Argonauts left Heracles behind for a similar reason; the ship Argo would not take him because she feared that he would have been too much for the rest of the crew" (1284a, 23–25).[9] Thus, the ban's entrance into Western political philosophy is by way of *an abandonment of the state from an individual*, rather than the expulsion of an individual from the state. This is essential, for only by viewing banishment from the vantage of the state's refusal to rule can we begin to understand the gravity of the threat posed to the state by those worthy of being banished.

As we have seen, the state maintains order not through law but through obedience. The law merely stands in to obscure the constant possibility that this obedience may at any moment collapse, rendering feeble even the most draconian statutes. The order of the state is only as robust as the order of obedience that embraces it. The biopolitical question, the question which for Agamben lies at the heart of politics, is therefore always a question of obedience and order, not law. Consequently, it is not those who break the rules of law that are banished from the *polis*; rather, it is those who wield political influence, those who "predominate too much," either directly or indirectly, that are ostracized. As the passage demonstrates, ostracism is not employed against those who break rules, but against those who, through monetary or social influence, threaten to alter the political order itself.

Continuing the discussion of banishment, Aristotle recounts the parable of Periander:

The story is that Periander, when the herald was sent to ask counsel of him, said nothing, but only cut off the tallest ears of corn till he had brought the field to a level. The herald did not know the meaning of the action, but came and reported what he had seen to Thrasybulus, who understood that he was to cut off the principal men in the state; and this is a policy not only expedient for tyrants or in practice confined to them, but equally necessary in oligarchies and democracies. Ostracism is a measure of the same kind, which acts by disabling and banishing the most prominent citizens. Great powers do the same to whole cities and nations, as the Athenians did to the Samians, Chians, and Lesbians; no sooner had they obtained a firm grasp of the empire, than they humbled their allies contrary to treaty; and the Persian king has repeatedly crushed the Medes, Babylonians, and other nations, when their spirit has been stirred by the recollection of their former greatness. (1284a, 29–1284b, 3)[10]

It is against the possibility of a different political future that banishment is marshaled, and it is within this same context that Hobbes tells us in chapter 18 of *Leviathan* that "the people of Athens, when they banished the most potent of their Commonwealth for ten years, thought they committed no injustice; and yet they never questioned what crime he had done, *but what hurt he would do.*"[11] Thus, even when no criminal action has taken place, and in the complete absence of malicious intent, the banished individual threatens to bring about, from the point of view of the current order, a destabilized future. The subversiveness of these individuals is therefore not achieved by breaking the law but by threatening to establish new ones, or more accurately, by threatening to become a law unto themselves. For these individuals, recognized by Aristotle as "gods among men," there is no law, for "they are themselves a law." In being-what-they-are, these individuals obtain autonomy and, most dangerously for the state, command admiration. It is this influence that is most threatening. They are models, exemplars of behavior, and consequently represent an alternative principle of order. It is a point I will return to.

We know from Aristotle, of course, that justice is possible only if proportionality is possible. In his remarks on banishment, the removal of the most successful and influential should be read as a means of achieving what the rules themselves cannot—namely, a proportional society. But one can push this reading further. It is not for the sake of being too wealthy or having too many friends that these figures are candidates for ostracism, rather it is because they play the game too well, follow the rules too cleverly, or with too much good fortune, that they call to attention the essential frailty of rules—their essential limitation when it comes to fair play and, ultimately, to justice—and thereby invite exile. And so, before ending his discussion, Aristotle draws the following, equally unanticipated, conclusion: "where there is an acknowledged superiority," he writes, "the argument in favor of ostracism is based upon a kind of political justice" (1284b, 15–17).[12] Justice, of course, can never exist independently of context—we know this, at the very least, from the writings of Hobbes—because justice and the proportionality it strives to maintain are inextricably associated with a "frame of life" that precedes justice. If it is true that the banishment of "influential" citizens is one means by which political justice is preserved, then we have in this passage one of the earliest, and certainly one of the most incisive, statements regarding the political utility of banishment. The state resorts to banishment when the social order within which one can decide on, or measure, the relative justness of an action is threatened by an influence that the law is powerless to regulate. Once again, it is not because these individuals are too wealthy or have too many friends that they are banished. It is because extraordinary amounts of wealth or friendship engender influences that threaten to *overwhelm* the law, not by breaking it, but by challenging the orderly ground upon which it rests and in reference to which it is capable of adjudicating. In these cases, when the everyday "frame of life" that holds chaos in check is threatened, the exercise of banishment serves the aims of justice, which is to say, the aims of order, for the ban is uniquely qualified to preserve order when the law no longer can.

Loss of *status*

Although important in the Greek context, it is in Rome that the most significant use of banishment occurs. Among the civil penalties of the Roman republic, exile was unquestionably among the most important, but in order to understand its significance we must first consider the basic political ideas upon which the concept was based and from which its punitive nature was derived. In 1901, A. H. J. Greenidge outlined the two prevailing ideas of the Greco-Roman world upon which the concept of *exilium* rested. The first was the principle that legal rights were the result of membership in a *civitas* and could not be derived from any other sources. Second, these rights were exclusively granted and honored by one *civitas* and, consequently, no one could hold citizenship simultaneously in two different states. Within the Roman context, the act of taking citizenship in a second state implied the automatic removal of citizenship in the first.[13] These two basic principles created the conditions necessary for the introduction of banishment, largely because both principles hinge on the concept of citizenship. But to properly understand the meaning and function of citizenship we must situate it in relation to another concept: *persona*.

Under ancient Roman law, *persona* referred to anyone or anything capable of bearing rights, and the technical term for the position of any individual regarded as a *persona* was *status*. In the Institutes of Justinian (535 C.E.), we have the definitive explication: "The *status* of a Roman citizen was composed of three elements: *libertatem, civitatem, familiam* [freedom, citizenship, and family]."[14] First, *status* entailed liberty. A *persona* was free and, unlike a slave, could bear rights. Secondly, *status* consisted of citizenship. For the Romans, the state was a privileged body separated from the rest of the world by the exclusive possession of certain public and private rights that were granted to its citizenry. It was an essential part of the *status* of a Roman citizens that they possess citizenship in the state, beyond which were the citizens of other states and the *barbari*. Finally, *status* involved membership in a family. In Rome, family ties were established not through blood but through a system of legal privileges that granted to the head of the family alone, usually the father, an independent will (*sui juris*). The head of the family held absolute authority over all other members through the exercise of *patria potestas*, and since persons under the power of another could not hold property, the father was sole property owner of the family and, accordingly, what the son acquired was de facto acquired for the father. Moreover, the son himself was a real possession of the father and in some cases could be killed by the father without it being considered legal homicide.

The sum of all legal capacities accorded to a *persona*, the possession of which gave one *status*, was collectively indicated by a term that had once referred to the mention made of the citizen in the registers of the census, *caput*, meaning head. These legal capacities flowed from the three basic elements of *status* mentioned above, and if a citizen ever changed his *status*, that is, if he lost one of these three elements of *status* through the loss of liberty, the loss of civic rights, or a change in family position, he underwent what was termed a *capitis deminutio* (i.e., loss of *caput* or *status*). As we learn from the Institutes, *capitis deminutio* took three forms—greater, middle, or lesser—depending on which of the three elements of *status* was primarily affected. Thus, the three elements of full Roman *status* were not permanent, and it was quite possible for a person to undergo significant changes in one or all of these elements.

Chapter 16 of the Institutes directly addresses the manner in which a change in *status* was brought about:

The *capitis deminutio* is a change of *status*, which may happen in three ways: for it may be the greatest *capitis deminutio*, or the less, also called the middle, or the least. 1. The greater *capitis deminutio* is, when a man loses both his citizenship and his liberty; as they do who by a terrible sentence are made "the slaves of punishment;" and freedmen, condemned to slavery for ingratitude towards their patrons; and all those who suffer themselves to be sold in order to share the price obtained. 2. The less or middle *capitis deminutio* is, when a man loses his citizenship, but retains his liberty; as is the case when anyone is forbidden the use of fire and water, or is deported to an island. 3. The least *capitis deminutio* is when a person's *status* is changed without forfeiture either of citizenship or liberty; as when a person *sui juris* becomes subject to the power of another, or a person *alieni juris* becomes independent.[15]

In the middle variant of *capitis deminutio*, as well as in the greater, the loss of citizenship also entailed the loss of position within the family, because only citizens held the right of belonging to a family. However, unlike the greater form of *capitis deminutio*, in which liberty is lost, in the middle variant, liberty is preserved but the person who undergoes this change of *status* loses citizenship and thus, before the eyes of the Roman judiciary, is made a stranger (*peregrinus fit*).

But making a stranger of a citizen did not proceed directly, as we learn from an important passage in Cicero's oration Pro Domo. Here we are told that it was an established maxim of Roman law that no one could cease to be a citizen against his will: "Has not this principle been handed down to us from our ancestors, that no Roman citizen can be deprived of his liberty, or of his *status* as a citizen, unless he himself consents to such a thing?"[16] Consequently, the loss of citizenship required by the middle form of *capitis deminutio* could not be brought about by force, because, as Cicero testifies, the state was prohibited from compelling anyone to abandon their citizenship against their will. Since the middle variant of *capitis deminutio* did not entail a loss of liberty (free will), the question arises as to how the loss of civil *status*, and the banishment entailed in it, was enforced.

The answer to this question is telling. Those condemned to banishment—those who lost citizenship without loss of freedom—were *indirectly* compelled to abandon citizenship by their own choosing. The means used to bring this about can be found in the passage from the Institutes quoted above, and specifically in the reference to being "forbidden the use of fire and water." The reference is to an ancient *interdictio* prohibiting Roman citizens from providing the sentenced person with the necessities of life.[17] Unable to access food, fire, and shelter, the sentenced person was driven *to withdraw himself* from the city—by his own volition. In Pro Domo we are given the following explanation:

The Roman citizens who left Rome and went to the Latin colonies could not be made Latins, unless they themselves promoted such a change, and gave in their names themselves. Those men who had been condemned on a capital charge, did not lose their rights as citizens of this city before they were received as citizens of that other city to which they had gone for the sake of changing their abode. Our ancestors took care that they should do so, not by taking away their rights of citizenship, but only their house, and by interdicting them from fire and water within the city [*Id autem ut esset faciendum, non ademptione civitatis, sed tecti, et aquae et ignis interdictione faciebant*].[18]

Accordingly, those who were condemned in this manner did not lose their citizenship until they were admitted as citizens of another state, in accordance with the legal principle that forbade Roman citizens from holding dual citizenship. Compelling an individual to find refuge in another state was therefore accomplished, not by depriving them of their civil standing within Rome, but by literally forbidding them access to the basic necessities of life. The "forbidding of fire and water" (*aquae et ignis interdictio*) thus served as an indirect means of inflicting a sentence of banishment. While exile (*exsilium*) was not explicitly included in the *interdictio*, and the person was technically free to remain within the city and submit to the penalty of being a domestic outcast, in effect the *interdictio* was banishment. The individual was placed outside of the law even within the confines of the state—removed from the order and protection of the sovereign field even while residing within the territory of Rome. The origin of exile under the *interdictio* was, therefore, *not* the physical removal of the individual from the state, but the abandonment of the individual to the dire consequences of the law's complete withdrawal.

By simply refusing to rule, the Roman judiciary brought about the desired end without ever commanding it. Indeed, in the case of those subject to the *interdictio*, as opposed to the forceful banishment to, for instance, an island, it was the individuals themselves who bore ultimate responsibility for their own exile. The law, by refusing to rule over certain individuals, by deciding not to include them within the sovereign field, effectively placed the fate of each individual into his or her own hands. As was the case for Aristotle, banishment is here the consequence of a refusal to rule, a withdrawal of the state from an individual.[19]

Civil Death

Speaking of the punitive effects of exile, and specifically of deportation, the Institutes equates banishment with civil death (i.e., the fate of those no longer living under law): "If a man, convicted of some crime is deported to an island, he loses the rights of a Roman citizen; whence it follows, that the children of the person thus removed from the list of Roman citizens cease to be under his power, exactly as if he were dead."[20] And in modern times, exile remains equated with civil death, for example, in Cesare Beccaria's *On Crimes and Punishments* (1775):

> He who disturbs the public tranquility, who does not obey the laws, who violates the conditions on which men mutually support and defend each other, ought to be excluded from society, that is, banished. . . . The whole should be forfeited, when the law which ordains banishment declares, at the same time, that all connections or relations between the society and the criminal are annihilated. In this case the citizen dies; the man only remains, and, with respect to a political body, the death of the *citizen* should have the same consequences with the death of the *man*.[21]

The importance of these passages rests in the parallel that is made between death and exile—a theme that can be found throughout the history of the ban. From the vantage of the state, whose concern is with political order, not justice, the civil death brought on by exile is as effective as bodily death. The death of the citizen leaves standing "the man only," a condition that draws us back to Agamben's discussion of biopolitics.

Because *only* citizenship is removed, the life of the person that is left corresponds neatly with Agamben's onto-political category of bare life. Whereas the removal of liberty requires either incarceration or bondage, and consequently an intensification of the relation between the individual and the state, the loss of citizenship alone does just the opposite. As Beccaria writes, far from being intensified, in the case of civil death "all connections or relations between the society and the criminal are annihilated." When liberty is lost through incarceration or bondage, the person remains within the sovereign field insofar as the law continues to apply. In the case of the exile, however, freedom is preserved precisely because the law ceases to apply. For Agamben, in such cases, "*the rule applies to the exception in no longer applying, in withdrawing from it*" (*HS*, 18; emphasis in original). And the life which remains—stripped of citizenship, deprived of the barest necessities of "fire and water," and abandoned to foreignness even within the heart of the state—is bare life, a life for which the withdrawal of the law is on the one hand deeply punitive, on the other hand full of potential.

The relation between banishment and death, seen clearly in the *homo sacer* (one who can be killed without committing homicide), is established not only with respect to the *aquae et ignis interdictio*, in which the public's complicity in withholding the necessities of life is a de facto sentence of death—either real or civil—but also appears in a more direct manner. In a passage from book 38 of the *Roman History* of Cassius Dio, and in reference to Cicero's own banishment, the logical conclusion of those who are no longer within the law is made clear: "Against Cicero himself a decree of exile was passed, and he was forbidden to tarry in Sicily; for he was banished five hundred miles from Rome, and it was further proclaimed that if he should ever appear within those limits, both he and those who harboured him might be slain with impunity."[22] And in Hobbes, echoing ancient jurisprudence, wherein one who threatens sovereign power is punished not by a penalty of death carried out by the formalities of state but by exposure to life unconditioned by law, chapter 18 of *Leviathan* reads,

because the major part hath by consenting voices declared a sovereign, he that dissented must now consent with the rest; that is, be contented to avow all the actions he shall do, or else justly be destroyed by the rest. . . . whether he be of the congregation or not, and whether his consent be asked or not, he must either submit to their decrees or be left in the condition of war he was in before; wherein he might without injustice be destroyed by any man whatsoever.[23]

In this early modern example we find sovereignty protected by a targeted suspension of law, permitting any citizen to exercise the sovereign right to kill with impunity against those who would challenge sovereign power. The "condition of war" in which those who refuse to consent to sovereign power find themselves parallels the abandonment of those who, like Cicero, find themselves in exile.

In a similar fashion, in Jean Bodin's *On Sovereignty* (1583), we are told that, according to Roman civil law, "anyone who assumed the authority reserved to the sovereign merited death,"[24] and that in response to such an act the Roman Lex Valeria, drafted at the insistence of Publius Valerius, "permitted homicide if one could make out a reasonable case for supposing that the dead man had indeed *aspired* to sovereign power," arguing, "it was better to have to resort to violence than to risk the destruction of both law and government in an anxiety to maintain the rule of law."[25] With striking clarity, Bodin recognizes within Roman jurisprudence what is true of all manifestations of sovereign power, namely, the suspension of the law for the sake of order. When placed in crisis, either by dissent, violence, or even by those who possess too much influence, sovereign power responds with the law's suspension, because what is at stake, what is always at stake but remains hidden until moments of crisis, is the contingent connection that binds the sovereign right to rule and make laws, with the territory over which it exerts its power and on whose obedience it depends. When this "frame of life" is disrupted, be it by regicide or public dissent, or by economic instability or strong social influence, sovereignty risks losing its power precisely because the legitimacy of the bond between authority and territory risks being undone. Whenever this bond is placed in doubt, the law will be suspended, either in whole or in part.

Those caught in this suspension, those who find their lives conditioned by the law's withdrawal, are, Agamben observes, not "simply set outside the law and made indifferent to it but rather [are] abandoned by it, that is, exposed and threatened on the threshold in which life and law, outside and inside, become indistinguishable" (*HS*, 28). Given the importance of this threshold between the inside and the outside, that is, the boundary necessary for the possibility of both banishment and sovereign rule, it is certainly no coincidence that among the most ancient prohibitions associated with banishment we find a prohibition against the moving of boundary stones. Before concluding, then, it will be instructive to briefly consider the role boundary stones played in the ancient context.

Boundary Stones

At the outset of this chapter it was stated that sovereignty requires a boundary. The boundary structures political relationships both for that within the sovereign field and for that which lies beyond it. It has also been argued that when the legitimacy of this boundary is challenged, when the edges of the sovereign field are made to appear arbitrary, sovereignty responds with banishment. It should not surprise us, then, to find that within ancient sources the displacement of boundary markers is included among the few original infractions that warrant exile. But the moving of boundary markers is not to be mistaken for theft of property. If this were the case, more obvious forms of property crimes would also be punishable by banishment. They are not. Instead, the moving of boundaries represents a very literal disruption of the relation between authority and territory—a point made clear when we understand the role these stones played in the very earliest narratives of the founding of Rome.[26]

In book 1 of *History of Rome*, Livy explains that at the founding of Rome on its seven hills, the city was surrounded with a mound and wall. In this way, he writes, the *pomoerium* was extended. Investigating the etymological origin of this term, Livy explains its reference to, "the space which the Etruscans of old, when founding their cities, consecrated in accordance with auguries and marked off by boundary stones at intervals on each side." He continues,

The part where the wall was to be carried, was to be kept vacant so that no buildings might connect with the wall on the inside, and on the outside some ground might remain virgin soil untouched by cultivation. This space, which it was forbidden either to build upon or to plough, and which could not be said to be behind the wall any more than the wall could be said to be behind it, the Romans called the *pomoerium*. As the city grew, these sacred boundary stones were always moved forward as far as the walls were advanced.[27]

According to Livy, the *pomoerium* signified a line running by the walls of a city but did not consist of the actual walls or fortifications themselves.[28] It was a symbolical wall, and the path of the *pomoerium* was marked by *termini*, or boundary stones, which served to demarcate the limit, that is, the *limen*, within which all things were under the authority of Rome and an object of Roman law (in effect, the sovereign field).[29] *Termini* also marked the boundaries of a property, and the owner of a property might use *termini* to divide his property for his children. In either case, there was a sacred quality to the stones and the *pomoerium* they traced, and it is for this reason that their disruption is catalogued among crimes punishable by banishment, *eliminium*, literally to take beyond the *limen*.[30]

In *Homo Sacer*, Agamben refers to Roman boundaries only briefly—one of the few instances where he mentions deeds that warrant the imposition of the ban:

> The crimes that, according to the original sources, merit *sacratio* (such as *terminum exarare*, the cancellation of borders; *verberatio parentis*, the violence of the son against the parent; or the swindling of a client by a counsel) do not, therefore, have the character of a transgression of a rule that is then followed by the appropriate sanction. They constitute instead the originary exception in which human life [bare life] is included in the political order in being exposed to an unconditional capacity to be killed. (*HS*, 85)[31]

Along with the breach of duty resulting from the relation between patron and client and the maltreatment of a parent by a child, the ploughing up or displacement of a boundary stone constituted a capital offence punishable by the withdrawal of the law's protection. Once again we find banishment pronounced, not against those who have broken the law, but against those who upset the order upon which the law is founded.

Exemplars

As we have seen, exile is far from a simple consequence of criminality. As Agamben correctly observes, what is at stake in the ban is not the application of the law to a crime, the determination of the illicit from the licit, but the ground (*solum*) of sovereign rule. What shows the ban to be "more ancient" than the law is its concern, not with the application of justice (the judicious exercise of law), but with the constituting authority of sovereignty, the ground upon which something like justice can appear and remain plausible.

Banishment, far from being mere punishment for a crime, is enacted when an individual life is deemed virulent to a community, when a life is understood to be *bane*ful. Banishment is primarily a response not to an unlawful action and its agent, but to a broad-reaching conceptual threat, to the very conceivability of establishing a *new* law.[32] An act that is merely criminal, no matter how despicable, is thoroughly acceptable to the law; it can be accommodated by the law and mitigated by punishment. The threat, to which the ban most typically responds, however, is not of this nature, for the ban, by expelling the body, also forfeits the law's claim over that body. If we refer back to Schmitt, what the ban responds to is not the breaking of a law but the threatening of order, be that through an excess of friends or wealth, as in Aristotle; or by disturbing "the public tranquility," as in Beccaria; or by threatening the life of the ruler directly; or even by displacing boundary stones that mark the limits of sovereign power. In each case, it is Schmitt's "regular, everyday frame of life" that is at risk. When this primary coherence is threatened, when it is challenged either by another ordering principle seeking to replace it, or more commonly, and which amounts to much the same thing, when sovereign authority risks being exposed as arbitrary, there appears a response that analytically cannot be the same as the punitive response that follows the breaking of a law. This response is the ban—a state action for which it is not at all clear, nor can it be clear, whether it is punishment or an escape from punishment.

It is for precisely this reason that we find in Cicero a discussion concerning whether exile is to be regarded as a release from punishment or a punishment in its own right.[33] In more modern times, we find this point referenced in *Leviathan*:

Exile (banishment) is when a man is for a crime condemned to depart out of the dominion of the Commonwealth, or out of a certain part thereof, and during a prefixed time, or for ever, not to return into it; and seemeth not in its own nature, without other circumstances, to be a punishment, but rather an escape, or a public commandment to avoid punishment by flight. And Cicero says there was never any such punishment ordained in the city of Rome; but calls it a refuge of men in danger.[34]

In *Homo Sacer*, Agamben likewise refers to the ambiguity of banishment as a form of punishment. He remarks, "the age-old discussion in juridical historiography between those who conceive exile to be a punishment and those who instead understand it to be a right and a refuge . . . has its roots in this ambiguity of the sovereign ban" (*HS*, 110). In each case, it is because banishment is not an act of law, and therefore, is outside the judicial logic of crime and punishment, that the ambiguity of exile appears. Life in exile is dire because the law is absent. The exposure to threats without the possibility of redress—no longer being an object for justice—compels the exile to seek shelter under the jurisdiction of another state. Yet life released from the law, despite the civil death this implies, is also, potentially, and in an extreme manner, a kind of liberty—namely, the potential ground of a new law, or more provocatively, the potential to be a law unto oneself.[35]

This, of course, leads us back to Aristotle. What the ban properly responds to is not that which perpetrates a crime but that which has influence. The ban responds not to the criminal but to "those who seemed to predominate too much," those whose paradigmatic presence is potentially an alternative to the law and therefore threatens the sovereignty of the law itself—something that obligates not a punishment but a forgetting. The ban is that penalty reserved not for a deed, but rather for a way-of-life whose threat is driven by the capacity to be a model (example) for a new system of order, thereby showing the current order to be violable. When, early in *Homo Sacer*, Agamben argues that "exception and example are correlative concepts that are ultimately indistinguishable and that come into play every time the very sense of the belonging and commonality of individuals is to be defined" (*HS*, 22), it is arguably this life-worthy-of-being-banned, and its paradigmatic character, that he has in mind. The banished individual (just as in the case of banned books or political parties) threatens the state by standing as an alternative to it, and in doing so places the entire logic of law into question. The example is forceful in a way the law is not, for exemplary individuals normalize a community without commanding that this normalization take place. The order produced by law depends on the obedience of the citizenry over which it is applied, and it is the example, for better or worse, that makes this obedience both plausible and possible. Consequently, when there appears within the sovereign field an individual whose influence becomes too great, that is, whose exemplarity becomes too persuasive, the state is compelled to respond, because not doing so would risk exposing the contingency of its own influence. The work of nationalism and patriotism are the most obvious instances of the state's attempt to shore up its own exemplarity, and it is no coincidence that in both these cases, the expulsion of foreigners and foreign influences is common—as is the strengthening of the boundaries that define the sovereign field.

When Aristotle speaks of those "gods among men" who are the targets of banishment, their presence within a sovereign territory is disturbing precisely because they upset the givenness of obedience. Aristotle claims that "gods among men" are "themselves a law," and it is in these figures, and these alone, that sovereignty finds its most potent foe. It is not those who break the law, but those who deny the legitimacy of its reach, that is, *the legitimacy of its field*, that represent a genuine alternative to the politics of sovereignty. Once again Aristotle provides insight:

Again, superiority is a cause of revolution when one or more persons have a power which is too much for the state and the power of the government; this is a condition of affairs out of which there arises a monarchy, or a family oligarchy. And therefore, in some places, as at Athens and Argos, they have recourse to ostracism. But how much better to provide from the first that there should be no such preeminent individuals instead of letting them come into existence and then finding a remedy. (1302b, 15–21)[36]

The management of obedience has always been the primary task of sovereignty, and it is in the disruption of this obedience that an alternative to sovereignty appears: not a disruption that leads to a new order and a new obedience upon which a new set of laws are erected, but a disruption that remains open. The task for a politics beyond sovereignty, a difficult and perhaps ultimately impossible task, is to realize a community of those who, by consensus or custom, are laws unto themselves—exemplars or exiles. This vision has, of course, often been ruled out as a political impossibility, but if a community beyond sovereignty is to be realized, this issue must be addressed. The ways-of-life subject to banishment suggest a place to begin.[37]

Whatever Politics

Jenny Edkins

In the opening pages of *The Coming Community*, first published in 1990, Giorgio Agamben sets out his notion of "whatever being" as the foundation of a "coming politics," the characteristics of which he outlines in the concluding section of the same book. This theme is taken up in his later writings, particularly the *Homo Sacer* tetralogy,[1] though in the subsequent work, and in his more recent commentaries on contemporary politics,[2] it is eclipsed for many readers by his concern with the diagnosis of sovereign power and biopolitics. It is Agamben's analysis of sovereignty, bare life, and the state of exception that has dominated the at times very critical uptake of his work in politics and international politics so far.[3] His analysis of the camp as the *nomos* of contemporary political life has proved very fruitful, as has his discussion of the state of exception, but his overall prognosis is taken by many to be a pessimistic one. In the context of the spread of the zone of indistinction and the reduction of politics to biopolitics, there seems to be no space left for political action: "politics today seems to be passing through a lasting eclipse" (*HS*, 4).

However, the pessimistic conclusion overlooks a significant facet of Agamben's work, where he seeks to propose an alternative to, and indeed a contestation of, sovereign biopolitics. In his review of *The State of Exception*,

Antonio Negri argues that there are indeed "two Agambens," one recognising and denouncing the state of exception, the other traversing it "with a feverish utopian anxiety" and grasping "its internal antagonism."[4] Stefano Franchi argues that the positive side of Agamben's work has received little attention in politics because of a "double reduction": first, his work has been seen as an investigation of contemporary political conditions, and in particular forms of governance; second, the spotlight has been on his *diagnosis* of sovereignty.[5] This rather overstates the case, however: several writers in international politics at least have acknowledged Agamben's positive move.[6] Others have recognised it but are uncomfortable with it: according to R. B. J. Walker, Agamben wants "to escape from the problem of sovereignty as fast as possible."[7] William Connolly emphasises the messiness of biocultural life and argues that the form of tight logical analysis that Agamben adopts is what leads to the eschatological move with which he ends.[8]

In this chapter I elucidate the way in which Agamben's challenge to a rethinking of politics goes beyond his analysis of the camp and exceptionalism to a thinking of *form-of-life*, in other words beyond a consideration of sovereignty and the sovereign ban to a consideration of subjecthood and ways of being other than those set up or set out by sovereign politics. One of the values of Agamben's discussions is the way in which politics is considered in terms of the subjectivities as well as the practices of power that it entails. It is this aspect that, for me, makes his work so interesting: it traverses the territory between sovereignty and subjectivity in ways that are thought-provoking and useful. As in Foucault's thinking,[9] for Agamben, forms of power are not merely constraining but productive, with specific forms of control or governance entailing particular forms of life. He calls for a rethinking of political categories in light of the contemporary relation "between sovereign power and naked life" (*MWE*, x).

Homo Sacer is intended to comprise four volumes in total. In an interview in *Süddeutsche Zeitung* on April 6, 2004, Agamben commented:

The last and most interesting for me will not be dedicated to an historical discussion. I would like to work on the concepts of forms-of-life and lifestyles. What I call a form-of-life is a life that can never be separated from its form, a life in which it is never possible to separate something such as bare life. . . . What an archaeology could be, whose object is a form-of-life, that is to say an immediate life experience, this is not easy to say.[10]

In the present chapter, I trace this element as it emerges in Agamben's work to date. Agamben offers a provocative analysis of ways in which being and politics might be rethought in conditions where the sovereign biopolitical machine has produced life as bare and has removed the possibility of politics. He argues for a community of whatever being, being such as it is, without identities, as the foundation for a coming politics. His concern with forms of life and their production is developed first through discussions of the biopolitical machine of sovereignty, which produces the figure of *homo sacer* through a distinction drawn between politically qualified life and bare or naked life, and the life of the *Muselmann* in the camps, where the distinction is between the human and the inhuman. It is elaborated further in his consideration of the anthropological machine that produces the life of man, as opposed to animal life. His concern throughout is with stopping or interrupting the machine. He proposes that *form-of-life* or whatever being, being such as it is, in itself, would evade capture by either machine; ironically, *form-of-life* is closely related to the very form of life, bare life, produced by the machine, which thus, it appears, contains the seeds of its own destruction.

It remains unclear to what extent Agamben is advocating the refusal of all distinctions between forms of life; although he seems to be moving in that direction, disturbing remnants of an anthropomorphism persist. He does not in any case take more widely into consideration other forms of being; his anthropogenic machine is confined in its operation to the man/animal distinction. Agamben's work points towards a coming politics in which ontologies of potentiality and actuality are rethought alongside a form of being together of whatever singularities that involves no form of belonging other than being thus. I argue that this entails a refusal of distinctions between forms of life, including in particular, in contemporary political circumstances, those between the human and the non-human, and, ironically, an embracing of the very indistinctions that sovereignty imposes in order to function.

Whether Agamben's work calls for an overarching eschatological move of redemption, or a patient politics that moves step by step within the constraints of existing power, is also debatable. Despite his emphasis on a community of beings that share no identity and no political project, he continues to see community in terms of a *coming together* of whatever singularities in some form, in contrast to the *being-together* proposed by Jean-Luc Nancy.[11] This demonstration of being in common, he argues, would be something that sovereignty could not tolerate.[12] Whether this could or would provide an effective, practical political action in response to the sovereign machine, and what form it might take, remains in doubt. I argue, alongside Nancy and Jacques Derrida, that such practices are in any case already taking place, in the here and now.[13] Sovereign distinctions do not hold; to refuse them, and to demonstrate being in common, is not to make a new move but only, yet most importantly, to embrace that insight and to call sovereignty's bluff.

Whatever Singularity

In *The Coming Community* Agamben writes: "The coming being is *whatever* being" (*CC*, 1; my emphasis). Here "whatever" is "that which is neither particular nor general, individual nor generic" (*CC*, 107). Whatever being is being *such as it is*, with all its properties. In other words, to use terms that occur later in Agamben's writings, it is immaterial whether whatever being is human or inhuman, politically qualified or excluded. But there is more to it than that. Whatever being is "reclaimed" or "freed" (*CC*, 1) from the dilemma of the universal and the particular; the question of its belonging or not to a class or set becomes irrelevant, as do the paradoxes of belonging (*CC*, 9). Instead, whatever being or being-such "which remains constantly hidden in the condition of belonging" to the nation, to humanity, to a class, "comes to light" as such (*CC*, 2). Moreover, "the singularity exposed as such is . . . loveable" (*CC*, 2). Agamben elaborates: "Love is never directed toward this or that property of the loved one (being blond, being small, being tender, being lame), but neither does it neglect the properties in favour of an insipid generality (universal love): The lover wants the loved one *with all of its predicates*, its being such as it is" (*CC*, 2).[14] Whatever being or whatever singularity implies desire, a desire of "the *as* only insofar as it is *such*" (*CC*, 2).

The question that then arises for Agamben is: what form of politics could be conceived that would provide for whatever being, for being *such as it is*, or, in other words, "what could be the politics of whatever singularity?" (*CC*, 85). Whatever being is "a being whose community is mediated not by any condition of belonging . . . nor by the simple absence of conditions . . . but by belonging itself" (*CC*, 85). The community of whatever singularities is not based on a sharing of properties ("being red, being Italian, being communist"), but neither is it an absence of such shared

properties, "a negative community" (*CC*, 85). It is a community of singularities who share nothing more than their singularity, their being-such or
their "whatever-ness" as such.

The coming politics, as a politics of whatever being, is not then the
same as a politics of social movements or an identity politics; it is not
"a simple affirmation of the social in opposition to the state" (*CC*, 86).
According to Agamben, it seems that social movements either share a call
for the recognition of particular claims or demands (the environmental
movement, the anti-Apartheid movement), or are formed explicitly on the
basis of a claim to shared identity (feminist, gay, black). Whatever singularities cannot form a social movement of this type because "they do not
possess any identity to vindicate or any bond of belonging for which to
seek recognition" (*CC*, 86). There is considerable discussion in the literature as to whether social movements or identity politics do in practice
require or imply such forms of belonging, or to what extent they entail,
rather, an articulation of a form of counter-hegemony or political frontier for temporary strategic political purposes.[15] There is significant debate
about the implications for practices of inclusion and exclusion that are
entailed. However, Agamben's more important point here seems to be the
larger one that states "can recognise any claim for identity . . . in the final
instance" (*CC*, 86). Such a claim is a demand for inclusion in or recognition by the state, not a claim that contests or disrupts the notions of inclusion and exclusion upon which sovereign power depends.[16]

The state has to have a form of belonging that affirms an identity,
and it may be that any identity, even a temporary strategic one, will do;
indeed, perhaps even an identity as human. What sovereign power "cannot
tolerate" is "that humans co-belong without any representable condition
of belonging," or "that singularities form a community without affirming
an identity" (*CC*, 86). In other words, "the possibility of the *whatever* itself
being taken up without an identity is a threat the state cannot come to
terms with" (*CC*, 86).

Bare Life

The reasons why this might be the case are elaborated in *Homo Sacer*,
which discusses how the sovereign state, and indeed sovereign power in
any form, operates through the drawing of distinctions between forms of

life. In contradistinction to Michel Foucault's contention that biopolitics emerged in the eighteenth century, with "the emergence of the problem of population,"[17] as a form of governance distinct from sovereignty, Agamben argues that *"the production of a biopolitical body is the originary activity of sovereign power"* (*HS*, 6).[18] In other words, "biopolitics is at least as old as the sovereign exception" (*HS*, 6).

The "protagonist" of the book is bare life, the form of subjectivity or personhood produced by, and captured in, sovereign power (*HS*, 8). The basic argument is well rehearsed by now in diverse contexts, including a number of writings in international politics.[19] Sovereign power, since its inception, has operated through the distinction of bare life (*zoē*), the life of the home (*oikos*), and politically qualified life (*bios*), the life of the public sphere (*polis*).[20] The structure of the sovereign ban,[21] or the state of exception, is such that bare life is included in the sovereign sphere precisely through its exclusion from it. The life set outside the law is nevertheless subject to and of the law through the very (legal) process of the setting outside of that life. Bare life in such a state of inclusive exclusion is described as *homo sacer*, a form of life that can be killed without accusations of homicide but that cannot be sacrificed.[22] This life excluded from the *polis* initially inhabits zones of indistinction between fact and law, zones such as the Nazi concentration camp; later such zones of indistinction come to extend beyond the camp. At this point, the exception becomes the norm and all life becomes bare life; life under the sway of sovereign power in the contemporary world is no longer politically qualified. Crucial to the whole process, and to its apparent unassailability, is the way in which bare life or *homo sacer* is both the object of sovereign power and the subject of democratic attempts to hold that power to account, first through citizens' rights and democratic accountability, then through human rights and humanitarianism. This means that humanitarianism and sovereignty, to pick on one pairing as an example, share a "secret solidarity": "Humanitarian organisations can only grasp human life in the figure of bare or sacred life, and therefore, despite themselves, maintain a secret solidarity with the very powers they ought to fight" (*HS*, 133). Both sovereign power and that which presents itself as opposed to it take bare life as their object or subject.

At this point, it becomes possible to see why a coming politics, if it is to be other than a sovereign politics, cannot be a form of identity or social movement politics. Such politics rely on the drawing of lines or the making of distinctions similar to those drawn by sovereign power. As such, they form part of the same logic, a logic of sovereignty that separates this and that according to their supposedly distinct qualities. Sovereign power is happy to negotiate the boundaries of the distinctions that it makes; what it could not tolerate would be the refusal to make any distinctions of this sort.[23]

Not only does sovereign power rely from the start on the separation between *zoē* and *bios*, but the structure of this separation reflects and subsumes important logics. It is the logical structure of sovereignty that must be delineated, Agamben claims (*HS*, 67). The paradox of sovereignty appears clearly in the attempts to distinguish constituting power (that founds sovereignty) and constituted power (that exists when sovereignty is in place).[24] Agamben argues that "this unresolved dialectic between constituted power and constituting power opens the way for a new articulation of the relation between potentiality and actuality" (*HS*, 44). What is more, he insists that "until a new and coherent ontology of potentiality . . . has replaced the ontology founded on the primacy of actuality and its relation to potentiality, a political theory freed from the aporias of sovereignty remains unthinkable" (*HS*, 44).[25]

The sovereign ban and the structure of potentiality are closely interrelated. In the same way as the sovereign ban "applies to the exception in no longer applying," potentiality "maintains itself in relation to actuality precisely through its ability not to be" (*HS*, 46). Agamben's analysis of potentiality is central to his understanding of sovereign power.[26]

Agamben argues for the indistinguishability of pure potentiality and pure actuality, a move that entails "nothing less than a re-thinking of the ontological categories of modality," the categories describing states of being or manners of existence, "in their totality" (*HS*, 44). Potentiality, as the potential to be or to do, can be shown to require also im-potentiality, that is, the potential not to be or to do,[27] and "it is precisely the relation to an incapacity that, according to Agamben, constitutes the essence of all potentiality."[28] Since, in addition, the passage from potentiality to actuality can be said to involve not the destruction of potentiality (as impotentiality) but rather its conservation, the distinction between potentiality and actuality disappears, and "actuality is itself nothing other than the full realisation of the potential not to be."[29] Or, as Agamben puts it, "What is potential can pass over into actuality only at the point at which it sets aside its own potential not to be. . . . To set im-potentiality aside is not to destroy it, but, on the contrary, to fulfil it, to turn potentiality back on itself to give itself to itself" (*HS*, 46). Rather than potentiality and actuality being distinct modes of being, then, they enter a zone of indistinction.

Importantly, Agamben then argues that "the sovereign is precisely this zone of indistinction" (*HS*, 47). In the sovereign act, "potentiality . . . suspends itself, maintaining itself in a relation of ban (or abandonment) with itself in order to realise itself as absolute actuality (which thus presupposes nothing other than its own potentiality)" (*HS*, 47).

To understand sovereignty and the sovereign ban, then, it is necessary to think potentiality without any relation to actuality. The long-standing distinction between potentiality and actuality must be abandoned, and instead potentiality must be conceived as a form of actuality and vice versa. What Agamben proposes is "nothing less than thinking ontology and politics beyond every figure of relation, beyond even the limit relation that is the sovereign ban" (*HS*, 47). What he challenges here is what he calls "the ontological root of every political power" (*HS*, 48). Being as currently conceived, as sovereign being, is trapped within the principle of sovereignty; any attempt to rethink politics beyond sovereignty requires a rethinking of being as such. However, in the end Agamben admits that this is not so much a logical problem as a political one, a cutting of the Gordian knot "in the service of a politics in which bare life is no longer separated and excepted, either in the state order or in the figure of human rights" (*HS*, 134).

It is not possible, then, to return to the distinction between *bios* and *zoē* in its old form: "there is no return from the camps to classical politics" (*HS*, 188). Agamben proposes rather a transformation of the "biopolitical body that is bare life" into the site for the constitution of a being "that is only its own bare existence" and a life "that, being its own form, remains inseparable from it" (*HS*, 188). Agamben calls this being *form-of-life*. It appears to resemble the *whatever being* of *The Coming Community*, "which wants to appropriate belonging itself, its own being-in-language, and thus rejects all identity and every condition of belonging" (*CC*, 87). This *form-of-life*, then, is whatever singularity, "the principal enemy of the State" and of sovereign power as such (*CC*, 87). The coming politics "*will no longer be a struggle for the conquest or control of the State, but a struggle between the*

State and the non-State (humanity), an insurmountable disjunction between whatever singularity and the State organisation" (*CC*, 85).

Ironically, then, the very form of being that is produced by sovereign power turns out to be that form of being that sovereign power finds intolerable. The distinction between *bios* and *zoē* that forms the basis of the sovereign ban produces bare life or *homo sacer*, the life included in the *polis* only by its exclusion from it. Sovereignty itself is produced by this act of exclusion of bare life, a life that returns, however, to haunt sovereignty and indeed to threaten its ultimate dissolution. Modernity "necessarily creates within itself" a bare life "whose presence it can no longer tolerate in any way" (*HS*, 179). In other words:

It is as if the bare life of *homo sacer* . . . now became—in assuming itself as a task—explicitly and immediately political. . . . If life . . . is immediately politics . . . this unity . . . appears as an indissoluble cohesion in which it is impossible to isolate something like a bare life. In the state of exception become the rule, the life of *homo sacer*, which was the correlate of sovereign power, turns into an existence over which power no longer seems to have any hold. (*HS*, 153)

Whereas, at one point in *Means Without End*, Agamben claims that *form-of-life*, a life he calls there *happy life*, "cannot be . . . the naked life that sovereignty posits" but should rather be "an absolutely profane 'sufficient life' that has reached the perfection of its own power and of its own communicability," making it "a life over which sovereignty has no hold," here in *Homo Sacer* what he seems to be saying is that naked or bare life itself,[30] if *assumed as a task* in this way, can be that very *form-of-life* that challenges sovereignty.

Sovereign power has to produce a homogenous and pure "people" by the exclusion of all that do not count as people in its terms. "To produce an undivided people" is a project that has as its impossible aim overcoming the "biopolitical fracture" (*HS*, 179). As a project it is aporetic, since "the constitution of the human species in a political body . . . always already carries the fundamental biopolitical fracture within itself" (*HS*, 177–78). However, it has now become "the implacable and methodical attempt to overcome the division dividing the people, to eliminate radically the people that is excluded" (*HS*, 179). In this context, a group that refuses assimilation or integration into the national body cannot be tolerated. It has to be exterminated, as in the Nazi final solution, not merely excluded (*HS*, 153, 179).

The *Muselmann*

In *Remnants of Auschwitz*, Agamben explores how this attempt to resolve the biopolitical fracture through extermination operated, and considers the forms of life produced in the camps, in particular the figure of the *Muselmann*. In doing this he points to the paradoxical breakdown of the biopolitical project, even in this extreme circumstance. He draws extensively on the testimony and reflections of Primo Levi.

Auschwitz is what Primo Levi calls "the grey zone," where those involved could not be reduced to victims and persecutors. Although newcomers to the camps expected to find "a terrible but decipherable world," what they encountered was "indecipherable: it did not conform to any model, the enemy was all around but also inside, the 'we' lost its limits, the contenders were not two, one could not discern a single frontier but rather many confused, perhaps innumerable frontiers, which stretched between each of us."[31] It is a zone of indistinction, where oppressed becomes oppressor in a "gray, incessant alchemy in which good and evil and, along with them, all the metals of traditional ethics reach their point of fusion" (*RA*, 21).

Primo Levi does, however, make one important distinction central to his descriptions of the *Lager*: a distinction among the camp inhabitants between the saved and the drowned. The saved are those who stay alive through a variety of means, for example by becoming camp officials or through their own struggles. The majority of the camp inhabitants do not survive more than three months:

Their life is short, but their number is endless; they, the *Muselmänner*, the drowned, form the backbone of the camp, an anonymous mass, continually renewed and always identical, of non-men who march and labour in silence, the divine spark dead within them, already too empty to really suffer. One hesitates to call them living: one hesitates to call their death death, in the face of which they have no fear, as they are too tired to understand.[32]

Auschwitz is the place where "the state of exception coincides perfectly with the rule and the extreme situation becomes the very paradigm of daily life" (*RA*, 49–50). The camps are the ultimate biopolitical machine; however, they turn out to be more than that, and this gives them their paradoxical character. Extermination in the camps is not just a question of killing; rather, it entails the production of the non-human from the human, the

point at which bare life becomes not only life that is not politically qualified but life that is not human. Auschwitz, in other words, is "the site of . . .
an experiment beyond life and death in which the Jew is transformed into
a *Muselmann* and the human being into the non-human" (*RA*, 39). It is
not a question of which humans live within the *polis* or are excluded from
it as bare life or *homo sacer*, but which humans are humans at all. The
boundary between the human and the non-human is at stake.

The attempt to bear witness to this situation reveals the paradoxes
that it entails. There is an imperative to bear witness: the survivor "cannot *not* remember" (*RA*, 36). What has to be born witness to is meaningless and unimaginable. But there is another difficulty, one to which Levi
draws our attention: "we, the survivors, are not the true witnesses."[33] The
survivors are "an anomalous minority . . . those who by their prevarications
or abilities or good luck did not touch bottom."[34] Those who did touch
bottom "have not returned to tell about it or have returned mute"; they
are the *Muselmänner*, "the complete witnesses."[35] Agamben calls this Levi's
paradox. The survivors "speak in their stead, by proxy."[36] They "must bear
witness in the name of the impossibility of bearing witness" (*RA*, 34).

The distinction between the human and the non-human is revealed
as paradoxical and impossible. The survivors were not just a minority, they
were not "the best . . . the bearers of a message."[37] On the contrary: "Prefera-
bly the worst survived, the selfish, the violent, the insensitive, the collaborators of the "grey zones," the spies. It was not a certain rule (there were none,
nor are there certain rules in human matters), but it was, nevertheless, a
rule. . . . The worst survived—that is, the fittest; the best all died."[38] Those
who survived, then, those who seemed to have preserved their "dignity" and
their "humanity," were the ones who were inhuman. It was "not decent to
remain decent" in Auschwitz; to remain decent was shameful in this context (*RA*, 60). The drowned, those who lost all their dignity and self-respect,
they were the human. In this situation, Agamben argues that Levi's paradox
can be rewritten: "*The human being is the inhuman; the one whose humanity
is completely destroyed is the one who is truly human*" (*RA*, 133).

Does this mean that in Auschwitz the assumption as *form-of-life* of
that very extreme of bare life to which the *Häftlinge* were reduced, the
becoming *Muselmänner*, would be a contestation of the biopolitical project? Is this the sense in which the one whose humanity has been totally
destroyed is truly human? Certainly, beyond the *Muselmann* no further

biopolitical division is possible. The biopolitical project has reached its limit: "the non-Aryan passes into the Jew, the Jew into the deportee . . . the deportee into the prisoner (*Häftling*), until biopolitical caesuras reach their limit in the camp. This limit is the *Muselmann*" (*RA*, 85). What emerges is "an absolute biopolitical substance that cannot be . . . divided by another caesura" (*RA*, 85).

In an interesting analysis in *Homo Sacer*, Agamben draws out parallels between Heidegger's writings and Nazi ideology, and identifies where, for him, they part company. The crucial divergence is described as follows:

Nazism determines the bare life of *homo sacer* in a biological and eugenic key, making it into the site of an incessant decision on value and nonvalue in which biopolitics [a politics of life] continually turns into thanatopolitics [a politics of death] and in which the camp, consequently, becomes the absolute political space. In Heidegger, on the other hand, *homo sacer*—whose very own life is always at issue in its every act—instead becomes Dasein, the inseparable unity of being and ways of Being, of subject and qualities, life and world, "whose own Being is at issue in its very Being." (*HS*, 153)

As we have seen, in the extreme state of exception become rule, "the life of *homo sacer*, which was the correlate of sovereign power, turns into an existence over which power no longer seems to have any hold" (*HS*, 153). In other words, it becomes a form of life that as *form-of-life*, perhaps, is impervious to the sovereign move to isolate bare life from politically qualified life. At this point, there seem to be two, perhaps inseparable, possibilities: Nazism, where biopolitics becomes the death camp, and the assumption of being as such, or the assumption of bare life, as Heidegger's Dasein.

After rephrasing Levi's paradox as we saw above, Agamben argues that "if the one bearing witness to the human is the one whose humanity has been wholly destroyed," then "the identity between human and inhuman is never perfect and . . . it is not truly possible to destroy the human. . . . Something always *remains*" (*RA*, 133–34). What remains, this *remnant*, is the witness.[39] This leads him to a new definition of the human, not, he claims, in terms of an essence: "the human being exists in the fracture between the living being and the speaking being, the human and the inhuman. . . . The human being is the being that is lacking to itself and that consists solely in this lack and the errancy it opens" (*RA*, 134).[40] The human being, then, Agamben concludes, "is a potential being" (*RA*, 134).

The categories of modality (possibility, impossibility, contingency, necessity) are not harmless operators having to do only with logic or epistemology; rather they are "devastating weapons used in the biopolitical struggle. . . . They divide and separate, in the subject, what is possible and what is impossible, the living being and the speaking being, the *Muselmann* and the witness—and in this way they decide on the subject" (*RA*, 146–47). In Auschwitz, these processes collapse; the *Muselmann* is "the catastrophe of the subject . . . the subject's effacement as the place of contingency and its maintenance as existence of the impossible" (*RA*, 148).

The *Muselmann*, then, demonstrates the effectiveness of biopower, but also reveals its hidden secret: it sought to produce "a survival separated from every possibility of testimony, a kind of absolute biopolitical substance that, in its isolation, allows for the attribution of demographic, ethnic, national and political identity" (*RA*, 156), or in other words, "a bare, unassignable and unwitnessable life" (*RA*, 157). To treat Auschwitz as unspeakable is to repeat this gesture. Testimony refutes it.[41]

Human Animal

In *The Coming Community*, Agamben talks of the coming politics as a struggle between the State and the non-State, equating the latter (in parentheses) with "humanity." In his later work "the State" is reconceptualised or reappears as sovereign power. The question of "humanity" appears again in *Homo Sacer*, where Agamben points to the "secret solidarity" between humanitarianism and sovereignty, and, as we have just seen, in *Remnants of Auschwitz* the question of the distinction between the human and the inhuman is revisited in depth.

In *The Open*, Agamben returns to the question of the human and the non-human, in this case in the form of the distinction between the human, or the "man,"[42] and the animal. He identifies an anthropogenic or anthropological machine, which, in a manner parallel to sovereignty, works through processes of exclusion and inclusion and produces a state of exception (*O*, 26–37). Indeed, perhaps the anthropological machine is sovereignty. There are two variants of this machine, that of the moderns, which functions "by isolating the nonhuman within the human," and that of the ancients, where "the non-man is produced by the humanisation of an animal." Whereas the former produces the Jew as "the non-man produced within the man," the latter produces "the slave, the barbarian, and the foreigner, as figures of an animal in human form" (*O*, 37).

The "anthropological machine of humanism" is an ironic one "that verifies the absence of a nature proper to *Homo*," where he is produced as "being always less and more than himself" (*O*, 29). Both machines produce a zone of indistinction, and a form of life—*bare life*—that inhabits that zone. The zone of indistinction (here translated as a "zone of indifference") is "perfectly empty, and the truly human being who should occur there is only the place of a ceaselessly updated decision in which the caesurae and their rearticulation are always dislocated and displaced anew" (*O*, 38). The life that inhabits this zone, then, is "neither an animal life nor a human life, but only a life that is separated and excluded from itself— only a bare life" (*O*, 38).

According to Agamben, what is at stake is not determining which of the two machines is "better and more effective—or, rather less lethal and bloody," but rather understanding how they work, "*so that we might, eventually, be able to stop them*" (*O*, 38; my emphasis). At present, we are living in an aporia where "for a humanity that has become animal again, there is nothing left but the depoliticization of human societies by means of . . . the taking on of biological life itself as the supreme political (or rather impolitical) task" (*O*, 76). However, this is only one of the two outcomes that Agamben suggests are possible from Heideggerian perspective. In a time when "the machine is idling" there is an alternative: "man, the shepherd of being, appropriates his own concealedness,[43] his own animality, which neither remains hidden nor is made an object of mastery, but is thought as such, as pure abandonment" (*O*, 80).

What he means by this remains ambiguous, although he elaborates somewhat in the remaining pages of the book. When the machine is stopped, he says, "in the reciprocal suspension of the two terms [nature and man], something for which we perhaps have no name and which is neither animal nor man settles in between nature and humanity" (*O*, 83): "To render inoperative the machine that governs our conception of man will therefore mean no longer to seek new—more effective or more authentic—articulations, but rather to show the central emptiness, the hiatus that—within man—separates man and animal, and to risk ourselves in this emptiness" (*O*, 92). Agamben's argument in *The Open* remains contentious and difficult to unravel.[44] The text can be read as advocating a taking up or assumption of bare life as such, as *form-of-life*, as being as such, and as whatever singularity. This entails a refusal of the anthropological machine, a machine that is continually defining and redefining the distinctions between forms of life, and as such is complicit in, necessary for, and even perhaps equivalent to sovereign power. It means a return to the idea of a coming community.

What is crucial here is whether the alternative Agamben proposes is radical enough. Does it entail a refusal of the machine, or merely a reinstatement of it with a different "definition" of what it means to be human? In *The Open*, Agamben does seem to reject Heidegger's problematic separation of Dasein, as a being that can see the open, from the animal, poor in world, that cannot.[45] Ultimately, Agamben appears to be arguing that any negation of the machine cannot be accomplished on a philosophical plane, but only in terms of practice. In the end, practice or human action, not philosophy, is what counts. Ontology and philosophy are to be considered only to the extent that they are political operators and, specifically, biopolitical weapons in the service of the anthropological machine of sovereignty.

In order to try to stop the biopolitical machine that produces bare life, what is needed is human action, "which once claimed for itself the name of 'politics'" (*SE*, 88). It is because there is no necessary articulation "between violence and law, between life and norm," that it is possible to attempt to interrupt or halt the machine, to "loosen what has been artificially and violently linked" (*SE*, 87). This opens a space for a return not to some "lost original state" but to human praxis and political action (*SE*, 88).

Whatever Politics

What would such action look like? How might we envisage or work toward a politics of whatever being—a whatever politics—from such a starting point? How would we respond to Agamben's own question, "What could be the politics of whatever singularity?" (*CC*, 85).

Agamben gives us one example in response to this question: Tiananmen. In the demonstrations in Beijing in May 1989, there was a relative absence of specific demands, and yet the non-violent protests led, after a period of standoff and apparent vacillation, to a strong and violent reaction by the state. Agamben sees these demonstrations as emblematic of a gathering of whatever singularities. The result was not encouraging: resistance of this type merely provokes the state to violence. It is a form of protest that the state as sovereign power cannot tolerate. Agamben concludes: "Wherever these singularities peacefully demonstrate their being in common there will be a Tiananmen, and, sooner or later, the tanks will appear" (*CC*, 87).

This example and Agamben's discussion of the coming politics as a struggle between the state and "humanity" provoke a number of questions. Is it always the case that sooner or later the tanks appear? Or, as Connolly argues, is politics messier and more subject to negotiation than Agamben asserts? The Tiananmen gatherings were not the only large demonstrations that year. They were followed in November by a series of demonstrations in East Berlin and elsewhere that led to the fall of the Berlin Wall. In this case, the tanks did not appear, though the ultimate outcome was not a whatever politics or a "third way" as advocated at the time, but the reinstallation of sovereign politics in a different form. Connolly argues that a focus on either the logics or the paradoxes of sovereignty leads to the reduction of the complexities of social and cultural life to an abstraction.[46] These complexities, in particular, are what allow for challenge and negotiation.

There are comparable disparities between Agamben and Derrida, summarized by Catherine Mills.[47] They differ on whether the conditions of contemporary politics call for an overcoming or a living-with, or as Mills puts it, "whether undecidability and deferral constitute the condition of political futurity or the condition to be overcome . . . through the inauguration of . . . the *ethos* or proper dwelling place of humanity that has not yet been."[48] Whereas "we wish only to think that we are on the track of an impossible axiomatic that remains to be thought," Derrida warns that such moves fail perhaps because "darkness is falling on the . . . very desire for an *axiomatic*, a consistent, granted or presupposed system of values."[49]

If a logic of sovereign power is identified that relies for its very operation on the production and generalisation of bare life as a form of life that is hospitable to its operation, then it is in a sense obvious that a challenge to sovereignty might be framed in terms of a refusal or de-stabilisation of that very form of life itself. This can take place as a grand challenge to and attempt to overthrow sovereign power itself as a form of power. This certainly seems to be what Agamben envisages at times: he talks of stopping the machine in *The Open*, assuming bare life as a task in *Homo Sacer*, and "severing the nexus between violence and law" in *State of Exception* (*O*, 38; *HS*, 153; *SE*, 88). However, can the process of challenge operate more modestly as a means of finding space alongside sovereignty for the installation of *form-of-life* as life that is not defined or definable in sovereign terms? Does Agamben's work have to be seen as leading to a grand eschatological move?

Agamben himself emphasises the irony and excess implicit in sovereign power. Although sovereignty operates through the production of bare life, this life is both the constitutive outside of sovereignty and the element that threatens its disruption from within. It is the life it cannot do without, but at the same time, ultimately, the life it cannot tolerate. Bare life, the destitute *homo sacer* of sovereignty, becomes, when assumed as *form-of-life*, the whatever singularity that sovereignty can no longer tolerate or contain. It is the excess that threatens to disclose the paradoxical instability and impossibility of sovereignty in its claim to be a form of governance or administration of life. The remnant, like the repressed, returns. The argument that Agamben proposes could then be presented in an alternative form. Bare life, the form of life produced by biopolitical, anthropological machine of sovereign power, is an undecidable. On the one hand it is trapped in a wasteland of indistinction between fact and law; on the other it is the rogue component that can bring to a halt the mechanism that produces it. Seen in this way, Agamben's work could be taken as a call for a micro-politics of action and engagement, which would be messy, certainly.

Agamben's discussion of Tiananmen and the coming community also provokes the question of whether politics is best thought of as entailing ways of being in common or community at all.[50] In *Politics of Friendship*, Derrida remarks that "we *belong* . . . to the time of . . . a harrowing tremor in the structure or experience of *belonging*. Of communal belonging and sharing: religion, family, ethnic groups, nations, homeland, country, state, even humanity, love and friendship," and stresses his discomfort with "mad and impossible pleas . . . such as these recurrent syntagms: 'relation without relation', community without community . . . 'inoperative' community . . . and all the 'X without X' whose list is, by definition, endless, finite in its infinitude."[51] Does politics necessarily entail a being together or being in common, in the sense of a coming together of beings into a community of beings? Jean-Luc Nancy argues, in contrast to Agamben, that all being is inevitably being together. Nancy proposes a new ontology, not of potentiality but of being-with, expressing it as follows: "Being cannot *be* anything but being-with-one-another, circulating in the *with* and as the *with* of this singularly plural coexistence."[52]

Significantly, in view of the discussions in this chapter so far prompted by Agamben's work on distinctions, for Nancy

this circulation goes in all directions at once, in all the directions of all the space-times . . . opened by presence to presence: all things, all beings, all entities, everything past and future, alive, dead, inanimate, stones, plants, nails, gods—and "humans", that is, those who expose sharing and circulation as such by saying "we", by *saying we to themselves* in all possible senses of that expression, and by saying we for the totality of all being.[53]

There are interesting parallels here with Agamben's thinking of testimony and language, where the speaking one speaks on behalf of the complete witness, the one who cannot speak. Nancy's framing is refreshingly inclusive; he argues that language speaks for the world "in order to lead the one who speaks . . . to all of being, which does not speak but which is nevertheless."[54] Though "humans" may speak, and by speaking expose existence, "what is exposed there also holds for the rest of beings."[55] In other words, our understanding of Being is "an understanding *that* we share understanding between us and, at the same time, *because* we share understanding between us: between us all, simultaneously—all the dead and all the living, and all beings."[56]

For Nancy, then, unlike Agamben, there is no question of a struggle for a coming politics, or of human action to interrupt the anthropological machine. There is always already community: "community is given to us with being and as being, well in advance of all our projects, desires and undertakings."[57] Even in the camp, community resists the attempt to annihilate community. Community can be equated with resistance, resistance "to all the forms and all the violences of subjectivity."[58] Again, we are drawn away from some grand eschatological move of overcoming to a recognition of the way in which whatever politics may already be taking place.

A final and important question that must be raised is the question of the human. What role does human being play in Agamben's thinking of politics? According to the Agamben of *The Coming Community*, "there is no essence, no historical or spiritual vocation, no biological destiny that humans must enact or realise" (*CC*, 43). However, he makes it clear that he does not mean by this that humans are thereby consigned to freedom. On the contrary, "there is in effect something that humans are and have to be, but this something is not an essence or properly a thing: *It is the simple fact of one's own existence as possibility or potentiality*" (*CC*, 43). In other words, "the being most proper to humankind is being one's own possibility or potentiality" (*CC*, 43). This means "exposing . . . in every form one's own amorphousness and in every act one's own inactuality" (*CC*, 44). This reading of the human is repeated, as we saw, in the discussions of Auschwitz.

Despite this refusal of an essence proper to human being, it seems there still remains in Agamben's formulation something proper to human life that sets it apart from other forms of life—animal life, for example. If this is a correct reading, then it is deeply problematic. Given that he has shown how the separation of politically qualified life from bare life is productive of and produced by sovereign power, and given that this distinction leads in the extreme situation of the camps to the attempt to separate the human from the inhuman and exterminate the inhuman, it is surprising that Agamben does not seem to advocate, in his notion of *form-of-life*, a life that cannot be distinguished even in this manner. To me it seems that the ultimate protest against sovereignty's production of its subjects as bare life would be the unconditional taking up of that designation, the setting aside of the social fantasy, or what we call social reality,[59] and the acceptance of the ungroundedness and indistinguishability of being.[60] This assumption of bare life would entail, as Véronique Pin-Fat and I have argued elsewhere,[61] the refusal of all distinctions between forms of life of the sort sovereign power proposes, including the distinction between the human and the non-human.

Distinctions between forms of life have operated differently in different historical periods. At one time, women were considered not to be full members of "the human race"; for example, in ancient Greece, women were not "politically qualified" as members of the public sphere. At another time, different "races" were considered primitive or savage, without full capacities as "human"; colonization was legitimized on the ground that such peoples were not yet able to take charge of their own political affairs. Each of these exclusions were, in their context, considered obvious, unproblematic, and even unchallengeable. In the contemporary world, the exclusion of non-human animals from the realm of politics is deemed obvious in much the same way. The exclusion of other forms of being is not even noticed as such.

However, as Agamben has so clearly demonstrated, exclusions of this type form communities based on sovereign violence. A *whatever politics*, if it is to be a politics without conditions of belonging, cannot operate as a politics of humanity or human being, however broadly drawn. It has to be a politics of being as such. It is by no means just a question of including that which is currently excluded—women through a discourse of women's human rights, or animals, for example, through an insistence on animal rights. Such inclusions, as Derrida has pointed out, are always on "human" terms.[62] It is rather a question of a refusal to draw the line between forms of life as such. It is to take literally Agamben's call for a *form-of-life* "that, being its own form, remains inseparable from it" (*HS*, 188). Otherwise, I suspect, the *form-of-life* risks remaining at root a sovereign move.

To be faithful to Agamben's analysis of the dangers inherent in the operation of sovereign power, then, we are drawn to the conclusion that any drawing of lines between forms of life has to be refused. Indeed, this call could be extended: it entails, for obvious reasons, a refusal to draw lines or make distinctions between *forms of being*. The line between the living and the dead, as Agamben points out (*HS*, 160–65), or that between the animate and the inanimate, as Nancy argues, is as problematic as the line between man and animal. Such a drawing of lines constitutes a sovereign move. A proper rethinking of ontologies of potentiality and actuality, such as Agamben advocates, would entail a rethinking of all being as potential being: not just human-being but cat-being, stone-being, god-being, or whatever-being as well.

Is this refusal another grand eschatological move, hopelessly utopian? Or could what is read as an eschatological move also be read as a call for a return to the here and now, in Derrida's sense? Derrida's response to the critique of his work as utopian is instructive here. He insists that the messianic experience that he speaks of "takes place here and now; that is, the fact of promising and speaking is an event that takes place here and now and is not utopian. This happens in the singular event of engagement."[63] He is concerned to differentiate this notion of the here and now from a present that is present or has presence in itself. It does not fall within a notion of a linear temporality of past, present, and future, and yet it is the location in which action takes place: "I try to dissociate the theme of singularity happening here and now from the theme of presence and, for me, there can be a here and now without presence."[64]

If we turn our attention to the here and now, we find that although the drawing of lines between forms of life is a sovereign move, an attempt to produce clarity and stabilisation, it is a move that cannot succeed, as both Derrida and Agamben have demonstrated. There is always a remainder that threatens the stabilisation from within. As Derrida reminds us, "it becomes necessary to stabilise precisely because stability is not natural . . . it is because there is chaos that there is a need for stability."[65] The stability, produced by the drawing of lines, the production of enclosed communities, the establishment of rules, is comforting: it is a bulwark against a fundamental chaos and indistinguishability that is "fundamental, founding and irreducible."[66] However, the fact that it does not work, that it is immediately prone to destabilisation, opens the possibility of change.

The call for a refusal to draw lines can, then, be seen in a different light. The drawing of lines always already fails. Attempts are continually made, in the here and now, in philosophy and in politics, to make distinctions, but these only ever partially or temporarily succeed. We do not need to look to the future to find out what a *whatever politics*, a politics without distinctions between forms of life, would look like: it is to be found, and fought for, in the here and now. The line-drawing strategies of sovereign power are themselves failing all the time. And alongside the practices of sovereign power there are other practices of politics that, acknowledging the impossibility of distinguishing between forms of life, attempt to live with the chaos, that work with negotiation and invention, that are open to the vulnerability and the exposure of being, and that forego the fantasy of an unattainable stabilisation and security.

Sovereign power is effective precisely because it incorporates into its logic the bare life or form-of-life that would subvert it, and successfully conceals its own fragility. But this incorporation entails the emplacement of disruption at the heart of power. To oppose sovereign power directly is to enter into its line-drawing strategies—themselves doomed to failure—and ironically to make disruption or destabilisation less likely or at least more easily concealed. A refusal to enter these strategies can take place within or alongside, yet independently of, sovereign power. We, whatever "we" are, are already exposed to the open—the trick is not to be captivated by the possibility of escaping that exposure, but rather to acknowledge the inevitable chaos of a world without lines. One of the most difficult things of all to give up, however, but the one it is possibly most necessary to relinquish, is the notion of the significance or importance of human-being. This particular distinction seems to be one of the most tenacious in contemporary political and philosophical thinking and practice.

From Sovereign Ban to Banning Sovereignty

William Rasch

The Logic of Sovereignty . . .

Poor Bertrand Russell, what a mean father. He was such a splendid procreator of paradoxes, but he cared so little for his offspring, always wishing they would deny their own existence or acknowledge their illegitimacy. But they have not gone away, and they still entertain us today. Who can forget—as some compiler of Russell's greatest hits might say—who can forget the Sicilian barber, the barber who shaves only and all those in his village who do not shave themselves?[1] Does the barber shave himself? If he does, then he does not *only* shave those who do not shave themselves; and if he does not, then he does not shave *all* those who do not shave themselves. So what does the perplexed Russell do with our paralyzed barber? He exiles him and condemns him to live outside the city walls, up in the foothills, alone, traveling to town every day to shave those who do not shave themselves. Poor Barber of the Outskirts of Town, he loses his birthright and his citizenship. Poor Bertrand, what a mean father—he subjects yet another of his unruly children to the paternal law of the excluded middle.

But what about that law itself? To what is the law of the excluded middle subject? Even asking the question raises the specter of another paradox, as Russell clearly recognized. Stated in the form of a proposition, the law of the excluded middle is a proposition about all propositions. It says: "All propositions are either true or false." The law, then, would seem to include itself within the set it adjudicates. It would seem to require that the law undergo its own scrutiny and pass judgment on itself. This Russell finds to be a vicious and therefore meaningless and illegitimate circle. "If from this law," he and Whitehead write in the *Principia Mathematica*: "we argue that, because the law of excluded middle is a proposition, therefore the law of excluded middle is true or false, we incur a vicious-circle fallacy. 'All propositions' must be in some way limited before it becomes a legitimate totality, and any limitation which makes it legitimate must make any statement about the totality fall outside the totality."[1] But where such a fallen statement lands remains a problem. Russell recommends his theory of types,[2] to the effect that statements about totalities must be made from a hierarchical level higher than the level occupied by the now limited totality under discussion—from the extra-urban foothills, as it were. A totality of totalities, therefore, becomes incommunicable. To many observers, however, including eventually Russell himself, the arbitrary and ad hoc nature of the theory of types has always been disquieting.[3] Indeed, favoring self-exemption over endless stairways to heaven, Wittgenstein provocatively points to the superfluity of the theory of types. "Clearly," he writes in 6.123 of the *Tractatus*, "the laws of logic cannot in their turn be subject to laws of logic," adding in parenthesis: "(There is not, as Russell thought, a special law of contradiction for each 'type'; one law is enough, since it is not applied to itself)."[4] Accordingly, it is not so much that the proposition "All propositions are either true or false" falls *outside* the set of all propositions; rather, remaining inside, the proposition excludes itself from its own workings. It simply cannot be subject to the same judgment that it exercises—which is to say that for the law of the excluded middle to operate, it must *be* the excluded middle, neither true nor false. Thus, self-exemption "solves" the paradox of totalizing propositions by rudely and insolently *becoming* the paradox. The barber who shaves only and all those who do not shave themselves, is not only *not* excommunicated from his Sicilian village, he is chosen to *rule* it. He is, at one and the same time, *of* the town and *over* it.

In a word, the barber is sovereign, for the paradox that both Russell and Wittgenstein ponder is the neat trick of sovereign self-exemption, which makes a necessary asymmetry out of an impossible symmetry. The sudden emergence of this figure—the figure of the sovereign—at first seems arbitrary and mysterious. When personified as an individual, an institution, or a general will, sovereignty appears as if it *precedes* the law, giving the law its force. Yet, the sovereign is simply the name given to a logical effect. Rather than prior or opposed to the law, the sovereign is law's shadow, its included and excluded double. In the set we call Sicilian village, law is universal. All are equal before the law. Whoever applies the law is also subject to the law. But the law itself is not subject to the law. The law lays down the law and demands obedience in exchange for protection *under* the law. In a world organized hierarchically, this Sicilian law might be subject to a "higher" law, a "natural" or "moral" law, but such a world must eventually arrive at God, who then becomes the sovereign source of law by the self-same self-exemption that hierarchical ordering means to avoid. Without God, deferral to higher levels must eventually lead to a classically bad infinity of provisional sovereigns whose sovereignty is forever relative to the next higher, yet equally provisional, equally relative sovereign. Ironically, then, for law to be absolute, it must be limited, it must be immanent to the set in which it rules and stand in no hierarchical relation to the outside. The distinction of levels is displaced—or rather—re-placed, re-entered into the set itself. The result is not a hierarchy of sets, but a simultaneous symmetry and asymmetry of propositions within the set of all propositions. The law does not derive its power from an external source, but rather achieves its power by distinguishing itself from itself—an act of logical nuclear fission, as it were. Thus, the proposition that maintains that all propositions are either true or false claims for itself the *authority* of truth precisely by refusing to subject itself to the mechanism of truth-testing. It is sovereign simply because it is sovereign.

. . . and the Rule of Law

The figure of the sovereign makes nervous those who are democratically inclined, because the democratically inclined hope to avoid asymmetry at all costs. They do so by replacing sovereignty by the rule of law, as if the rule of law had no need of the personified sovereign because it made use of impersonal reason, that is, as if reason were not itself another name for the figure of sovereign self-exemption. As if, in other words, the operation of even the most basic law, such as the law of the excluded middle, were not a sovereign operation. Therefore, that the domestic and international rule of law replaces an older reliance on both state and, to a lesser degree, popular sovereignty, is a commonplace of twentieth-century liberal, constitutional thought. In its most basic form, the rule of law, as opposed to the rule of men, allegedly supplants the naked and arbitrary force of a willful sovereign power or majority mob. The subjects of the rule of law are individuals who are said to form a collective entity called humanity. As late as 1934, the American legal scholar James Brown Scott could still unhesitatingly claim that what we now call "humanity" is but an extension of an older, inclusive community of Christian believers. With the discovery of the New World, Scott wrote, the old European, Christian community was "replaced by an international community today universal and embracing all peoples of all continents; the law applicable to members of the Christian community was found to be applicable to non-Christians; and the law of nations, once confined to Christendom, has become international."[5] More recently, and in a more secular vein, liberal theorists like Jürgen Habermas and John Rawls have grounded popular will formation and a Law of Peoples on liberal human rights, such that, ideally, we are left, in Habermas's words, with a "cosmopolitan law" that "bypasses the collective subjects of international law [i.e., states] and directly establishes the legal status of the individual subjects by granting them unmediated membership in the association of free and equal world citizens."[6] In other words, a global legal order based on human rights, which, as Rawls states, forms a "proper subset of the rights possessed by citizens in a liberal constitutional democratic regime,"[7] is but a nearly seamless, universal extension of the liberal domestic sphere. Instead of the traditional anarchy of sovereign states jealously guarding their autonomy, we have a single community of individuals who obey the law—not because of its arbitrary and authoritarian sovereignty, but because the law is said to represent every individual's reasonable interests. With human rights established as the normative origin of all law, war is outlawed, rogue states policed, and violations of these rights punished in a global domestic sphere. The rule of law, we are told, governs all human relations.

Against this background, Carl Schmitt's famous definition—"Sovereign is he who decides on the exception"[8]—sounds, at best, anachronistic. After all, the decision has already been made, and that decision dictates that there will be no more decisions, that decisions will be replaced by universally valid, because rationally achieved, norms. Under the law, there will be no exception, just rule. Thus, from the universalist point of view, the concept of sovereignty, with its recognition of an irreducible and indeterminate conflict of state interests, is not just an outdated but also an outlaw concept, for it attempts to subvert the normative order that enlightened modernity is said to have achieved. But Schmitt's definition, though unpopular, is not all that anachronistic. And if it is illegal, it is not because it *op*poses the liberal order so much as it *ex*poses it. Indeed, it seeks to explain it *as* an order, as one possible order among many—in short, as a political reality, and not merely a legal or moral ideology. "Like every other order," Schmitt writes, "the legal order rests on a decision and not on a norm."[9] It can therefore be said that Schmitt's definition of sovereignty—again: "Sovereign is he who decides on the exception"—is itself an answer to a question, namely: When push comes to shove, who decides? Who is this he, she, or it? Accordingly, the liberal denial of sovereignty necessarily prompts the paradoxical query: What or which sovereign power determines that there will be no sovereign power? Or, more politically theological: what or which sovereign power declares, "Thou shalt have no other sovereign powers before me"?

Why is decision unavoidable? It is unavoidable, Schmitt answers, because of the limits of logic. Simply put, Schmitt argues against the possibility of determining logically or rationally a "highest, legally independent, underived power," because any attempt to do so leads, as our Sicilian barber showed us, either to infinite regress or to paradox. It leads to infinite regress because reality is governed by the law of causality, and the law of causality is infinite. Every cause is the effect of a prior cause. It is paradoxical because if the highest, underived power is the norm that establishes the rule of law, it too must be under the law, it must be in the field of its own operations—else it would commit the same self-exemption characteristic of sovereignty. But if it too is under the law, it cannot be the highest, underived power, because its actions can then be determined (by what? by whom?) to be legal or illegal. The problem cannot be solved logically. It must be solved "existentially." To cut the chain and fix a point of origin to serve as an underived norm, or to establish procedures for determining where to cut the chain, or to establish discursive rules for establishing procedures for determining where to cut the chain, is, ultimately, to commit a political act. More important than the question of where the chain is cut is the question of who cuts. Liberal human rights, from which Habermas and Rawls wish to derive popular will formation and the Law of Peoples, are precisely what they say they are—liberal—because they are the manifestation of a liberal political order, and *not* because liberal ideology vibrates at the same frequency as the dynamo at the heart of the universe. The universality of human rights is directly linked to the extent of the political hegemony that serves as *their* starting point. Establishing norms does not precede politics and evade sovereignty; it *is* politics, sovereign politics.

When, therefore, Giorgio Agamben, following Schmitt, states that the "paradox of sovereignty consists in the fact the sovereign is, at the same time, outside and inside the juridical order" (*HS*, 15), he does not exclude the force of law from this rule. Classically, the paradox of sovereignty is resolved—but certainly not solved—by the distinction between a constituting and a constituted power, a distinction that Schmitt endorses and that constitutional liberals attempt to evade. As Agamben says, "Today, in the context of the general tendency to regulate everything by means of rules, fewer and fewer are willing to claim that constituting power is originary and irreducible, that it cannot be conditioned and constrained in any way by a determinate legal system and that it necessarily maintains itself outside every constituted power" (*HS*, 39–40). Liberal theorists, like Hans Kelsen in Schmitt's time and Habermas in our own, try to derive the rule of law painlessly from norms that are said to be objectively, consensually, and/or procedurally universal. They assume that objectivity or universality takes the sting of sovereignty out of constitutional rule, that, because necessary and thoroughly internalized, their norms exert no force but only instantiate freedom. Thus, a liberal constitution simply embodies in legal form what, in Habermas's words, "could be *jointly* accepted by *all* concerned without coercion."[10] Agamben replies "that *the constitution presupposes itself as constituting power* and, in this form, expresses the paradox of sovereignty in the most telling way" (*HS*, 40–41). Though written as law, it is as if the constitution existed outside the law in a state of nature. It legitimizes the rule of law but cannot itself be legitimized except by way of a sovereign self-exemption—the sovereign self-exemption of norms or procedures that are deemed (again: by whom?) universal and thus incontestable.

Like Schmitt, Walter Benjamin also saw through this liberal sleight of hand and recognized that if one wished to transcend sovereignty, one needed to transcend law itself. For this reason, Benjamin analyzed the force of law in terms of a dual, but linked, violence that is but another version of the distinction between constituting and constituted power. The violence that demands obedience to the existing law is *rechtserhaltend* (law-preserving), while the violence that founds the law, that establishes the necessary asymmetry by means of self-exemption, is *rechtsetzend* (law-positing). This latter violence opens up an ordered space that the former preserves. Benjamin names both types of legal violence "mythic." Taken together, they sovereignly establish a historically given social, legal, and political order.[11] Regarding Benjamin's distinction, Agamben notes: "If constituting power is, as the violence that posits law, certainly more noble than the violence that preserves it, constituting power still possesses no title that might legitimate something other than law-preserving violence and even maintains an ambiguous and ineradicable relation with constituted power" (*HS*, 40). Benjamin, it can therefore be said, emphasizes the unity of the distinction between constituting and constituted violence by labeling them, collectively, "mythic."

There is, however, a second type of violence, categorically different from mythic violence. Divine violence, which cannot be defined positively, is nonetheless all that mythic violence is not. In Benjamin's words: "If mythic violence posits law, divine violence destroys it; if the former sets boundaries, the latter destroys them boundlessly; if mythic violence brings with it guilt and atonement, divine violence redeems; if the former threatens, the latter strikes; if the former is bloody, the latter is bloodless in a lethal way."[12] Accordingly, mythic violence is mundane. It establishes a contingent political order that is built on the forced, provisional suspension of the originary paradox. It can define that ordered space only from within that ordered space. It is, for example, an order in which something called "justice" prevails, not because justice is absolutely just, but because justice is an effect of the sovereign self-exemption and thus a necessary component of the contingently determined political order. In the court of reason, all propositions are judged to be true or false, except the proposition that states that the court is a court of reason. Divine violence, on the other hand, comes as if from the outside to limit the space of the political, indeed, to mark that space for demolition. It too recognizes that the paradox at the origin of the mythical world cannot be solved peacefully, but it assumes that the perplexing knot of asymmetry at the source of the political can simply be cut by a single, simple act of violence that will "found a new historical age,"[13] one in which the sovereign self-exemption will be rendered null and void. Divine violence does not replace one political order with another, it replaces one order of *the political*, based on the sovereign self-exemption, with another, yet-to-be-determined manifestation of the political beyond all exception.

The State of Nature as the State of the Political

On this, then, they all agree: that the paradox of sovereignty, no matter how resolved, is the common structure of all modern political life—indeed, perhaps all political life since Aristotle. Where they differ—where, that is, Agamben, taking Benjamin with him, differs from Schmitt—can be seen in this complaint: "The problem of sovereignty," Agamben writes, "was reduced to the question of who within the political order was invested with certain powers, and the very threshold of the political order itself was never called into question" (*HS*, 12). Where they differ, then, is over the possibility of calling the logical structure of sovereignty into question; for calling into question the very structure of sovereignty is what Agamben wishes to do, and it is what he says Benjamin wishes to do. But calling sovereignty into question is not what Schmitt is after. Thus, this is the great distinction that organizes the work of Schmitt, Benjamin, and Agamben—not totalitarianism versus democratic rule of law, but the metaphysics of the West, which is characterized by the ontology of sovereignty, versus a post-metaphysical ontology of the political yet to be realized. Whereas Schmitt locates himself firmly within the political as defined by the sovereign exception, both Benjamin and Agamben imagine the possibility of a politics that exceeds the political. Yet neither Agamben nor Benjamin can say what the grand Other of the structure of sovereignty may be, only that it *ought* to be; that if and when it comes, it will come with an all consuming but bloodless violence that, in Benjamin's terms, will be divine, not mythic, neither law-making nor law-preserving; and that if and when it comes, it will institute a new, post-sovereign, post-rule-of-law, historical epoch. It will be, as Agamben, referring to Benjamin, intimates, "capable of releasing man from guilt and of affirming natural innocence" (*HS*, 28).

Agamben translates what we have treated as logical inevitability into a metaphysical mistake, or rather, into the mistake of metaphysics itself. The fall into metaphysics is occasionally historicized and discussed as the sin of modernity. When Agamben writes that the "inclusion of bare life in the political realm constitutes the original—if concealed—nucleus of sovereign power," and when he then goes on to assert that it "*can even be said that the production of a biopolitical body is the original activity of sovereign power*" (*HS*, 6), one can think of Bodin, absolutism, and eventually the French Revolution, with its inclusion of the "social question," as Hannah Arendt called it—that is, the introduction of poverty and happiness into the realm of the political.[14] One can, and Agamben does, refer to *The History of Sexuality*, where Foucault notes "the entry of life into history" in the eighteenth century. "For the first time in history," Foucault writes at the end of the first volume,

biological existence was reflected in political existence; the fact of living was no longer an inaccessible substrate that only emerged from time to time, amid the randomness of death and its fatality; part of it passed into knowledge's field of control and power's sphere of intervention; . . . [indeed,] it was the taking charge of life, more than the threat of death, that gave power its access even to the body.[15]

But when Agamben laments the "24 centuries" within which "Western politics" has not been able to "heal the fracture" that lay exposed and bare already in Aristotle (*HS*, 11), then we know the argument is structural, foundational, and historical only in the most apocalyptical sense. What reveals itself in the sovereign ban, as Agamben calls the move of self-exemption, is the long, slow, but inevitable telos of the West, an ingrained imperfection that inheres as much in the democratic tradition as it does in absolutism or twentieth-century totalitarianism.

Agamben's claim, briefly, is this: the sovereign decision, exception, or ban—the sovereign self-exemption, in other words—places the sovereign (again, as person, institution, or collective will) both within and without the space or system that the sovereign decision demarcates. Recall: the proposition about the set of all propositions both is and is not a proper member of that set. But this ambiguous zone of inclusion and exclusion in which the sovereign finds himself is also occupied by the sovereign's logical or structural analog, the enigmatic figure of *homo sacer*—sacred life—who incorporates bare life in all its exposed fragility. "The sovereign sphere," Agamben writes, "is the sphere in which it is permitted to kill without committing homicide and without celebrating a sacrifice, and sacred life—that is, life that may be killed but not sacrificed—is the life that has been captured in this sphere" (*HS*, 83). Thus we have "two symmetrical figures" in this sovereign space "that have the same structure and are correlative: the sovereign is the one with respect to whom all men are potentially *homines sacri*, and *homo sacer* is the one with respect to whom all men act as sovereigns." This space, Agamben notes, is "the first properly political space of the West distinct from both the religious and the profane sphere, from both the natural order and the regular juridical order" (*HS*, 84). This claim—namely, that the Western notion of the political is both historically and logically marked by a master-slave relationship far more radical than any Hegel imagined, one that is devoid of recognition and doomed to unavoidable death—is a claim in need of examination.

If one turns to Hobbes, surely the most interesting and influential early-modern philosopher of sovereignty, one notices that what Agamben calls the political, Hobbes calls the "state of nature," that is, the pre-political and pre-historical situation that calls the political into being in the first place. In the Hobbesian state of nature, each person has the same right, the right to self-preservation, thus each person has the same absolute power over the other—and, of course, each person is also subject to the same absolute power of the other. The condition of the human individual in the state of nature is the condition of war. In this war of all against all, nothing is unjust because there is no law, no distinction between good and evil, right and wrong, justice and injustice. The state of nature, it could therefore be argued, is the state in which "life may be killed but not sacrificed," indeed, the sphere in which the roles of sovereign and *homo sacer* are forever interchangeable. Agamben dehistoricizes the Hobbesian construction.[16] The state of nature, Agamben says, "is not a real epoch chronologically prior to the foundation of the City but a principle internal to the City" (*HS*, 105). Thus, the realm of the political is not, as in Hobbes, founded on a contract in which rights are transferred to a sovereign in exchange for peace and protection. Rather, the state of nature as the state of war is directly constituted by the political. "It is not so much a war of all against all," Agamben writes, "as, more precisely, a condition in which everyone is bare life and a *homo sacer* for everyone else" (*HS*, 106). The political, that is, does not replace nature; it creates it. The state from which Hobbes's sovereign rescues us is the state into which Agamben's sovereign plunges us.

The contrast is instructive. The primal scene in Hobbes shows man in a fallen state. Or rather, a natural state is one in which nature is indifferent and man is left to fend for himself. Any attempt to overcome this natural state and create a political commonwealth for mutual security is forever threatened with failure, and failure is defined as the return of the state of nature in the form of a catastrophic and bloody civil war. Thus, the political, however temporary and flawed it may be, is cherished because it establishes the hope for civil peace. The principle of sovereignty, based on a constitutive asymmetry, is consequently seen as a necessarily imperfect but nevertheless still *necessary* solution to a perpetual problem. In the absence of divine intervention and an ultimate theory of types leading back to the sovereignty of an immortal God, the *mortal* God produced by the sovereign self-exemption will have to do. Left by an absent God to our own devices, we create the political. For Agamben, on the other hand, the problem that Hobbes thinks he solves is in reality the *product* of the political space he creates and the *consequence* of the sovereign ban. The existence of *homo sacer*, the life that may be killed but not sacrificed, is not a political problem but a problem of the political. Consequently, any strictly political action undertaken in the space defined by the sovereign ban is undertaken in vain. "Until a completely new politics . . . is at hand," he writes, "every theory and every praxis will remain imprisoned and immobile, and the 'beautiful day' of life will be given citizenship only either through blood and death or in the perfect senselessness to which the society of the spectacle condemns it" (*HS*, 11). Much like Adorno and Horkheimer, on the one hand, and Heidegger, on the other, Agamben sees the trajectory of the political in the West heading inexorably toward totalitarianism or facile consumerism. In either case, thoughtless political action simply replicates and expands the horrific space of the modern. To think the political from within the political, in Agamben's view, is to "remain inside nihilism" (*HS*, 60).

It is a fascinating dilemma that faces us. Hobbes's pessimistic view of human nature, his belief in natural or anthropological evil, allows, oddly enough, for human fallibility, but only at the expense of accepting human incorrigibility. The fact of original sin compels tolerance of imperfection. The political is the realm in which the effects of fallibility are contained and minimized. Sovereign self-exemption is the mechanism by which this containment is achieved. To Agamben, however, this toleration of the political as defined by the sovereign ban can be nothing but a fatalistic acquiescence in the *creation* of the social nightmare called the state of nature. In order to transcend this nihilism, we are urged to embark on a quest for metaphysical transfiguration. Intolerant of what we are, or what we have been forced to become, we are charged with becoming other than what we are, becoming, perhaps, truer to what we *really* are, or what we ought to be. Consequently, we are faced with a staggering Heideggerian task—no mere reconfiguration of the political, but a thorough rethinking of Being. Simply to think "the form of law," Agamben tells us, "does nothing other than repeat the ontological structure that we have defined as the paradox of sovereignty (or sovereign ban). . . . Only if it is possible to think the Being of abandonment beyond every idea of law . . . will we have moved out of the paradox of sovereignty toward a politics freed from every ban" (*HS*, 59). If mythic violence establishes and preserves the law, then a "politics freed from every ban" must arrive, if and when it does arrive, on the wings of a thoroughly divine, thoroughly bloodless, but lethal, violence.

Messiah or *Katechon*?

The line is clearly drawn between the presumption of guilt and a fallen politics, on the one hand, and, on the other, a reclaimed innocence based on being abandoned by the law. Agamben marks this distinction with a neat contrast between Walter Benjamin and Carl Schmitt—between, that is, the messiah and the *katechon*. "For Benjamin," Agamben notes,

the state of demonic existence of which law is a residue is to be overcome and man is to be liberated from guilt (which is nothing other than the inscription of natural life in the order of law and destiny). At the heart of the Schmittian assertion of the juridical character and centrality of the notion of guilt is, however, not the freedom of the ethical man but only the controlling force of a sovereign power (*katechon*), which can, in the best of cases, merely slow the dominion of the Antichrist. (*HS*, 28)

For Benjamin, according to Agamben, guilt does not precede law and call it into being; rather, guilt is introduced into the world with the demonic rule of law. Thus, to be liberated from the structure of sovereignty is to be returned to a natural state of innocence. Agamben's Schmitt, on the other hand, is a firm believer both in the priority and irreducibility of original sin. Sovereignty is the result of and compensation for guilt, not its cause.

In short, Benjamin's messianic, divine violence would bring us back to the garden from which we have strayed. Schmitt's *katechon*, on the other hand, condemns us to a long, lonely vigil, a fearful wait, first for the Antichrist and then for the eventual cataclysmic redemption, a redemption that does not restructure political life on earth but relieves us from having to live on earth at all.

The theological scene of battle evoked by Agamben is not gratuitous, for we are reminded of medieval debates concerning natural law (*ius naturale*), debates that culminated in a thirteenth-century battle between the pope and radical Franciscans. Roman legal theorists of the early Church held the view that in the state of nature there was no dominion, no private property, and no mastery of one human over another. Rather, everything was held and used in common. It is only with the introduction of the law of nations (*ius gentium*) that private property and the political sphere, with its separation of nations and resultant wars, come into being. By espousing "apostolic poverty," which stated that one had the right to use the earth and its products for survival but had no rights of dominion, no property or ownership rights, the Franciscans wished to re-occupy this state of nature and thereby reclaim a measure of innocence, even in the midst of a fallen and sinful world. But, as Richard Tuck states in his study of the origin of natural rights theories, the Franciscan theory of apostolic poverty was not just the self-justification of a religious order; it had "a normative point: if it was possible for some men to live in an innocent way, then it should be possible for all men to do so."[17] The image of the entire world as an enormous commons, open to all and owned by none, has nourished utopian thought ever since, and continues to do so today. One need only think of Linebaugh and Rediker's *The Many-Headed Hydra* or Hardt and Negri's *Empire*.[18] And, I would add, one need only think of Agamben's work as well, his injunction to move "out of the paradox of sovereignty towards a politics freed from every ban," and his evocation of a "coming community" that has never heard the call of the law.

But one could ask: why has this new community, freed from every ban, never been realized? It is, to be sure, an unfair question. Utopias should never be scrutinized. But it is a necessary question, for any answer will inevitably bring us back to the issue of guilt.

As the melancholic and self-pitying champion of the *katechon*, the delayer, who preserves an imperfect social order in the absence of the *par-*

ousia, Schmitt is made to stand for the political nihilism Agamben deplores. Schmitt becomes the embodiment of guilt, the guilty, disciplined body that waits for the Antichrist. But more: Agamben accuses him of a guilt of a higher order, for Schmitt is not simply the representative of an unavoidable guilt, he is not simply guilty; rather, he is guilty of his guilt. As the apologist for a natural or anthropological notion of evil, Schmitt, like Hobbes, finds humans to be fundamentally incorrigible. We live, to invoke again the language of Hobbes, in an indifferent state of nature in which the guilt of our imperfection manifests itself as violence. As a consequence, the political is constituted as a realm in which this violence can be contained, limited, and redirected, but never abolished. The political, on this view, is not a utopic space of individual or social self-actualization, but an imperfectly human space of infinite negotiation. A natural or anthropological notion of original and ineradicable sin, therefore, relieves us from the impossible pressures of perfectibility and compels tolerance of imperfection. Guilty of our imperfection, we atone for our sins imperfectly within a social space that acknowledges our imperfection.

Thus, to argue for the political as currently configured, with its recognition of a social and legal order constituted by a necessary mythic violence, is to embrace the oddly comforting notion of guilt. This, the acceptance of a natural and inevitable guilt, is the *higher-order* guilt Agamben labels nihilism. We are commanded therefore to deny the political as delineated by the sovereign ban, to free ourselves from guilt by rejecting the metaphysics that, in Agamben's view, supports it. Overcoming the metaphysics of the sovereign ban clearly cannot occur from within the political space of that metaphysics. Any step out of our fallen state must be a step initiated by a divine violence—this time a truly bloodless violence, because it is to take place in the non-corporeal world of thought. Ironically, if we do *not* reject the political and the metaphysics that grounds it, then we are burdened with an even greater guilt than the simple guilt of the political; if we do not reject the paradox of sovereignty, then we are charged with the guilt of accepting guilt, the theological guilt of rejecting redemption. It is as if willfully inhabiting the political were like staring into the face of God—and denying Him. The symbol of this greater guilt is Agamben's dramatic equation of modernity with Auschwitz, that is, his characterization of the camp—the death camp, the work camp, the internment center—as the "*nomos* of the modern" (*HS*, 166), the "political space of modernity itself"

(*HS*, 174), where "all life becomes sacred and all politics becomes the exception" (*HS*, 148). With the essence of modernity reduced to a technological killing field, embracing the political is equivalent to building concentration camps while awaiting the Antichrist.

But denying God—or at least denying His intervention in the world of the political—is precisely what the *katechon* does. The word *katechon* refers to a perplexing figure in the second letter to the Thessalonians, in which Paul attempts to dampen overeager expectations. Christ's return, Paul assures us, is imminent, but will be preceded by signs. Only after the Antichrist has usurped God's place in the temple will Christ come again to claim his own. Waiting for Christ entails waiting for the Antichrist, yet the time of the latter's arrival is also not known, for there is, Paul says, a *katechon*, a delayer or restrainer, whose task it is to prevent the Evil One's arrival. Christ will come at some unknown future time when the Antichrist has prevailed over the *katechon*. The unsolved riddle of the *katechon* lies not only in who or what this figure might be, but *why* Paul would want to delay the coming of the Antichrist when the coming of the Antichrist signals the final battle and the triumphant return of Christ. If we longed for the *parousia*, should we not be impatient with the interference of the *katechon*?

But what if, after two thousand years and untold promises, we have lost our faith in the *parousia* and grown weary of waiting for the arrival of divine violence? Then would not delaying the Antichrist be what we should hope for? What if the *katechon* were not primarily a theological figure, but a political one, or rather a figure of the political itself? Attempting to come to terms both with the seemingly infinite deferral of the Second Coming and with the existence of a universal yet non-Christian, secular authority, the early Church assumed that the *katechon* represented the Roman empire. Thus, in the absence of any imminent ascendancy into the City of God, the mundane space of the political as such is designed to prevent the coming of the Antichrist, and with him, the end of the world. The political, on this early Christian view, must be imperfect but beneficial—were it perfect, it would not be the *katechon*, but Christ, and were it demonic, to use Agamben's term, it would be the Antichrist, which is precisely what the political attempts to hold at bay. The *katechon*, as a figure for the political, rejects the promise of the *parousia* and protects the community from the dangerous illusions of both ultimate perfection and absolute evil. Embracing the political, therefore, can only be considered nihilistic if one entertains the hope of replacing the City of Man with the City of God here on earth itself.

So, if we commit what in Agamben's eyes can only be seen as the sin of embracing the political, perhaps it is because we do not fear the arrival of the Antichrist as much as the arrival of Christ Himself. We are like the stubborn Pharisees who denied Christ, and perhaps we can now see that they were right! In an odd but compelling way, we know that Christ and the Antichrist are really the same—figures who promise us perfection, figures who offer us redemption and bestow upon us the guilt of failing perfection or rejecting their offer. The *katechon*, the political, those human institutions that keep us human, that keep us ensnared in our many, ordinary guilts— perhaps this is all we have. And to long for the divine destruction of the imperfect world of the political—perhaps this is the greater nihilism.

Coda

Agamben offers us an alternate vision of the political, a vision of the political that cannot be recognized as such by one who seeks to delay the Antichrist. In his book *The Coming Community* Agamben confronts us with a fascinating theological question: What happens to the souls of unbaptized babies who have died in ignorance of both sin and God? What is their punishment? "According to Saint Thomas," Agamben reports:

The punishment of unbaptized children who die with no other fault than original sin cannot be an afflictive punishment, like that of hell, but only a punishment of privation that consists in the perpetual lack of the vision of God. The inhabitants of limbo, in contrast to the damned, do not feel pain from this lack: since they have only natural and not supernatural knowledge, which is implanted in us at baptism, they do not know that they are deprived of the supreme good. . . . The greatest punishment—the lack of the vision of God—thus turns into a natural joy: Irremediably lost, they persist without pain in divine abandon. God has not forgotten them, but rather they have always already forgotten God. (*CC*, 5–6)

This, then, is the state of the ideal community, the community not based on identity or law but on being blissfully abandoned.

Like the freed convict in Kafka's *Penal Colony*, who has survived the destruction of the machine that was to have executed him, these beings have left the world of guilt and justice behind them: the light that rains down on them is that irreparable light of the dawn following the *novissima dies* of judgment. But the life that begins on earth after the last day is simply human life. (*CC*, 6–7)

Simple, human life is not bare life; it is not the life that is constructed by the sovereign ban, nor the life that is structured, as Schmitt's, by the primacy of the friend/enemy distinction. It is not sacred life, and thus is not exposed life. Rather, in this description of limbo, we have the vision of a community that has never heard of the gods and thus is in no need of the law; a community that knows no friendship, has no need of friendship, because it has never known enemies; a community that cannot conceive of innocence because it has never experienced guilt. In limbo we await no one and wait for nothing.

It would be nice to be one of those dead and unbaptized babies who float, in limbo, between the polarities that trigger the paradox and the guilt of sovereign logic. But I wonder: Can they remain suspended indefinitely? How long would it take for the sin of the political to make its presence felt again? After all, what would the members of this community do if at their borders—and those borders could be internal as well as external—a messenger arrived, an apostle with an apple, as it were, who spoke of God and Satan, of good and evil, of salvation and damnation, of friend and enemy? What would they do? Would they listen to this emissary from another world? Could they *avoid* listening to this tempting apostle? Would it be possible to close one's ear to the sound of the political coming as if from the outside? Would it be possible to forget what one has heard immediately upon hearing it? If not, would it be possible to close the mouth of this political emissary in a non-political way? Or can the political only be silenced politically? Do you suppose that in an attempt to protect itself from this message, the community of abandoned souls would be tempted to silence the messenger? Do you suppose these souls would be tempted to kill the messenger for the sake of the community, much like the Young Comrade must be killed, and must agree to his killing, in Bertolt Brecht's *The Measures Taken*? If so, what kind of killing would this be? Would it be a sacrifice? A homicide? Or would it be a killing that was neither a sacrifice nor a homicide?

Giorgio Agamben

The Discreet Taste of the Dialectic

Antonio Negri

Translated by Matteo Mandarini

1. What has immanence (the thought and life that—according to Deleuze—has no "outside") to do with the dialectic (a thought that always has an "outside" to construct or to subsume in the *Aufhebung*)? Nothing, from the standpoint of immanence in the strict sense of the term. But dialectics, that is, the thought of a continuous movement that absorbs the transcendent in the real and raises the real to the absolute, claims that this movement represents the actual definition of immanence. From the standpoint of philosophical terminology, it certainly does not, but the question of the relationship between immanence and dialectics is familiar from the standpoint of philosophical opinion and historiography. In different forms and at different levels—metaphysical in Plato, logical in Aristotle, theological in Aquinas, ontological in Hegel—the question of the relationship of immanence to dialectics was, at least in these cases, answered largely in the affirmative. The numerous distinctions of transcendent and/or transcendental mediation were formulated and exhibited for this reason. In the course of the restless genealogy of our time, the philosophy of modernity—from the Renaissance to German Idealism and its epigones—has been the strange bedfellow of dialectics. It is as though, at the end of

the modern era, we re-awoke to philosophy, feeling that the relationship between immanence and dialectics was legitimate and its positive resolution necessary.

It was essential that this tradition be broken. The thought of Giorgio Agamben—like that of the post–World War II generation—is born precisely of the theoretical negation and the ethical refusal of this relation. The reaffirmation of that relation represented not only the death of God but of Man as well. Whatever form this move beyond dialectics took, it was considered the very mark of "doing philosophy." Dialectics could no longer be considered a thought that sublated the negative. It was to be understood as the experience of a movement that is violently wrecked on the rocks of madness and death, of senseless capitalist totalitarianism and of the genocides of modernity. It was judged to be a thought that merged with the new destinies of domination, of war and extermination, that the universally acclaimed technologies of modernity had constructed. If it was impossible to write poetry after Auschwitz and Hiroshima, it was equally doubtful that it was possible to continue doing philosophy through the mere repetition of dialectical forms. From here springs the dialogue between the "negative philosophy" of the last dialectical philosophers in crisis and the radical immanence of the first postmodernists (poststructuralists), between the *Dialectic of the Enlightenment* and *The Order of Things*—as does the radically nondialectical solution adopted by the new philosophical generations and the intention to avoid every philosophical exercise that includes or justifies death, which is encapsulated in ferocious secular theodicies. From here, also, stems the decision to reconstruct an open, extended, universal path of redemption. This is where Giorgio Agamben is born.

Language and Death (1982), which could equally have been called "Hegel's Dialectic and the Idea of Death in Heidegger," is Agamben's first fully philosophical and substantially metaphysical book after a long literary apprenticeship. The confrontation with Hegel's dialectic is at the forefront. This first work constituted a veritable introduction to philosophy, in which he proposed, in contrast to the insatiable gluttony of the dialectical method, an analytical one that would typify his approach in subsequent years. This involved *constructing* critically on the terrain of being and ploughing a path to *redemption* along the *margin* of the existential and the linguistic. Redemption was entirely immanent, never failing to remember the mortal condition of existence. Working in the discipline of philosophy meant endeavouring to ethically traverse being, eliminating all dialectical residues (which were, at that time, widespread among the epigones of idealism and in the twilight of socialism). The point of this was to produce true, politically directed, and ethically characterised knowledge that would be directed toward a possible redemption of humanity. At first sight it looked as though Agamben, like Derrida and Nancy, was perusing a point of being that is desirous of the Other and that was, nonetheless, always illusory. It was not so. The more Agamben deepened his phenomenological analysis of being, the more he worked through the possible, presenting/configuring a new horizon (as Blanchot had occasionally done) and traversing the linguistic world in the terms of a critical ontology. In so doing, Agamben's thought, and the description of the reality that he shadowed, approached the Marxist idea of the *General Intellect*, that is, to the positive idea of the linguistic labour of the common, traversed by struggles, by processes of exploitation, and by tremors of liberation.

Of course, things were not simple. In the pursuit of the path we have described, which involved introducing and working with the hints of linguistic and existential "possibility" we have alluded to, Agamben drew on elements that emerged from within Italian Marxist philosophical culture at the time of his philosophical apprenticeship.[1] At the same time, displaying enormous critical courage, he went on to produce a breakthrough on the plane of ontology, a sort of "Copernican revolution" within the figure of being constructed by Heidegger. Heidegger's ontological realism (his materialism?) was, in fact, adopted as the inevitable horizon of the experience of life, of knowing and doing. Agamben separates out experience and language from the morass in which Heidegger had placed them, as if smeared across the horizon of being, and redefines them as possibility. Whereas, in Heidegger, they were undifferentiated, Agamben introduces difference. "Possibility" or, rather, the totality of the possible was included in this immersion in being. Being was absolutely immanent. It was the *infinite plane of immanence*, as both Deleuze and Agamben would go on to define it. Redemption was not any "outside" but an always determinate "inside." This world, this being in which we were immersed, was also a source of possibility. *Sein und Zeit* was read again in the Tuscan light. The barbarous Teutonic and Nazi inclinations were torn from it. But was this possible?

. . .

2. Let us return to the philosophical climate in Italy during the tumultuous 1960s and 1970s. The thought of *Krisis* represented the theoretical point of reference for the crisis of Marxism in Italy for quite some time. The erosion of the Marxist theory of value, and the attendant impossibility of bringing it back into line with the rational schema of economic planning or to the political *dispositifs* that attached themselves to it, determined the—typically Italian (that is, imposed by the high level of struggle)—demand to save communist politics beyond the crisis of communist theory. The philosophy of *Krisis* unfolded within this framework.

The crisis of the theory of value, that is, of that which had formed the rational foundation for revolutionary theory, became the focus for the effort to found anew the project of that theory. In other words, it led to a Prometheanism of politics in the absence of science or, rather, in the presence of the radical crisis of its foundation. Science, therefore, became science of the project to the extent that it could not be science of the foundation. Thus, a form of acute schizophrenia grasped a considerable part of the theory of Italian communism. As the skepticism advanced and led back to the origins of the modern philosophical and political thinking of the West, one was confronted with the unfolding of a kind of pure science of the political. The foundation was plunged into mysticism, thereby indicating the absence of any validation for that technical rationality by which one, nevertheless, acceded into the disenchantment of politics.

First, *Language and Death* has a valuable historical-critical function: that of situating itself "in the place of the negative," as the theorists of *Krisis* liked to depict it. It grabs the thought of *Krisis* by the horns and tears it from the political mystification that consumes it. From this perspective, it resituates negative thought in the philosophical discourse of its time and gives it the status of a critical passage. In what respect? In respect to the problem of the definition of the foundation. The second merit of Agamben's book is that it attacks with great determination the problem of the foundation itself and resolves it, not by hypostasising *Krisis*, but by rediscovering the link between being and practice.

Agamben sets out from the conviction that the birthplace of Western philosophy, its search for an ontological foundation (necessarily articulated by the language that expresses it), is essentially a mystical one. The search for an ontological foundation circles, fatally, around the definition of the sayable, which can be nothing but the repetition of the being-said.

The foundation is reduced to the means of expression: the foundation can be only insofar as it is said. But the being-said is not thereby a foundation, it is pure *voice*. The ruse of the philosophy of *Krisis* was to accept the crisis of the foundation and to certify its sinking into mystical thought, but to simultaneously adopt the voice and the logic of expression as intentions autonomous and independent from those of the mysticism of the foundation. In this way, the logic of the project not only claims to be without foundation but—by the cunning of the gods—is truly so. However, on these grounds, the thought of the project ends up being ineffective. It is under the illusion that it can take on the logical power of an unresolved problem. But a logical power is an insubstantial one.

In his historical reconstruction of the development of the problem of the foundation, that is, of the relation between ontological foundation and the voice that expresses it, Agamben simultaneously cuts through two knots represented by Hegel and Heidegger. In Hegel, the identification of the problem of the foundation and of the logical dimension of its expression is total. But—as Agamben notes—it is precisely this radical assumption of the problem of the foundation within the logical dimension that explodes the problem. Hegel takes the indefinite circularity of the problem as foundational. The bad infinite that he wanted to avoid becomes the beginning. The foundation becomes the unfounded—and, in logic, it can only be thus. The insignificance of the voice claims to be the foundation of being. But the voice is only a modality of being and does not found it. The ontological-linguistic circle remains open, as Heidegger demonstrates that this circle can never close. He pushes Husserlian intentionality to the point of identity with the time of being. The sense [meaning] of being can only issue into the undermining of all sense [direction] to being,[2] occurring in the declaration of the completely inessential character of the existent and, therefore, resulting in a completely negative ontological status for the voice that expresses being as well. Hegel's attempt to think being as the relation of all relations is undermined by the recognition that every relation is unfounded. Hence, the sense of metaphysics is to grasp the nullity of relations. Ironically, the oldest systematic programme of German Idealism, which consisted in drawing the negative—through the dialectic—into the process of the totality, was brought to completion by Heidegger in nihilism.[3]

Indeed, Agamben emphasises that this nihilistic self-dissolution of being frees the voice—but *another* voice, an absolute voice, absolved of the negativity of which it had been the bearer. Effectively, it is now *poiesis*, inasmuch as it endures as the only power of this dissolved universe.[4] The voice is freed from the genealogy of negativity. First, it is left in desperate solitude, then, it attempts to reorganise itself in the linguistic relation, and, finally, it endeavours to comprise the existent in the ethical relationship. Is an absolution of the voice possible that posits it as the basis for a metaphysics of Man? It is possible when the voice does not try to logically comprise metaphysics within itself. When, instead, it presents itself as ethical and, on this basis, it sets out the rationale of being. The value of nihilism can only be grasped in this way.

Can nihilism be overturned as well? Can the voice—having been the key to the attempt to make being logical and, thus, having constituted the ground of the dissolution of sense, of the foundation itself—become the horizon of sense? And where would this occur?

It seems to me that a third thinker intervenes here. I am referring to Marx. Referring, that is, to a Marx dragged to the level of real subsumption and, so, to the horizon of the complete reduction of being to the voice, of the chain of productive relations to the community of linguistic relations. Here the theory of the voice presents itself as a coining of being in ethical terms. Enough logical coining of being! Enough positing of *Krisis!* Only the voice, insofar as it is collective, ethically meaningful, productive, and constitutive represents the basis of a "philology" capable of reconquering being. From Hegel to Heidegger, the tradition of Western metaphysics dissolves. Its completion is its end: the "end of the days" [*fine dei tempi*] that Kojève saw in Hegel. But the end of days is the opening of a new time dominated by the ethical voice.[5] Marx intuited its significance. Negative thought is no substitute for Marx, as it is unable to put politics in place of theory. It is simply the introduction to a rereading of Marx within real subsumption, and therefore it is an introduction to founding theory anew.

· · ·

3. As we can see, Giorgio Agamben's original choice has other merits, aside from that of allowing him to stand outside the relation of immanence to dialectics posited by idealism. We shall consider these other advantages before turning to the question of whether or not it is possible to read Hei-

degger positively (and perhaps adhere to his ontology)—in other words, whether (as one used to say) a "progressive use" (or better still, as one says today, "an alternative use") of Heidegger is possible.

What are the other merits of Agamben's first ontological decision? I think that they stem from the fact that, armed with his potent ontological determination, Agamben is able to critically engage with the other dimension of his thought (its source of inspiration or ground of comparison): the French poststructuralist experience. Let us pause and take one step at a time. Where structuralism—as a Marxist heresy—had defined a world that tightly, integrally unified production and reproduction, reality and ideology, constructing a "process without a subject,"[6] poststructuralism has above all attempted to transform the structural field into a vital field of immanence. It has attempted to acknowledge, in its untranscendability, not only motors, articulations, dynamisms, senses, and differences of ontological movements but the power that produced this field as well. The process had to have a subject somewhere, even if no one knew where. It is unnecessary to recount the numerous experiments and ruses that were tested in this laboratory. It is enough to reflect on the forms in which the horizon of poststructuralism intersected with the dimension of the living and the field of immanence began to be traversed by disseminative (à la Derrida) or generative (à la Deleuze) experiences, or in the way that a new vitalism began to be organised in biopolitical terms (à la Foucault). The fact remains that this formidable episode in contemporary thought, which corresponds to the liquidation of the modern and the invention of the postmodern, continues to be terribly fragile in its reference to being and history. Of course, Derridean phenomenology has constructive hiatuses that save it from any teleological tendency; Deleuze's Bergsonism is marked by conscious and recurrent oscillations protecting it against relapses into idealism; and Foucault's hermeneutic is nourished by a schizophrenia that is consciously directed toward the dissolution of all continuity, creatively exploding any form of relation between genealogy and the production of subjectivity. However, the experience of poststructuralism remains fragile, as is often the case with thought that is being intensively transformed.

We certainly do not wish to claim that Agamben's philosophical approach allows him to escape this fragility. In the unfolding of his thought, in its relation to French philosophy, Agamben risks all the dangers faced by Derrida, Deleuze, and Foucault (against whom he measures himself, as does every student against his teachers). But he has done so armed with that complex theoretical and practical experience that was forged in the struggles in Italy during the 1970s that formed the backdrop to his thought. However, he has the advantage of showing just how concrete is the ontology of the field in which he situates his analysis. Ontology, as the place and experience of investigation, no longer presents itself simply as a plane of immanence, as a space in which the determinations of thought are outlined. It is also expression. The ethical density of Agamben's thought turns the destruction of metaphysics into an operation, not a ruse. The subject knows itself to be ethical insofar as it is the agent of the destruction of metaphysics. The subject is immediately positive, inasmuch it grasps being as the absolutely open horizon to be traversed, despite being flattened onto the dimension of the destruction of metaphysics. In the *Oldest Systematic Programme of German Idealism*, to stick with one of Agamben's constant reference points, the totality of the ethical is a collective result. It is the *polis* to be reconstructed. In the same way, in French philosophy, the totality of the ethical is presupposed. It is the only presupposition, the true immanence formed by language, by production, by differences. If this appears still to retain Heideggerian dimensions, it is nevertheless in this dimension that thought must risk itself—knowing that the univocity of Heideggerian being is dissolved in equivocity. To traverse being does not mean to dominate it. It means taking it for what it is: destructuring it and displaying it as the figure of the collective voice and its continual dislocation in accordance with the rhythm of the voice. In this way, Agamben also ends up the most determined representative of the second generation of poststructuralism, and one will never be able to say that his thought is tenuously rooted in uncertain alternatives. Agamben is anything but a "weak" postmodernist. His concern will be to continually dissolve the ambiguity of the phenomenological reference of poststructuralist thought and bring it back to a new problematic and constructive tableau: that of deconstruction, desire, and politics.

Those who, like Agamben, have turned their attention to being, do not forget its consistency. Heidegger's materialism, in the same way as Nietzsche's dystopia, defines the backdrop of our present. Every strategy will be conditioned by them. Agamben's arrival on the philosophical scene occurs within such a constellation. It forms its backdrop but also its "strong" condition.

. . .

4. Therefore, the genesis of Agamben's thought is organised around an ontological choice. But this choice—whatever its initial course of development, its forms and articulations—is rooted in a kind of Heideggerianism. Being is given and destinal.[7] Agamben seems essentially to dwell on the given. Does this mean that the destining of Heideggerian being is absent from Agamben's standpoint, from his *initium philosophandi?* Let us try to deal with the question we posed previously: whether an "alternative use" (or, as one used to say, a "progressive use") of Heidegger is possible and, if so, to what extent.

In other words: how can one structure the world that Agamben's ontological approach initially constituted? How can one, bearing in mind—as Agamben always has done—Heidegger's definition of being (and, hence, the experience of death), construct a positive idea of redemption?

We must recognise that, in relation to this aspect of the project, Agamben's theoretical development has been marked by a series of ever more evident breaks. Perhaps *La comunità che viene* (*The Coming Community*) (1990), where the experience of redemption was presented as dystopia, is where the break was strongest. In this work, Agamben demanded that the edge of death be crossed by vital tensions and that Spinoza's maxim— "A free man thinks of nothing less than of death, and his wisdom is a meditiation on life not on death" (*Ethics* pt. 4, P67)—be turned into an aspect of method. The power of being began to be presented as central. Of course, it remained restless, perhaps vacillating, but it was a structurally innovative moment in Agamben's thought. Then Agamben took a variety of different paths, and in *Homo Sacer* (1995) this problematic appeared again in all its complexity and contradictoriness. It probably remained the unresolved condition of his thought.

It seems that there are two Agambens. There is the one who lingers in the existential, destining, and terrifying shadows, where he is perpetually forced into a confrontation with the idea of death. And there is another Agamben, who, through the immersion in the work of philology and linguistic analysis, attains the power of being (that is, he rediscovers pieces or elements of being, by manipulating and constructing them). In this second guise, Agamben at times appears—in his wavering between nocturnal aspects and creative upsurges of being—as a Warburg of critical ontology. Paradoxically, however, these two Agambens *always* coexist and, when you least expect it, the former reemerges and obscures the latter. The shadow of death spreads lugubriously over the desire to live, pitting itself against the excess of desire. Or the reverse.

Let us leap ahead to some of the most recent examples of his work. In *Stato di eccezione* (*State of Exception*) (2003), we are able to see both of these Agambens at once. First, Agamben recognises and denounces the fact that the state of exception (a state of death) has come to involve all structures of Power and renders absolutely empty every experience and definition of democracy. This is the imperial condition. This is a first line of interpretation. Indeed, this definition of the state of exception is situated within an undifferentiated—either cynical or pessimistic—ontological horizon, where every element is reduced to the empty play of an equivalent negativity. Here, the state of exception appears as the indifferent backdrop that neutralises and discolours all horizons, and reconnects them to an ontology unable to produce sense other than destructively. This being is entirely unproductive; it merges with law (or its absence), whereas only a radically innovative and revolutionary activity should be called upon to give sense to the real. But there is no sign of the latter. Thus, one witnesses an overvaluation of law (in the definition of the political) and an underestimation of ontology (in the definition of revolution). Therefore reality does not produce sense. It is clear that there is no difference between "state of exception" and "constituent power,"[8] since they both exist at the same level of indistinctness. The definition of the biopolitical—in this Agamben—is indifferent to antagonism and, probably, to the expression of the ethical "voice." To no avail will one affirm that the law of exception annuls being, when—in truth—resistance and constituent power create it! In contrast, here everything that occurs in the *bios* is bent to the indistinctiveness of nature, of the *zoē*. . . . One easily perceives the drift that compels all unilateral conceptions of the *bios* to a naturalistic reduction. The effect of this first cross-section of the analysis is paradoxical: all that occurs in the world today is as if fixed in a totalitarian and static horizon, as under Nazism. Naturally, one can object that things are not so. If we can be said to live in a state of exception, it is because we are experiencing a ferocious and permanent "civil war," where positive and negative *clash*. Their antagonistic power can in no sense be flattened into indifference.

Agamben, however, does not stop here. *State of Exception* provides us with a second, more original and powerful perspective—a Spinozist and Deleuzian one. Here, the analysis does not survey an inert biopolitical plane but traverses it with feverish utopian anxiety, grasping its internal antagonism. It is true, the philological weapon that Agamben utilises so dextrously in the face of the complexity that invests it becomes almost uncertain, in any case hesitant. Discoveries emerge as surprises—but they are still real discoveries, conceptual and linguistic innovations. The postmodern shows itself to be ontologically hard and creative. At this junction, the *genealogy of the biopolitical* lends continuity to the archaeology and philology. The utopian *dispositif* does not stand in synchronic contrast to the ontological horizon but surges up, penetrates, diachronically breaks down both legal institutions and development. The dialectic is truly overcome because the biopolitical is traversed internally. At this point in Agamben's thought, the biopolitical is no longer seen from without, as though it were an independent reality to be studied, to be recognised—a fruit to be picked. Hegelianism is definitively overcome by a critique that recognises the impossibility of the dialectical homology of opposites, as is any nostalgia for left Hegelianism. Even Benjamin, who also experienced this set of problematic hitches and painful dialectical reminiscences, is overcome. With a formidable gesture, Agamben goes—both conceptually and ethically—across and beyond the state of exception. In the same way, primitive Christianity or early communism went through and out the other side of imperial power and enslavement, destroying them by hollowing them out and dematerialising them from within. In this second scenario, Agamben's analysis shows how immanence can be both realist and revolutionary.

. . .

5. As frequently occurs—and not only in philosophy—it is a case of weights and measures. That is to say, if the hesitation between Heidegger or Spinoza, and the corresponding choice of the interpretation of being, are the signal of an ambiguity—or better still, an alternative— which is not simply an aspect of our thinking but of being itself, then this hesitation cannot last long. Or rather, it will not last when common being structures itself and shapes its power—that is to say, when being is presented concretely, historically, and phenomenologically as *biopolitical*. For a long phase of his philosophical apprenticeship, Agamben, in contrast to Deleuze, to whom he is in other respects very close, exalted the negative aspect of being in contrast to desire and to the constructive movement of *conatus*, and arranged the determinations of life within this

sundered horizon. This will become increasingly difficult—frankly impossible—once Agamben enters the field of biopolitics. *Homo Sacer* marks this point. *But why does Agamben accept the challenge of the biopolitical field?* This is not an extemporaneous or improper question. It could be an impertinent one, were we to forget how frequently Agamben approached the analysis of ways of life and developed a sort of sociology of lifestyles (à la Simmel or Benjamin). Having said that, it is still true that his approach to the life-world (*Lebenswelt*) has little in common with that dramatic ontological definition that lay at the basis of his thought. Taking nothing away from the intensity of his investigation of the phenomenology of the forms and styles of life, it must be said that these remained formal, that they avoided emphasising the political dimension, and also lacked a sufficient emphasis on the temporality of those forms. So why does Agamben choose to test himself on the biopolitical field? What induces him to interpret the immersion in lived being in terms of the comprehension of historically determined being, that is, of the experience of the *Erlebnis* in terms of *historia*—or rather, of the *res gestae*?

An initial answer could be: political passion, ethical indignation, and the "voice" of the alternative. Agamben is a revolutionary and he abhors the "existing state of things." That is unquestionable. But it remains insufficient to explain his conversion to biopolitics, since he is, above all, a philosopher. It is hard to trace his motivations back to political reasons. The influence of Foucault could be another reason, bearing in mind the importance of his thought for many young Europeans in the 1990s and, so, for many of Agamben's interlocutors. And without doubt it is. In those years, Foucault reemerged as a philosophical and political thinker of great importance. There is no doubt that Agamben frequently consulted his work at that time. But this also seems insufficient to me to explain Agamben's conversion from the problem of the experience of being to that of biopolitical expression. His cultural universe, which stretched from Heidegger to Benjamin, from the dialectic of mysticism to Deleuzian immanence, is too complex to speak of influences. The reason for Agamben's decision to test himself on the biopolitical terrain stems from contradictions within his thought, that is, from his irresoluteness in considering the dimensions and (positive) powers of being.

In Agamben, the translation of the idea of being into that of biopolitics occurs within the framework of an operation of *neutralization* of the biopolitical itself. Indeed, the definition of biopolitics that Agamben ascribes to (a) fixes the indistinctiveness of life and politics, between home and city, *zoē* and *bios*; and (b) introduces biological life into the calculations and mechanisms of Power and, thereby, allows biopower to define and organise the biopolitical terrain. What does all this mean? First, that it will no longer be possible to speak of being except in political terms and of body other than in biopolitical terms. But, second, that this new space is always invested by Power, and involved, therefore, in the destining, deathly dimension of being. It is important to note that, in his definition of *biopolitics*, Agamben not only denies that his concept can be isolated, outside and beyond *biopower*, but he also denies that the biopolitical can also be conceived as a dichotomous field. For Agamben, the logic of the biopolitical field is, at best, a field of forces that is bipolar and transitive: home and city, *zoē* and *bios*, life and politics flow from one to the other, and are situated within an ever reversible flow. In this way the absolute neutralisation of the biopolitical is imposed.

One is left wondering why Agamben ever wanted to use the term or assume the problematic of biopolitics. Had it been merely to construct the image of passive marginal resistance, as in the *Muselmann* in the concentration camp or that of Bartelby in his New York office, the nihilistic conception of being (and a "marginal" conception of resistance) would have been sufficient. There was no need to trouble the categories of the biopolitical to identify and shape the desperate and savage figure of the *homo sacer* (sacred in the sense of the assumption of a punishment that separated him from the common). Even in this case, the scandal of the separation from the *polis* was not so different, on the terrain of being, from the destinal break that humanity as such undergoes. Each one of us is *homo sacer*.

So why did Agamben feel the need to engage with the field of biopolitics? Is it because his ontology requires an outlet in life as well as a historical determination? Perhaps. But once this engagement takes place, his thought lacks the strength to separate (within the conception of being) that which Heidegger unified—the given and destiny—and that which, conversely, Spinoza separated: the given and love, *conatus*, *cupiditas*, and freedom. Agamben lacks the strength to throw out the modern (and the end of the modern) and thereby to discover and exalt life's moment of production.

. . .

6. We have now reached the crucial question: *can there be a concept of biopolitics that does not include the concept of productive force?* Can biopolitics be defined as a field? Is it not necessary to understand it in terms of production and endow it with a productive function? Agamben begins to define the notion by excluding all productive qualities and flattening it onto the ontological dimension. In other words, biopolitics is turned into a permanent *dispositif* of metaphysics. Agamben insists that since classical antiquity, it has been impossible to distinguish life from politics. Already with Aristotle, the concept of life is given an ethical and political configuration. The neutralisation of the concept of biopolitics could not have been carried out more radically. Thus, the criticism directed against many of the contemporary champions of biopolitics, that they do not understand how difficult it is, in Foucault himself, to separate the notion of biopolitics from that of biopower, becomes entirely redundant. For Agamben insists that it is useless to extract a positive and productive concept of biopolitics. Biopolitics and production, Agamben tells us, have nothing in common.

May we be permitted our right of reply. It would appear to us that Agamben's exclusion of the productive determination from the concept of biopolitics not only precludes a definition of biopolitics but even prevents us from grasping the concept of being. Agamben starts from the presupposition that productive power is to be attributed only to Power, or, better still, to biopower. This position could appear reactionary. It certainly is not, in Agamben. Nevertheless, it is Heidegger's position, taken up once again, not only in terms of the founding, exterior, formal dimension of his phenomenology, but in that of the qualifying, nihilistic aspect of his destruction of ontology. Once again, the only creative alternative in modernity, Spinoza's productive being, is set aside. The evolution of the very concept of being, in the relation of biopower to biopolitical freedom, is denied— not to mention the history of the concept of production and of the diverse and progressive productive fields that history has registered. To outline this history in *Time for Revolution* (2003), I insisted upon a tripartite definition of production in Western philosophy that crosses the field of ethics, politics, and biopolitics. In antiquity (the era of the *centaur*), the relation of production finds human activity entirely conditioned by nature. In the modern era (that of *man-man*), production is found to mould life itself. In the postmodern era (that of the *man-machine*), the biopolitical relationship is one in which metamorphosis and production not only determine the object but become the very subject of the movement of being. Therefore, far from it being possible to flatten production onto an eternal idea of a being assumed within a continual mystification of Power, production is the key and engine of development and of the ever new configuration of the being of life. When one alludes to the ontological experience of Spinozism as the great alternative within modernity (and which prefigures the post-modern), one is speaking of productive being, of a being as the indefinite singularisation, reproduction, and, therefore, construction of new being.

New problem: from Agamben's perspective, having flattened the reality of the biopolitical field onto the fabric of an indefinite negative ontology, and having excluded production from the biopolitical context, innovation, progressive development, and the productive excess of life become useless and irksome. If you wish for something new, you will find it on the margins of being. The event will be mystical rather than a hard ascesis within being. You will be left with vision and contemplation rather than activity and construction; ecstasy, in place of enjoyment. Once again, we see here how the height of resistance is interpreted by Agamben as passivity rather than as rebellion, represented by Bartleby rather than Malcolm X, by *homo sacer* rather than the slave or the proletariat. Agamben's biopolitics is not only neutralised once it is flattened onto a negative metaphysics of being, but it is also disincarnated in the exclusion of history— or rather, of the *res gestae*—it produces. For Agamben, the "concentration camp" or the "state of exception" have nothing in common with the constellation of forces and ideologies that wanted and constructed them. The theoretical intuition risks becoming merely a literary trope. In respect of this, the later Agamben constitutes a regression when compared to the Agamben of *Language and Death*.

We come now to another point. By inserting the ontological dimension into the framework of the definition of the real, Agamben had given a solid image of the postmodern. Given the criticisms that we have made, it appears that we are now denying him the role of ferryman of the postmodern, in the passage from deconstruction to ontology.[9] This is not so. What we object to is the weakness betrayed by his inability to bring his work to a close. We are no longer interested in the moment when Agamben reveals his inability to reach the other shore and stops halfway across. We are interested in the reasons why he is unable to do so. Our suggestion is that it is because Agamben is prisoner of the "fetishism of the commodity"; that is, of that catastrophist conception (typical of the Marxism of the 1920s) that considers the production of commodities as the production of a reified world (and only of a reified world). More precisely, without tracing once again the genesis of that notion of the postmodern that—from Guy Debord to Lyotard, by way of Socialism or Barbarism—deduces the inevitable reduction of all value to exchange value, to commodity or money from the description of the "real subsumption of society by capital." Although it is true to say that the notion of the postmodern is also born of this theoretical experience, it is also certain that Agamben (among others) opposes to it, or rather imports an ontological *dispositif.* This is a crucial point. But once he has done this, what significant effects does it produce? First, that of situating being at the heart of politics and eliminating the fragility or inconsistency of the lateral, insubstantial, aleatory paths from the postmodern tragedy of fetishism, inauthenticity, and alienation. Second, Agamben's thought leads us to the reaffirmation of *use value.* It is a reaffirmation that is typical of leftist Hegelianism and of the young Marx. It is a discreet dialectical rediscovery (à la Benjamin) that opens the way, not to the triumph of the *Aufhebung,* but to the heroism of the negative.

We can only applaud Agamben's stance. However, it is singularly unproductive. Behind this heroism lies the chasm of the return to nothingness, to the destinal insignificance of being, to the marginality of refusal. There is a sort of naturalistic or fundamentalist terrorism (the restoration of use value) that we really have no use for in an age in which the problem is not that of the return to nature but of constructing another one, of manipulating the existent so as to construct a new world and to move—in a wholly dystopian way—on this terrain. If there are only exchange values, it is with them that we must reconstruct the world. We do not know where we shall arrive, but we know that we can only move in a world of commodities, of reified things and bodies—to submit them to production and to invent the common through production. It is only in production that life and existence intersect, and it is only through it that this relationship can and must be continually revolutionised. This is not utopia but daily life.

. . .

7. It is sad to see the dialectic reappear in Agamben's thought and to see it do so—discreetly—on the basis of an image of being that has been unable to become productive. Agamben reminds me of an obscure (but

very interesting) philosopher of the 1600s: Arnold Geulincx. Geulincx's problem was theodicy, not only inasmuch as it constituted the justification of God but insofar as it was a justification of being, that is, of a world that the transcendent divine cause had so totally invested that it closed down all spaces for freedom and production. Epistemological occasionalism had become ontological. The consequence of this was a sort of determinism organised by a dialectical hierarchy of causes, which shaped the framework of the world through the unbreakable conditioning of every event. By reconstructing the framework of the world in this way, Geulincx stood in opposition to the immanent ontology of Spinozist inspiration that spread in the centuries leading up to the *Aufklärung*. Geulincx stood in opposition to the concept of a being that produced new—excessive and singular, living and expressive—being. In contrast to Spinoza's notion of immanence, determinism is as free as life itself. We have a few questions for Agamben. If being, life, biopolitics are not productive, what is this world if not a "camp," an "exception" (not excess, not innovation) always imposed by Power over life? What is the difference between this and Geulincx's notion of God, which entails that if we kill, then God is a "homicidal God"? If we die, is it because the "Lord of Death" willed it? If being is unproductive and each of its movements are given by the geometrical "extension" of Power, if our body is a "life sentence," where can one find the "voice" of redemption? Will our praxis be an "I act because it is absurd," in the same way as for Geulincx it was a *credo quia absurdum*? Will this not be a desperate pessimism of reason and a terrorist optimism of the will?

The experience of resistance; the desire that is always newly exercised in the production of subjectivity; the capacity to produce (from the perspective of the common) a revolution that does not delude itself into thinking it can evade the world of commodities but wants instead to transform it—all this constitutes a rejection of all forms of determinism and enables us to see the world from the standpoint of challenges and creative *dispositifs*. If there is being, ontological determination, it cannot express itself other than as power, as potent ethical and not mystical "voice."

Approaching Limit Events

Siting Agamben

Dominick LaCapra

At issue in many approaches to the Holocaust and other extreme or limit events, situations, and experiences are two perspectives with problematic relations to one another. One affirms a notion of redemption as absolute recovery with no essential loss, even with respect to so traumatic a past as the Shoah. The second involves the denial or absolute negation of such redemption and a view of redemption in general as unavailable, absent, or repeatedly and aporetically in question. An initial way to see these perspectives is as formulations of working through and acting out—working through as redemption of meaning in life and transcendence of problems toward mental health and ego-identity; acting out as often melancholic, compulsive repetition in which any notion of redemption or full recovery is out of the question and problems reappear in disguised or distorted form. If there is any hope of recovery in this second perspective, it is through radical negation of hope in redeeming the past or making sense of it in the present. Instead one affirms a decisive disjunction vis-à-vis the past, pure utopian possibility, creation ex nihilo, and a (post)apocalyptic leap into an unknown future or state of being. One may even apprehend a glimmer of a totally other form of life—even a redemptive *Augenblick*—in the shadow cast by radically negative critique itself. What tends to be excluded in both perspectives (neither of which I agree with) is a view of working through, not as full redemption, total recovery, or unmitigated caesura, but as a recurrent process that, with respect to extreme trauma or limit events, may never totally transcend acting out or compulsive repetition but that does provide a measure of critical distance on problems and the possibility of significant transformation, including desirable change in civic life, with its responsibilities and obligations.

In changing registers in a manner that does not imply total discontinuity with the previous considerations, I would observe that another way to view these two perspectives is as approaches to the sacred or the sublime. I would like briefly to explore this other way (if only because I have discussed more thoroughly the earlier one—that in terms of acting out and working through—in my writings).[1] Here I am suggesting that the sublime and the sacred can be seen as displacements of one another—one in a secular, the other in a religious key—or at least that, in discussions of the sacred and the sublime, one may have a comparable role for the distinction between the immanent and the transcendent. Indeed, in discussions of limit events or situations that invariably seem to bring up (if only to resist) issues typically related to the sublime, one may often be moving in the difficult and somewhat uncomfortable area of secular or displaced theology even when one attempts to give to that theology the name—perhaps the misleading name—of ethics, of literature as an ethics of writing, or even (as in certain discussions of Claude Lanzmann's film *Shoah*) of autonomous art.

In the first perspective (involving full redemption or recovery) we have a modality of the immanent sublime, and in the second perspective (denying the very possibility of such redemption or recovery, even seeing it as taboo, sacrilegious, or "barbaric"), a modality of the radically transcendent sublime that at the limit (with the "death of God") may be erased or repeatedly held in abeyance (for example, in the form of a messianism without a messiah or messianism as a structure of expectation that intrinsically requires continual deferral). Yet both perspectives intimately relate trauma and the sublime. The sublime involves a transvaluation or transfiguration of trauma with more or less destabilizing effects for any conventional or harmonizing notion of sublimity and perhaps for any normative conception of ethics or politics whatsoever. The sublime is related to excess or, conversely, lacuna or lack—that which is disconcertingly, perhaps ecstatically, other and aporetically beyond (or beneath) any ability to name or to know. It may also be related to radical transgression, at times in sado-masochistic and/or sexual form. It may even approximate disaster and be approached only in a self-effacing writing of disaster marked by a repeated recourse to the paradox, double bind, and *mise en abîme*.

I would note that the immanent sublime finds one of its most unsettling manifestations in what I would term the Nazi sublime. This variant can be detected in the words and actions of at least certain perpetrators during the Shoah. Indeed, I think the primary locus of the sublime during the Nazi genocide itself was in this group of perpetrators. A much-discussed document in which it is active is Himmler's 1943 Posen speech, and one finds traces of it in the endlessly repeated, at times elated or even carnivalesque dimensions of killing and torture in the Einsatzgruppen and their affiliates. One also finds it in certain forms of activity in the camps or the forced marches at the end of the war. Such "sublimity" involved a fascination with excess or unheard-of transgression, endlessly repeated yet adamantly endured traumatic scenes, a code of silence (or unsayability), and a quasi-sacrificial quest involving regeneration or redemption through violence and purification for the self and the community by eliminating "contaminating," phobic, even ritually repulsive presences. Here I shall cite some relevant passages from Himmler's Posen speech given to upper-level SS officers (hence intended for the initiated and not as propaganda for the general public):

I also want to make reference before you here, in complete frankness, to a really grave matter. Among ourselves, this once, it shall be uttered quite frankly; but in public we will never speak of it. Just as we did not hesitate on June 30, 1934 [the purge of Ernst Röhm and his SA leadership], to do our duty as ordered, to stand up against the wall comrades who had transgressed, and shoot them, also we have never talked about this and never will. It was the tact which I am glad to say is a matter of course to us that made us never discuss it among ourselves, never talk about it. Each of us shuddered, and yet each one knew that he would do it again if it were ordered and if it were necessary.

I am referring to the evacuation of the Jews, the annihilation of the Jewish people. . . . Most of you know what it means to see a hundred corpses lie side by side, or five hundred, or a thousand. To have stuck this out, and excepting cases of human weakness—to have kept our integrity [or decency: *anständig geblieben zu sein*], that is what has made us hard. In our history this is an unwritten, never-to-be-written page of glory.[2]

Paradoxically, one may also find another variant of the immanent sublime in the belated reactions of certain survivors or commentators who attempt to provide a redemptive, awe-inspiring, at times even sacralizing account of the Shoah itself and to convert it into a founding trauma that furnishes an affirmative identity for self and community. This gesture cannot be assimilated to, or viewed as simply "contaminated" by, the Nazi sublime; it is complex. In one sense it is an attempt to take back the Shoah from the perpetrators and make it serve the victims (perhaps figured as martyrs) or their descendants. In significant ways, however, the gesture remains within a certain logic of redemption and has many dubious dimensions, especially in the case of nonsurvivors who find sublimity through a transfiguration of the suffering of others. The transfiguration of trauma into a founding experience or occasion for saving sublimity may have a political and ethical role in justifying policies or practices that are open to question—from Holocaust memorialization in the United States to certain Israeli figurations of the redemptive nation and its hard-line right to defend itself in any way it sees fit.

The transcendent sublime, which may be hesitantly intimated or under erasure, has the appeal of counteracting the lure of the immanent sublime, which may include regeneration through violence and a quasi-sacrificial or totalizing logic. Indeed, the transcendent sublime would seem to serve as a bar to any mode of sacrifice, but at the cost of eliminating all forms of the immanent sacred, including the limits it sets on human assertion and its protective function for nature or human and other-than-human beings. There is also a sense in which the transcendent sublime remains within an all-or-(almost)-nothing "logic" of the absolute and a displaced theological frame of reference. It too stresses excess or what is (perhaps transgressively) beyond the limits of representation, naming, and normativity. The supplementary stress is on lacuna, lack, or loss, and what is beneath representation. Such an orientation may be accompanied by a bracketing or even denigration of knowledge (except for learned ignorance, in which knowledge aporetically returns time and again to its own limits and forms of undoing); it may have a dismissive, demeaning, or begrudging view of this-worldly activity (*divertissement*) in general or at least it seems to provide little viable space in which to develop such knowledge and activity. In a sense an orientation to the transcendent sublime remains fixated on the absolute in its very elusiveness, unavailability, or unpresentability. Jean-François Lyotard, at least in certain aspects of his thought, would perhaps be a paradigmatic figure here, but he is not alone.[3]

Whether Maurice Blanchot's writings, insofar as they bear on the Shoah, can be seen as engaging considerations associated with the sublime may be debatable.[4] Still, in Blanchot, a simultaneous attenuation and intensification of the contemplative life, and a hesitant, allusive intimation of what might seem to be an effaced or erased transcendent sublime, are related to endless waiting, patience, and an ascesis of style (or a self-effacing ethic of writing), even harrowing isolation in the wake of disaster. Blanchot's writings, insofar as they pertain to the Shoah, may be defensible as a personal, anguished response—a modality of impossible mourning undecidably close to (or sharing a threshold of indistinction with) endless melancholy and (im)personal bereavement. In a sense they may be read as based on an extreme, posttraumatic, empathic response to the abject plight of victims, even to the point of self-erasure. But one may doubt whether they should be taken as exemplary or whether their import for the response to limit events should be generalized. It is unclear whether they become exemplary in Derrida's reinscription of them. In any case, the understanding of ethics in the complex constellation of thought that includes Blanchot and Derrida (for example, in the latter's "The Force of Law: The 'Mystical' Foundation of Authority'" or *The Gift of Death*) tends in significant ways to be linked to the sublime—ethics in terms of excess or what is beyond the limit of normativity that articulates relations of people in groups or institutional settings such as the family, the school, the workplace, or the polity.[5]

Here what was traditionally seen as the supererogatory virtue—that which is above and beyond the call of duty or ordinary obligation—seems at times to lessen or even obliterate the significance of the latter or to cast it at best as a necessity made as a pragmatic concession in order to carry on in the world (just as human rights or the subject may be radically criticized in principle but conceded as a necessity of contemporary forms of political and social action). Civic life may even become ghostly or virtual, a spectral hope with at best a virtual agent or bearer, a question of an unavowable or coming community, or, in Derrida's recent formulation (in *Specters of Marx*) of endless longing, a seemingly blank utopianism that denies its own utopian status, a messianism without a messiah.[6] The relation to every other may even be figured on the model of the radically asymmetrical or nonreciprocal relation (or nonrelation) between the agonized individual (or singularity) and the radically transcendent divinity. This relation involves absolute respect for the Other/others, yet this respect in the seeming register of sublimity provides the sense of how to relate to others in terms of daily commitments, obligations, and mutual rights and duties. It provides a sense of justice not in terms of measure or limits but as an invariably supererogatory virtue that seems to take relations out of institutional settings and even make them transcend or systematically exceed institutions. Justice here is closer to grace or the excessive gift—the *acte gratuit* or the potlatch—than to norms and judgment related to a network of normative limits. The sense of normativity I am invoking should not be conflated with positive law, construed as amenable to programming and rigid codification, or collapsed into normalization (or taking the statistical average or the dominant as normative). Rather, it would relate to articulatory practices that would be open to challenge and even at times radical transgression but would nonetheless set limits to personal and group assertion that ideally would be affirmed and could be argumentatively defended as legitimate.

I think there is greater appeal in the second (transcendent) perspective on the sublime than in the first. But the problem that is occluded or at least insufficiently addressed in the second perspective is that of the transitional "space" or mediating and mitigating (but non-totalizable) links between absolutes or sublimities, that is, the sublunar or subastral space of ethical and political life. This is the space in which the primary question is the variable relation between limits and excess, including transgression and the limit event or situation, in various institutional settings and sociopolitical forms of activity. It is the space in which the distinction between the human and the nonhuman (which invariably serves invidious functions that often underwrite victimization of the other) may be radically problematized but not become a deceptive, self-defeating object of fixation—a space in which such problematization is related, not only to a notion of the split or disjunctive subject, but also to a notion of the human animal or being as a compromise formation of complex, interacting forces. It is also the space for developing forms of knowledge and understanding (involving affect, notably in the form of empathic response) that do not pretend to be identical with things themselves but that do provide some orientation in behavior and have a bearing on ethical judgment. (Hence empathy in the sense I am using the term involves not identification but respect for the other as other even when one's response is, in relation to the traumatic, itself unsettled and to some extent uncontrolled.) In this civic space, the ethical is not fully calculable or a matter of accounting, but it does involve the mutual ability to count on others in terms of one's fallible knowledge of how they have behaved in the past and may be expected to behave in the future.

Such knowledge is not fully redemptive, but it may confront the problem of transmitting trauma (or rather unsettlement) in a mitigated way that both indicates empathy with victims and—at least with respect to the Shoah—questions (without peremptorily dismissing) a "logic" of the sublime that transfigures trauma. Such constitutively limited knowledge may also help create the readiness to feel anxiety in the face of the unexpected or the uncanny in a fashion that does not assure nonrepetition of the past but that may provide some basis for a nonparanoid response to its displaced repetitions or reconfigurations. Moreover, I do not see the possibility of an ethics of daily life—an ethics with a critical distance on theology—that is not based on a sense of legitimate limits, however much such a sense may be problematic, tested by forms of excess, or open to continual questioning and supplementation (for example, by necessary economic and political concerns). It is in terms of ethics in this nonsublime or subastral sense—a social and civic sense that is remedial but not fully redemptive—that one may ask for an explicit acknowledgment of one's past, for example, in the (different) cases of de Man, Heidegger, or Blanchot. I think ethics is misconstrued as, or even sacrificed to, sublimity when Derrida, in what would seem to be an unguardedly transferential act of projective identification, writes these startling words: "Perhaps Heidegger thought: I can only voice a condemnation of National Socialism if it is possible for me to do so in a language not only at the peak of what I have already said, but also at the peak of what has happened here. He was incapable of doing this. And perhaps his silence is an honest form of admitting he was incapable of it."[7]

Without denying one's own implication in the ambivalent "logic" of the sublime and even recognizing its almost compulsive appeal, one may still insist on the need to develop thought and practice in the transitional civic "space" or modality that at times seems reduced to a vanishing point in an emphasis on either an immanent or a radically transcendent sublim-

ity. Or to put the point in deceptively simple nominal terms: after a generation devoted to exploring what was gained in the paradoxical mode of
pure waste or excessive expenditure (*dépense*), it may now be time to ask
whether something important was obscured or lost yet may still be recov-
erable (or "redeemable") in readings of Bataille, notably with respect to his
response to Durkheim, to wit, a sense of legitimate limits not only or even
predominantly as a pretext for, but rather as a strong countervailing force
to, excess and the allure of transgression.[8] (Of course the challenge would
be to articulate such limits, not in the abstract but in specific, variable,
contestable situations.) And the question I would raise is whether and to
what extent, with respect to the Shoah and perhaps to other limit events,
one should, in one's own voice, resist a "logic" of the sublime and, more
generally, whether one should engage in a careful, differentiated critique
of an aesthetic of sublimity. One may raise this question without subscribing to an indiscriminate hostility to the sublime, especially when its role,
notably in art and religion—is explored in its tense, mutually questioning relations to an affirmation of legitimate limits (including ethical and
political limits).

I would like to turn now to the work of Giorgio Agamben, particularly his *Remnants of Auschwitz*, in the light of the problems I have evoked.[9]
Agamben has recently risen to prominence in the field of critical theory,
and there is a sense in which he seems constrained to raise the stakes or
"up the ante" (which is already astronomically high) in theoretically daring, jarringly disconcerting claims if he is to make a significant mark as a
major theorist. This seemingly inevitable process of vying with, or even
trying to outdo, predecessors is one of the more problematic aspects of the
"race for theory" in the recent past, an inclination that becomes increasingly tempting to the extent that critical theory, both in general and in its
significant variations, is subjected to impatient dismissals or misinformed
understandings. (This context makes it all the more important to try to
develop informed and nuanced—albeit at times forceful—readings, interpretations, and critiques.) In Agamben, moreover, a sustained intricacy
of formulation and an insistently paratactic or "poetic" style in philosophy make it both difficult to understand him in a way that enables critical
exchange and possible for a sympathetic (or perhaps extremely generous)
reader (or overwriter) to gloss questionable passages in a quasi-theological
manner that always displaces attention to other, less dubious passages,

even if they are to be found in another work. The fact that Agamben is a writer who seems to elicit this response in some readers (even to generate a discipleship) is itself of interest, but it shall in general not characterize the approach I take. Rather, I assume that through critical analysis and exchange, at least aspects of Agamben's thought will be disclosed that might otherwise escape attention.

Agamben adamantly rejects the first perspective on limit events that seeks redemptive meaning, and he often seems to move toward the second perspective. But there are at least intimations of a transitional "space" or nonbinary network of possibilities—a "threshold of indistinction"—that cannot be reduced to the options allowed by my two perspectives or even conceived in spatial terms. (A closer analysis would disclose comparable dimensions in the thought of Blanchot or Derrida.) In *Means Without End* such a threshold of indistinction seems related, however problematically, to the form of life involving open possibilities that Agamben defends and opposes to the nexus of sovereign power and bare or naked life. The allusive status of this dimension in *Remnants of Auschwitz*—where, if anything, it should have been elaborated further with respect to Agamben's notion of ethics—is unfortunate. Moreover, Agamben in the latter book also refers to a state of exception (also invoked in his earlier works) and to a gray zone (a move made with reference to Primo Levi's *The Drowned and the Saved*) whose relations to the threshold of indistinction and to one another are not explicitly thematized and explored as a problem.[10] The larger question that arises is that of the way in which the transitional "space" or "threshold of indistinction" (close to Derrida's notion of undecidability) operates historically and transhistorically as well as empirically and ideally (or normatively); the way it problematizes, or even undoes, existing concepts or norms—indeed entire conceptual and normative orders, perhaps even the very concept of normativity; and the way it may help to generate newer conceptual and normative articulations explicitly recognized as problematic but nonetheless in important ways affirmed as legitimate.

Agamben clearly (and, I think, rightly) rejects the idea of any full recovery, redemption, or use of the Holocaust (a term he rejects for etymological reasons) for spiritual uplift or as proof of the essential dignity of the human being and the ability of the human spirit to endure all hardship and emerge on a higher level of spirituality.[11] Indeed, he even sees Auschwitz (a metonym he employs and apparently finds unproblematic) as radically undermining or delegitimating all preexisting ethics and all post-war discourses relying on traditional notions of ethics as well as any and every ethics related to dignity and conformity to a norm.

> Auschwitz marks the end and the ruin of every ethics of dignity and conformity to a norm. The bare life to which human beings were reduced neither demands nor conforms to anything. It is itself the only norm; it is absolutely immanent. And "the ultimate sentiment of belonging to the species" cannot in any sense be a kind of dignity. . . .
>
> The atrocious news that the survivors carry from the camp to the land of human beings is precisely that it is possible to lose dignity and decency beyond imagination, that there is still life in the most extreme degradation. And this new knowledge now becomes the touchstone by which to judge and measure all morality and all dignity. The *Muselmann*, who is its most extreme expression, is the guard on the threshold of a new ethics, an ethics of a form of life that begins where dignity ends. And Levi, who bears witness to the drowned, speaking in their stead, is the cartographer of this new *terra ethica*, the implacable land-surveyor of *Muselmannland*. (RA, 69)

In a sense, the provocation and promise of, as well as the problems involved in, Agamben's approach are condensed in this passage (including the unfortunate, dissonant use of "guard"). It signals the way Agamben offers what might be seen as a powerful but questionable conception of the relation between the post-Auschwitz and the poststructural (or perhaps the postmodern) that is of world-historical and fundamental philosophical importance. I shall begin with the issue of the relation of the historical to the transhistorical. Often Agamben seems to subsume Auschwitz as a complex historical phenomenon in a theoreticist or high-altitude discourse that eliminates its specificity and uses it to make points (for example, concerning the role of paradox and aporia) that might have been made without it. In any case, his understanding of the relation between history and theory does not set up a sustained, mutually interrogative relation, in which questions are posed in both directions without the hope of a final synthesis or reduction of one term to the other. In another sense, however, Agamben attributes uniqueness to Auschwitz that goes beyond any notion of specificity or distinctiveness and is related to the world-historical, even apocalyptic significance he attributes to it, both in placing in question and even eliminating the relevance of all preexisting or conventional ethics (whose nature he does not really investigate) and in posing the problem of rethinking ethics from the ground up, indeed from an indistinct point of virtuality that undercuts any conceivable ground.

Here I would mention a number of other features of Agamben's thought that one may accept, reject, or have mixed reactions to on the basis of one's own (often unexamined) assumptions. Indeed, how one describes these features or tendencies depends on how one reacts to them (my own reactions are mixed). Agamben has a sense of the apocalyptic and a penchant for the all-or-nothing response that help to induce the figuration of Auschwitz as a radical rupture or caesura in history.[12] This radically new state of affairs, signaled by the advent of the *Muselmann*, creates a sense of urgency and extreme insistence that might also be described as lending itself to a rhetoric of histrionic hyperbole—one that contrasts significantly with the general tone of understatement broken only at times by emotional upset and stylistic hyperbole in Primo Levi, who has a privileged place in Agamben's study of the remnants of Auschwitz. The privileged position is, however, somewhat equivocal, in that Levi is both taken as a paradigm and employed as an object of projective identification whom Agamben ventriloquates, just as he sees Levi ventriloquating or speaking for the *Muselmann*. In the former respect, Agamben can write: "Primo Levi is a perfect example of the witness" (*RA*, 16). In the latter respect, Levi serves Agamben as a prosthetic device (not to say a dummy-figure) in a covert process of identification with, and speaking for, the ultimate victim and instance of abjection, the *Muselmann*.

Agamben is concerned, not with delimited historical research that uncovers new facts about Auschwitz, but with its "remnants" or remainders construed in terms of the problem of the possibilities and limits of understanding it—"the ethical and political significance of the extermination" and "a human understanding of what happened there, that is, . . . its contemporary relevance" (*RA*, 11). One question, however, is whether certain forms of specificity are eliminated by the overly homogeneous view of Auschwitz as a unicum that marks a radical break in history or at least in the history of the ethical and political. For example, Agamben insists quite rightly on the need for a sustained inquiry into the *Muselmann*, which has not as yet been undertaken. He relates and contrasts the *Muselmann* and the witness. The *Muselmann* is one who cannot bear witness for himself or herself and hence needs to be supplemented by the witness, who nonetheless is paradoxically forced to bear witness to the (*Muselmann*) impossibility of witnessing. And the *Muselmann* is Primo Levi's drowned victim, the only true witness, the bereft witness unable to give testimony or bear witness. He or she is also the Gorgon whom others could not bear to behold but upon whom Agamben gazes and enjoins us all to gaze. The Gorgon is the antiprosopon, the prohibited face that does not give itself to be seen (*RA*, 53). And "the Gorgon designates the impossibility of seeing that belongs to the camp inhabitant, the one who has 'touched bottom' in the camp and has become a non-human" (*RA*, 54). (Here one broaches the question of the turn to a discourse of the sublime in the attempt to account for the most extreme form of abjection and victimization—a *coincidentia oppositorum* or meeting of extremes.) Yet there are a number of dubious dimensions in Agamben's ambitious and admirable attempt to affirm the importance of, and somehow come to terms with, the *Muselmann*.

Agamben takes the *Muselmann* in isolation from his or her context—the historical conditions of emergence, which cannot be seen only in terms of a homogeneous idea of Auschwitz or a few restricted references to the SS. Indeed, Agamben almost seems to come upon the *Muselmann* as one might discover a creature in the wild or on another planet—what has sometimes been called planet Auschwitz to distinguish it from anything we have hitherto known on planet Earth. And in Agamben the planets collide and interpenetrate to the point of indistinction. The difficulty is that Agamben offers no sustained inquiry into the ideology and practice of perpetrators in the creation of the historical state of affairs that brought the *Muselmann* into being. One gets almost no sense of the perpetrator-victim dynamic that was crucial in the emergence of, or the erosive process leading to, the *Muselmann*. One would think that the perpetrators and their role in the genesis of the *Muselmann* would also be among the remnants of Auschwitz that are deserving of contemporary understanding and relevance. Indeed, Agamben's use of the historical for transhistorical purposes postulates the *Muselmann* as the prototype of the split or divided subject, and in the process Auschwitz itself tends to become a paradoxically abstract counter or philosophical *Lehrstück*.

Agamben has a general conception of the modern age as one tending toward or even embodying the combination of sovereignty and mere, bare, or naked life of unlimited power and the reduction of the human being to a being denuded of possibilities and in a condition of ultimate abjection. (One might compare naked life to Heidegger's conception of the *Ge-stell*, or reduction of all things to a standing stock or reserve of raw material, perhaps even to Marx's notion of abstract exchange value.) Auschwitz and the *Muselmann* are the fullest realization to date of this extreme or excessive state of affairs, which Agamben both severely criticizes and at times seems to approximate or even replicate, at least in part, in his own all-or-nothing, insistently evacuating, postapocalyptic assumptions or assertions. Indeed, in Agamben, the immanent sacred is denuded of all traditional dimensions of the sacred (its ambivalence, its attraction-repulsion, its elation or ecstasy, its limit-setting and limit-transgressing power).[13] It is reduced to bare or naked life. Instead of seeing this reduction as one important effect of recent history (related to developments within religion and to modes of secularization, including capitalism and positivism)—an effect nonetheless countered by other significant forces—he at times seems to postulate it as a general theory of the sacred in transhistorical terms. Insofar as this postulation occurs, he discloses, apparently as a belated, posttraumatic effect of Auschwitz, what putatively was the case all along. The begged question is whether, to what extent, and in what specific ways it is the case even now.

Elaborating this theory is a basic project in *Homo Sacer*, where Pompeius Festus's *On the Significance of Words* becomes the basis of a conception of the "sacred man" as a victim or outsider, subject to being killed at will by anyone but not to sacrifice (in any traditional sense) or homicide (in any criminal or legal sense). The result in that book with respect to the Holocaust is a rather reduced understanding of it in terms of biology, medicalization, and eugenics related to a Foucauldian notion of biopower and biopolitics. This line of argument continues in *Remnants of Auschwitz* (see, for example, 82–86), where, as in the earlier book, it leads to an excessively one-sided or analytically reduced understanding of the victim as mere or naked life. Hence the camps are "the site of the production of the *Muselmann*, the final biopolitical substance to be isolated in the biological continuum. Beyond the *Muselmann* lies only the gas chamber" (*RA*, 85). Agamben's notion of mere, bare, or naked life may in important ways apply to the reduced state of the *Muselmann* and to one dimension of other victims (insofar as they were considered as mere raw material or stock, treated as pest or vermin, or hunted as "mere" game by perpetrators and bystanders). But, as I shall try to indicate, it eliminates or ignores other aspects of Nazi ideology and practice with regard to victimization. Agamben himself, moreover, also sees the *Muselmann* not as mere life but as a threshold figure: he or she "marks the threshold between the human and the inhuman" (*RA*, 55). How the notions of *Muselmann* as naked life and as marker of a threshold relate to one another is not clear, but in any case, for Agamben, "the sight of *Muselmänner* is an absolute new phenomenon, unbearable to human eyes" (*RA*, 51). In the *Muselmann* we presumably behold and bear witness to the absolutely, blindingly, even apocalyptically new. And in our relation to Auschwitz and the *Muselmann*, we are decidedly within a postapocalyptic condition of existence, a condition of remnants or perhaps of ruins.[14]

Here one may mention the importance for Agamben of Carl Schmitt's notion of the state of exception.[15] He does not examine to any significant extent Schmitt's ideas on secularization as the displacement of the religious in the secular, which, I think, might in certain ways inform a treatment of the sublime, including unthematized dimensions of Agamben's own thought, including its insistence, if not fixation, on the dubious human/ nonhuman opposition and its relation to the sublimely apocalyptic and postapocalyptic. In the runaway state of exception (which seems close to Schmitt's state of emergency), the exception becomes the rule (hence the distinction between rule and exception becomes blurred or breaks down), and preexisting normative and legal orders are suspended. (At the limit one is in a "state" of anomie or Hobbesian war.) The sovereign is one who declares and decides on the state of exception. Agamben sees this condition as generalized or rampant in the post-Auschwitz world, and this allows him to assert that the camp is the prototype of modern life and that Auschwitz is now everywhere. As he puts the point in one of his more resounding declamations: "Behind the powerlessness of God peeps the powerlessness of men, who continue to cry 'May that never happen again!' when it is clear that 'that' [Auschwitz] is, by now, everywhere" (*RA*, 20). The postapocalyptic Auschwitz-now-everywhere hyperbole is one insistently repeated and variously reformulated feature of Agamben's account that lends itself to an elated, seemingly radical, breathlessly ecstatic discourse of the sublime. Hence, in his chapter on "The Witness," after putting forth a pathos-charged, participatory evocation of Levi's discussion of the wordless child Hurbinek (who utters an "obstinately secret" word whose meaning is undecidable—the word *mass-klo* or *matisklo*, which Agamben approximates to "the secret word that Levi discerned in the 'background noise' of Celan's poetry" [*RA*, 38]), he ends with these intricately straining (unsayable?) words (reminiscent of certain passages in Foucault's *Histoire de la folie*): "The trace of that to which no one has borne witness, which language believes itself to transcribe, is not the speech of language. The speech of language is born where language is no longer in the beginning, where language falls away from it simply to bear witness: It was not light, but was sent to bear witness to the light'" (*RA*, 39).[16]

One might, however, also argue that the hyperbole (even the cryptic prophetic mode) allows for a justifiable sense of urgency and indicates the limitations of ethics or politics as usual or indeed of any useful, easy approach to problems. Indeed, if one agrees with Agamben, he is not being hyperbolic but, rather, lucid in the arresting manner of the child who sees that the emperor has no clothes—that the post-Auschwitz world is itself utterly bereft or bankrupt and in dire need of some inconceivably new politics and ethics. In any event, one (or at least I) would like to know more than Agamben provides about the usual or conventional state of ethics and its relation to traditions. One result of his procedure is that he offers little room for immanent critique or deconstruction based on a careful analysis of the past and the "unredeemed" possibilities it may offer for action in the present and future (the possibilities that interested Walter Benjamin in his historical and critical dimension—Benjamin's more decidedly apocalyptic-messianic moments are the ones that captivate Agamben). One may well argue, and this would seem to be Agamben's view, that Auschwitz itself provided no such possibilities either in itself or in its aftermath. But one may contest this view without going to the other extreme of spiritual uplift or fixation on the moments of resistance (the Warsaw ghetto uprising, for example) or mutual aid in the most dire of circumstances (some instances of which Levi recounts and which appear in many survivor testimonies). One may also contest Agamben's view while recognizing the importance of sustained reflection on the *Muselmann* and, more generally, on the question of posttraumatic repetition of the conditions and experience of victimization, including extreme disempowerment and harrowing isolation, even in survivors who have in certain significant respects reconstructed a life "after Auschwitz."[17]

One reason for what might be seen as a deficit of historical understanding and of immanent critique is Agamben's reliance on etymology, which tends to substitute for both historical analysis and argument. Agamben will often provide an etymology, at times lending it greater certainty than it may warrant, or he will cite some authority who has provided such an etymology and then proceed from the putative etymology to a conclusion, thereby omitting any analysis or argument linking the etymology to the point he wants to assert. This is a feature Agamben shares with Heidegger, the philosopher who has probably had the most formative role in his thought. Etymology, however putative or even fictive, can be thought-provoking when it opens up a line of investigation or reflection. But can it substitute for historical analysis or argument?

I would like to look closely at the way Agamben invokes etymology to dismiss any use of the term *Holocaust*. He is not alone in doing so, although he declares his dismissal in peremptory tones that seem to imply an unawareness of the extensive discussion of usage in this matter. But the more important point is that his appeal to etymology not only substitutes for historical analysis and argument but also ignores the way usage over time may deplete or even wash away etymological sediment in the meaning of a term. I think this process has occurred for many people who employ the term *Holocaust* largely because it is the one having currency in their society and culture, not because of any investment in a certain idea of sacrifice.

Agamben rehearses the well-known etymology of *Holocaust* in terms of a burnt sacrificial offering, and then he adds many less known, erudite details. The telos of his account is that the term is "intolerable" and he "will never make use of this term" (*RA*, 31). (The apodictic nature of his statements might suggest that his analysis and critique function subtextually as a ritual of purification with respect to a "contaminated" usage.) The intolerability of the term *Holocaust* derives from its ambiguity as a euphemism and an intimation that the events in question could possibly have sacred meaning. Agamben also makes reference to the use of *Holocaust* as a component of anti-Semitic diatribe. One may agree with these excellent reasons for suspicion and still question whether the use of the term necessarily entails them. One may also raise a question about a term Agamben seems to use as if it were unproblematic. "The Jews also use a euphemism to indicate the extermination. They use the term *so'ah*, which means 'devastation, catastrophe' and, in the Bible, often implies the idea of a divine punishment" (*RA*, 31). But what about the term *extermination*? Was this not a term employed by the Nazis—a term that is far from unproblematic? Is it not a component of the discourse of pest control, if not bare or naked life? The point I wish to make is that no term is unproblematic for "the events in question." The best (or "good-enough") strategy may be both to recognize that there are no pure or innocent terms (however "purified" by critical analysis) and to avoid fixation on one term as innocent or another as taboo. Instead, while being especially careful about unintentional repetitions of Nazi terminology, one might employ a multiplicity of terms (Holocaust, Auschwitz, Shoah, Nazi genocide, and so forth) in a flexible manner that resists fixation while acknowledging the problem in naming. Moreover, as I intimated earlier, the banalized use of the term *Holocaust* may be beneficial in eroding any sacrificial connotation, not only with respect to "Auschwitz," but even more generally as a process Agamben might also see as beneficial (and that could be taken as the desirable "demystifying" or delegitimating dimension of his own conception of homo sacer and bare or naked life). It is also noteworthy that the term *Holocaust* is used not only by anti-Semites, as Agamben seems to imply, but also by Jews, including survivors, and this could be another reason for its use more generally. (In a comparable way, the broader population of those who try to avoid prejudice or even to be "politically correct" tends to follow usage in self-designation within a relevant group, say, of "African Americans" or "Latinos" and "Latinas.") Agamben notes that Levi used the term *Holocaust* reluctantly "to be understood" and that he believed that Elie Wiesel "had coined it, then regretted it and wanted to take it back" (*RA*, 28). But whether or not Wiesel "coined" it (which I doubt), it came into general currency among survivors, Jews, and the general population with the varied effects I have tried to touch upon.[18]

I have noted that Agamben moves from a rejection of an immanent sublime or a redemptive reading of Auschwitz to a more transcendent sublime that is nonetheless complicated by certain movements in his thinking. Particularly problematic is his use of Primo Levi as privileged witness (or "example") in relation to the *Muselmann*. Agamben at first supplements his rejection of redemptive readings with a critique of the view that Auschwitz is unsayable (*RA*, 32). He also criticizes Shoshana Felman, who is often associated with an extremely sophisticated variant of this view. But his criticisms are, I think, local disagreements within a more general accord. Felman traces a labyrinthine paradox or aporia, whereby the witness cannot bear witness from either inside or outside the events of the Shoah but can only at best bear witness to the breakdown of witnessing. For Agamben,

Felman does not interrogate "the threshold of indistinction between inside and outside" the Shoah, and she aestheticizes testimony in appealing to the song as a performative event that "speaks to us beyond its words, beyond its melody" (*RA*, 36). But Agamben is in fundamental agreement with the view that she elaborates, in *Testimony*, of the Shoah as an event without witnesses or an event that paradoxically bears witness to the breakdown of witnessing, thereby leading to endless aporias.[19] He also invokes Lyotard's *The Differend* in noting that "there is something like an impossibility of bearing witness" (*RA*, 34). And like Felman and Lyotard, he stresses the excess and the lacuna at the heart of the limit situation or event. The question here is how his critique of the appeal to unsayability relates to his affirmation of what seems to be very close to it, indeed even within the same "threshold of indistinction": the notion that the Shoah in its excess and its lack (its supplementary uncanniness and disconcerting challenge) bears witness to the impossibility or breakdown of witnessing. In Lyotard and at times in Agamben, this paradoxical view prompts a dual movement: toward both the insistence on the paradox as paradox and the necessity of working or playing out new formulations to respond to the excess/lack that continually requires rearticulations that can never reach total closure. At other times, however, there seems to be a compulsively repetitive return to, or even presupposition of, the paradox or aporia to which one moves as does the moth to the flame.

Let us look more closely at these complex movements. While relying on the unexplicated notion of uniqueness, Agamben nonetheless puts forth a relatively rare appeal to caution:

Those who assert the unsayability of Auschwitz today should be more cautious in their statements. If they mean to say that Auschwitz was a unique event in the face of which the witness must in some way submit his every word to the test of an impossibility of speaking, they are right. But if, joining uniqueness to unsayability, they transform Auschwitz into a reality absolutely separated from language, if they break the tie between an impossibility and a possibility of speaking that, in the *Muselmann*, constitutes testimony, then they unconsciously repeat the Nazis' gesture; they are in secret solidarity with the *arcanum imperii*. (*RA*, 157)[20]

Agamben probably means "survivor" or "witness" rather than "*Muselmann*" in the last sentence. But such slippage aside, he elsewhere restricts the possibility of testimony to bearing witness to the impossibility of witnessing, or speaking "only on the basis of an impossibility of

speaking," which, mirabile dictu, presumably will be the ultimate rejoinder to negationism. In the light of such "undeniable" testimony, "Auschwitz—that to which it is not possible to bear witness—is absolutely and
irrefutably proven" (*RA*, 164). In addition, "the witness attests to the fact
that there can be testimony because there is an inseparable division and
non-coincidence between the inhuman and the human, the living being
and the speaking being, the *Muselmann* and the survivor" (*RA*, 157). What
Agamben adamantly resists is relating the threshold of indistinction to an
understanding of the human being as a compromise formation between
biological life (not reducible to mere life) and political or ethical life—a
supplementary understanding that contests without simply negating the
idea of an "inseparable division and non-coincidence between the inhuman and the human" and allows for more complex, nonabsolute interaction between the two.

At times Agamben formulates problems in a manner that itself seems
to eradicate the paradox in paradox and to lead to a pure, all-or-nothing
antinomy that eventuates in a stark decision and eliminates any tension
between a disjunction, radical difference, or internal alterity within the
human and an understanding of the human as a compromise formation:

> When one looks closely, the passage from language to discourse appears as a para-
> doxical act that simultaneously implies both subjectification and desubjectification.
> On the one hand, the psychosomatic individual must fully abolish himself and
> desubjectify himself as a real individual to become the subject of enunciation and to
> identify himself with the pure shifter "I," which is absolutely without any substan-
> tiality and content other than its mere reference to the event of discourse. But, once
> stripped of all extra-linguistic meaning and constituted as a subject of enunciation,
> the subject discovers that he has gained access not so much to a possibility of speak-
> ing as to an impossibility of speaking—or, rather, that he has gained access to being
> always already anticipated by a glossalalic potentiality over which he has neither
> control nor mastery. . . . He is expropriated of all referential reality, letting himself
> be defined solely through the pure and empty relation to the event of discourse. *The
> subject of enunciation is composed of discourse and exists in discourse alone. But, for this
> very reason, once the subject is in discourse, he can say nothing; he cannot speak* (116–17;
> emphasis in original)[21]

Such a formulation deprives one of an ability to ascribe responsibility and agency. It vastly oversimplifies the problem of language in use. And
it amounts to a philosophical analog of both the political idea of a post-

war *Stunde Null* (point zero) and the theological concept of creation ex nihilo. It also indicates Agamben's proximity to a variant of existentialism as well as a variant of structuralism.[22] One finds a comparable formulation in *Means Without End* (141), where options are restricted to the poles of the antinomy between the view of humanity as having one fully unified identity, telos, essence, or ergon and its construction in Agamben himself as pure possibility related to the absolute bankruptcy of the past and the irrelevance of every preexisting value (an enumeration of these values on page 124 lists "freedom, progress, democracy, human rights, constitutional state"). Such an antinomic and antinomian formulation eliminates the mediations provided by history in its relation to theory.

In *Remnants of Auschwitz*, via the universalization of the *Muselmann* and his or her identification with the divided or split subject, Agamben goes on to assert that

> the living being and the speaking being, the inhuman and the human—or any terms of a historical process . . . have not an end, but a remnant. There is no foundation in or beneath them; rather, at their center lies an irreducible disjunction in which each term, stepping forth in the place of a remnant, can bear witness. What is truly historical is not what redeems time in the direction of the future or even the past; it is, rather, what fulfills time in the excess of a medium. The messianic Kingdom is neither the future (the millennium) nor the past (the golden age); it is, instead, a remaining time. (*RA*, 159)

One may agree with Agamben's criticisms of teleology, foundationalism, and modes of redemption as fulfillment at the beginning or end of time but still raise questions about what he affirms (insofar as it is understandable) as a fulfilled time (in the key of excess) or perhaps an always already available remnant. Indeed, he seems to redefine the "truly historical" in terms of transhistorical, theoreticist notions of an "irreducible disjunction" and a paradoxical time-fulfilling excess that entail a construction of all history as a postapocalyptic remnant whose terms both bear witness to the apocalypse and hold out a saving grace in the form of an ever-present *Jetztzeit* ("remaining time").[23] Agamben's conception of the "truly historical" may even be residually indebted to a sacrificial logic involving substitution, in which the part that remains somehow saves or redeems the whole in however paradoxical or aporetic a manner.

Other movements in Agamben's account would seem to invalidate any notion of redemption or salvation.[24] The witness (Levi, for example) bears witness to the *Muselmann*, hence to the most extreme or abject impossibility or breakdown of witnessing. (Is the difference between the unsayability that Agamben criticizes and such paradoxical witnessing one of reflexivity: one now repeatedly says that there is unsayability rather than just saying the event is unsayable? Is Agamben's approach different from one—which I would accept—that does not begin with, or become fixated on, breakdown or aporia but is open and alert to such breakdown or aporia when it occurs in the witness's attempt to recount traumatic experience and perhaps in the commentator's empathic attempt to render such an attempt?) Such paradoxical or aporetic saying or witnessing, as Agamben discusses it, often seems close to a discourse of the sublime, which Lyotard has elaborated, and Felman enacted, in more explicit terms. Except for the sacrificial form the analysis at times seems to take, the sublime here is radically transcendent in that one can bear witness to it only indirectly or paratactically by indicating time and again, and in various repetitive formulations, the impossibility of acceding to it through representation. And it is now radically disjoined from any positive or affirmative senses of the sacred, from any intimation of the martyrological, or from any unspoken promise of parousia in the mode of negative theology. Yet the lowest of the low, the *Muselmann* as the limit of abjection, seems to evoke a discourse that, in its own excess and its insistent, at times intolerant, struggle with the aporetic limits of thought, seems at least like a specter of the sublime. If one may refer to sublimity at all (and one may conceivably argue that one may not), it now seems like the horizonless pale shadow of a god that has not died but been recognized as absent, perhaps endlessly.

Still, there are times in Agamben when the *Muselmann* himself or herself becomes sublime in effulgent yet chiaroscuro terms that outdo, while recalling, passages in Kant:

> This is language of the "dark shadows" that Levi heard growing in Celan's poetry, like a "background noise"; this is Hurbinek's non-language (*mass-klo, matisklo*) that has no place in the libraries of what has been said or in the archive of statements. Just as in the starry sky that we see at night, the stars shine surrounded by a total darkness that, according to cosmologists, is nothing other than the testimony of a time in which the stars did not yet shine, so the speech of the witness bears witness to a time in which human beings did not yet speak; and so the testimony of human beings attests to a time in which they were not yet human.

Or, to take up an analogous hypothesis, just as in the expanding universe, the far- thest galaxies move away from us at a speed greater than that of their light, which cannot reach us, such that the darkness we see in the sky is nothing but the invis- ibility of the light of unknown stars, so the complete witness, according to Levi's paradox, is the one we cannot see: the *Muselmann*. (*RA*, 162)

Even aside from the question of whether the *Muselmann* can or should serve as the occasion for a dark-winged lyrical flight into sublimity, one may ask whether there is a crucial dimension of bearing witness and giving testimony that Agamben occludes. He discusses the *Muselmann* as the ultimate victim, the one who died or was completely crushed, and yet who is also the true witness, the sublime witness whose testimony would be truly valuable but who cannot bear witness. He also discusses the sur- vivor-witness as ultimately bearing witness to the *Muselmann*. What he does not investigate with care is the arduous process whereby bearing wit- ness and giving testimony are themselves crucial aspects of the movement (however incomplete and subject to remission) from the victim—indeed the potential *Muselmann*—-to the survivor and agent. Agamben concludes his book with a series of quotations from former *Muselmänner*, and one may ask how it is even possible to refer to oneself as a *Muselmann* in the past tense given the utterly abject, disempowered position from which one has to emerge, at least to some extent or momentarily, to make this usage possible. Indeed, one might argue that part of the process elided by Agam- ben is crucial in understanding the witness who performatively is not only a victim but a survivor who lives on in part precisely by giving testimony or bearing witness.

This process is obscured, perhaps even devalorized (whether inten- tionally or not), by the relentless insistence on the aporias and paradoxes of bearing witness to the impossibility of witnessing—aporias and paradoxes that may indeed arise but should not be presupposed or converted into a vehicle for a repetition compulsion. In Agamben, one often has the sense that he begins with the presupposition of the aporia or paradox which itself may at times lose its force and its insistence in that it does not come about through the breakdown or experienced impasse in speaking, writing, or trying to communicate but instead seems to be postulated at the outset. In other words, a prepackaged form seems to seek its somewhat arbitrary con- tent. And the paradox and the aporia become predictable components of a fixated methodology. Indeed, the terms in which the aporia as assumed, self-negating telos are sometimes (not always) formulated may be rather unconvincing. For example, near the beginning of the book, one has the following:

What is at issue here is not, of course, the difficulty we face whenever we try to communicate our most intimate experiences to others. The discrepancy in question concerns the very structure of testimony. On the one hand, what happened in the camps appears to the survivors as the only true thing and, as such, absolutely unforgettable; on the other hand, this truth is to the same degree unimaginable, that is, irreducible to the real elements that constitute it. Facts so real that, by comparison, nothing is truer; a reality that necessarily exceeds its factual elements such is the aporia of Auschwitz. (*RA*, 12)

This formulation may give one an indistinct sense of a problem, but it is an indistinction that is more vague than indicative of one's implication in a threshold of indeterminacy or undecidability. "The only true thing," "irreducible to the real elements that constitute it," "facts so real," "a reality that necessarily exceeds its factual elements"—these formulations gesture offhandedly without evoking an aporia. Or, if the aporia is evoked, it is in rather routinized terms with reference to an excess in the limit event that others (notably Lyotard and Saul Friedlander) have discussed extensively.[25]

The relations between and among the threshold of indistinction, the gray zone, and the state of emergency are not elucidated in *Remnants of Auschwitz*—indeed the three seem at times to be conflated, at least "after Auschwitz."[26] The lack of elucidation may be abetted by postapocalyptic assumptions, the acting out of posttraumatic symptoms, and the fragmented, paratactical nature of Agamben's approach. (Reminiscent of Wittgenstein in the *Tractatus* and the *Philosophical Investigations* or Lyotard in *The Differend*, he employs numbered paragraphs.) I would suggest that the "threshold of indistinction" is a transhistorical concept that is evoked in variable ways by historical phenomena or "cases," while the gray zone and the state of exception as rule refer to more historically determinate situations that may nonetheless become a basis for transhistorical reflection, just as the historical figure of the *Muselmann* may become a basis for a general or transhistorical reflection on abjection. I would also suggest that the threshold of indistinction has an affirmative or at least an undecidable valence that both problematizes norms and may help in the generation of newer normative articulations. When approximated to or conflated with the state of exception, it is generalized and given a political and juridical inflection. As such, it may be related to a condition of normative dislocation that the sovereign, through a decisionist gesture, is supposed to determine and resolve. One may of course argue that a goal of social, political, and civic life is to avoid the rampant state of exception or to see it at best as an extreme condition in an intolerable state of affairs that may be a prelude to revolution. Hence one might even want to bring about something at least close to a state of exception in oppressive regimes, but the judgment concerning what regime falls into this "category," and whether collapse, panic, and disarray are more likely than revolution in any desirable sense, is debatable. The postapocalyptic Auschwitz-now-everywhere hyperbole would eliminate this problem in judgment by generalizing the state of exception along with the gray zone and the threshold of indistinction. Hence the routine yet surrealistic soccer match in Auschwitz between the SS and Jewish members of the Sonderkommando "repeats itself in every match in our stadiums, in every television broadcast, in the normalcy of everyday life. If we do not succeed in understanding that match, in stopping it, there will never be hope" (*RA*, 26). How would one go about stopping that match, and if one accepts the limited value of the afterimage of unsettlement projected forward by the match at Auschwitz but objects to the shrill yet leveling logic in Agamben's exclamation, is one condemned to hopeless complacency and business as usual?

One might also contend that the gray zone in its historical sense (as used by Primo Levi) is not so much a threshold of indistinction or even a state of exception as a condition of extreme equivocation that is created largely through the practices of perpetrators and imposed on victims, typically in the form of double binds or impossible situations. Moreover, as a historical condition, the gray zone need not be generalized but at least at times may exist as an intermediary zone between relatively clear-cut cases or groups of perpetrators and victims. Indeed, one may argue that the gray zone and, in different ways, the rampant state of exception may obviate confrontation with the threshold of indistinction as it exists and poses problems for everyone. This is because the gray zone and the state of exception (particularly when it gives way to an anomic state of emergency) typically involve, or devolve into, a binary opposition between self and other (perpetrator and victim, friend and enemy, us and them), in which anxiety may be projected from the (oppressing) self onto the (oppressed) other as well as localized invidiously in those placed in equivocal or double-bind situations (particularly perpetrator-victims or collaborators). Moreover, the generally applicable threshold of indistinction creates anxiety that normative orders may help mitigate but never entirely eliminate. It relates to the manner in which decisions, especially extremely difficult decisions, are never entirely predetermined by norms, although norms may indeed help guide decisions in many cases and to some extent in all but the most difficult and problematic cases. In addition, one may defend as desirable a condition of society in which the threshold of indistinction exerts pressure on everyone but is not generalized as a state in which the exception becomes the rule—a state that is of direct political consequence. The legitimate normative articulation of life in common would be such that one could in general distinguish between the exception and the rule and not expect everyone to live according to the extreme or excessive demands placed upon the exception (something that may be argued to occur in the state of exception). Within any concrete situation, one would of course have to further articulate these general considerations, for example, with reference to questions of equality and hierarchy involving specific economic, political, and social issues. The considerations on which I have touched all too briefly seem to have little place in Agamben's discussion, in *Remnants of Auschwitz*, of the gray zone, the threshold of indistinction, and the state of exception.[27]

Agamben not only sees Levi as speaking for the *Muselmann* but generalizes the gray zone in a manner that threatens to undo significant distinctions, eventuating in a view of all existence in terms of the limit event or situation as a state of exception, if not emergency or crisis, in which the exception becomes the rule. I have noted that, from Agamben's postapocalyptic perspective, "Auschwitz marks the end and the ruin of every ethics of dignity and conformity to a norm," and "Levi, who bears witness to the drowned, speaking in their stead, is the cartographer of this new *terra ethica*, the implacable land-surveyor of *Muselmannland*" (*RA*, 69). Of Levi, Agamben also writes: "He is the only one who consciously sets out to bear witness in place of the *Muselmänner*, the drowned, those who were demolished and touched bottom" (*RA*, 59). The problem here is not the argument that Auschwitz, or the *Muselmann* in particular, poses distinctive problems for ethics or that it is dubious to impute essential dignity to the *Muselmann*, especially for self-serving reasons. What is problematic pertains to the synecdochic use of the *Muselmann* as a theoretical cipher to disprove human dignity and to discredit all preexisting (perhaps all presently conceivable) forms of ethics. What remains of ethics (if it still can be called ethics) in Agamben is dissociated from law and voided of all forms of normativity (including responsibility and guilt). It seems to eventuate in an empty utopianism and a form of political romanticism ("as Spinoza knew, the doctrine of the happy life" [*RA*, 24]). In any case, Agamben takes a potential in humanity and, rather than examining closely its historical role in Auschwitz and comparing it carefully with other situations and possibilities, actualizes it in universal terms by generalizing the *Muselmann* as the prototype or exemplar of humanity. This *condition humaine*, as "life in its most extreme degradation," becomes "the touchstone by which to judge and measure all morality and dignity" (*RA*, 24).[28] The result is an unsituated, extreme mode of victimology or identification with the abject and utterly disempowered—something which, despite its transhistorical cast, might most generously be seen as a radical reversal of, or perhaps an overcompensation for, extreme victimization under the Nazis.

In his brief but trenchant reflections on ethics, Agamben apparently takes Auschwitz as an apocalyptic divide between past and present that delegitimates all uses in the present of past ethical assumptions or discourses. He even attributes such a view to Levi: "The *Muselmann*, as Levi describes him, is the site of an experiment in which morality and humanity themselves are called into question" (*RA*, 63). Moreover:

> The unprecedented discovery made by Levi at Auschwitz concerns an area that is independent of every establishment of responsibility, an area in which Levi succeeded in isolating something like a new ethical element. Levi calls it the "gray zone." It is the zone in which the "long chain of conjunction between victim and executioner" comes loose, where the oppressed becomes oppressor and the executioner in turn appears as victim. A gray, incessant alchemy in which good and evil and, along with them, all the metals of traditional ethics reach their point of fusion. (*RA*, 21)

There are many contestable features in these statements to which I shall return. Here I would point out the dubiousness of seeing total ethical meltdown in Levi, who drew from traditional culture and ethics both to provide him with sustenance in the camps and—in a manner that was, if anything, perhaps insufficiently informed by the concerns that preoccupy Agamben—to inform his postwar reflections on his experience.

If one recalls the quotation from Himmler's Posen speech, one may well sympathize with Agamben when he asserts of the *Muselmänner*: "To speak of dignity and decency in their case would not be decent." Sympathy wavers when he adds, in his prevalent turn to a kind of free indirect style or middle-voiced usage:

The survivors [including Levi as Agamben speaks with(in) and for him] are not only "worse" in comparison with the best ones, those whose strength rendered them less fit in the camp, they are also "worse" in comparison with the anonymous mass of the drowned, those whose death cannot be called death. This is the specific ethical aporia of Auschwitz: it is the site in which it is not decent to remain decent, in which those who believed themselves to preserve their dignity and self-respect experience shame with respect to those who did not. (*RA*, 60)

Auschwitz epitomizes the absolute impossibility of "death with dignity" in the modern world, the way in which death gives way to the fabrication or manufacture of corpses. "This means that in Auschwitz it is no longer possible to distinguish between death and mere decease, between dying and 'being liquidated'" (*RA*, 76). More generally, in the modern world one's unease about dying is related to its privatization, deritualization, and concealment from public view.

Agamben is touching upon important issues here—issues that should not be obliterated by any reservations about his approach. Still, he is so concerned with the problem of death that he pays scant attention to processes of killing among the Nazis and their relations to specific objects of victimization. In the relatively few references to the SS, even they undergo, rather than activate, processes and are often framed in the passive voice or in something approximating a bystander position or even a position that almost seems to place them (as in the soccer game) on a gray-on-gray, level playing field with victims. "The SS could not see the *Muselmann*, let alone bear witness to him" (*RA*, 78). Or again: "Both the survivor's discomfort and testimony concern not merely what was done or suffered, but what could have been done or suffered. It is this capacity, this almost infinite potentiality to suffer that is inhuman—not the facts, actions, or omissions. And it is precisely this capacity that is denied to the SS" (*RA*, 77).

There may be a worthwhile shock or scandal induced by accusing the SS of an incapacity to be inhuman—a shock relating to an attempt to rethink the threshold between the human and the inhuman or nonhuman and to reposition ethics as other than purely humanistic. Agamben does not make explicit and explore the implications of this unsettling, seemingly paradoxical idea, for example, concerning the "rights" or claims of other-than-human animals. (Indeed, one danger of Agamben's sharp binary between the human and the inhuman or nonhuman, which he maps onto the opposition between the speaking being and mere or naked life, is the exclusion or even scapegoating of nonhuman animals who, by implication, seem reduced to mere life or raw material.) Moreover, *pace* Agamben and whatever may be the case concerning almost infinite potentiality, the capacity to suffer is something humans share with other animals, and it is related to empathy, which the SS did not have with respect to victims. But this capacity (or Agamben's postulated incapacity, for that matter) was not simply denied to the SS as passive recipients. It was actively countered, blocked, or eliminated through ideological and related practical forces, as well as through the dynamic of victimization that brought victims to the abject state which Nazi ideology, in circular and self-fulfilling fashion, attributed to them. A particularly questionable feature of Agamben's orientation is that the deficit of the SS, in terms of a lack of inhumanity, is itself construed in terms of an almost infinite (quasi-divine?) capacity or potentiality for suffering. No known being, human or otherwise, has this infinite capacity. Beyond a certain threshold of suffering, one blacks out, and it would seem that Agamben strives to write from, or even from beyond, that threshold. Once again we seem to be in the vicinity of ethics understood in paradoxical terms as supraethical, supererogatory excess rather than in more socially and politically viable terms. Does empathy with respect to both human and other-than-human beings require an infinite capacity for suffering, or does the latter radically transcend empathy into an ecstatically indistinct realm of sublimity that would itself seem, in any social or political terms, to be isolating? (Almost involuntarily, I think of the unimaginably suffering but transfigured Christ ascending into heaven.)

Agamben's related understanding of the meaning of Himmler's Posen speech is curious at best. He sees it in line with his idea of the SS as not having the inhuman, almost infinite capacity to suffer. He relates the latter to another passive position with a paradoxical twist: the *Befehlnotstand*. "The executioners unanimously continue to repeat that they could not do other than as they did, that, in other words, they simply could not; they had to, and that is all. In German, to act without being capable of acting is called *Befehlnotstand*, having to obey an order" (*RA*, 77–78). Agamben then relates the perpetrator's claim to undergo orders that one must obey, thereby acting without really acting, to the passage from Himmler's Posen speech (which I quoted earlier in a somewhat different translation): "Most of you know what it means when 100 corpses lie there, or when 500 corpses lie there, or when 1,000 corpses lie there. To have gone through this and—apart from a few exceptions caused by human weakness—to have remained decent, that has made us great. That is a page of glory in our history which has never been written and which will never be written" (*RA*, 78).

Himmler himself has a preference here for passive or indeterminate constructions that veil somewhat the fact that those whom he addresses not only have beheld a scene but are responsible for having brought it about. One may analyze the functions of such a construction but not simply repeat it transferentially in one's own analysis. Moreover, Himmler in this passage is not altogether like Eichmann on trial appealing to a distorted Kantian sense of duty in doing one's job and obeying orders; he does not simply appeal to a *Befehlnotstand* or the inability to do otherwise. There are in his words an appeal to the sublime (notably a mathematical sublime in the geometrically increasing expanse of corpses), to the fascination with excess and radical transgression in the form of unheard-of mass destruction, to the glory which the uninitiated will never understand, to the quasi-sacrificial allure of victimization in the absolute injunction to kill all Jews without exception (by definition there is no such thing as a good Jew), and to the superhuman ability to become hard (interestingly mistranslated in the above quotation as "great"—"absolute greatness" characterized the sublime for Kant) by enduring (*durchstehen*) the aporia or combining in oneself the antinomic features of decency and radical transgression.[29] In other words, for Himmler, Nazis did look the Gorgon directly in the face, and this "sublime" gaze made them hard in a sense they desired. What is interesting is Agamben's inability to detect these aspects of the Posen speech and to focus instead on what would seem unaccentuated in, if not projectively inserted into, it.[30]

There is also a problem with respect to what might be termed, for lack of a better word, subject positions. For Levi as survivor to say that not he but the *Muselmann* is the true witness is, I think, an acceptable hyperbole. For Agamben to identify with Levi and hence speak for (or in the stead of) Levi and hence for the *Muselmann* (as he believes Levi does) may be hyperbolic in an objectionable sense. Moreover, the idea that Auschwitz radically delegitimates all preexisting ethics and all present appeals to them, including all notions of decency and dignity, paradoxically runs the risk of granting a posthumous (postapocalyptic?) victory to the Nazis. In any event, it obviates a careful inquiry into the uses of such concepts by victims and survivors themselves, as well as their attempts to preserve some sense of dignity and decency in impossible situations. It also risks handing the concept of decency over to Himmler as his heritage rather than struggling for and rethinking it (for example, by criticizing any invidious use of it to distinguish the human from the other than human, including the animal that cannot itself be reduced to bare or naked life or be understood in neo-Heideggerian terms as not having a world or a form of life).

One important feature of Agamben's notion of ethics is its radical disjunction from law—with responsibility and guilt placed squarely on the side of law. I would agree that ethics may not be identified with or reduced to law (or vice versa) and that protesters are evasive if they claim moral but not legal responsibility for their actions (*RA*, 22). But this does not imply a total disjunction between ethics and law or a relegation of responsibility and guilt to law and their elimination from ethics. Responsibility and guilt are concepts that are differentially shared by ethics and law, and Agamben does not provide any idea of a form of social life in which ethics would not involve these concepts. Nor need responsibility as answerability be reduced to a rigidly codified, quasi-legal formula, as Agamben seems to imply in his etymological analysis of *sponsa* and *obligatio*, as well as in a pseudohistorical just-so story that at most would apply to a restricted idea of the subject and subjectivity ("Responsibility and guilt thus express simply two aspects of legal imputability; only later were they interiorized and moved outside the law" [*RA*, 22]). The unstated horizon of his view would seem to be an ecstatic, anarchistic utopia that remains terra incognita and whose relevance to present problems or commitments is left utterly blank. Indeed, not only is it dubious to make Auschwitz the bomb that explodes the status quo; the sublime negativity and the hope against hope that combine to inspire such a gesture may all too readily become a license for evasiveness with respect to responsibilities and commitments in the present. Moreover, in Agamben's approach one loses sight of the tense, mutually engaging relation between the "law" or the strength of norms and what it fails to encompass—what indeed remains both as remnants and as possibly valuable irritants that indicate the limits of the law and areas demanding change. And generalizing the ecstatic, including the ecstatically transgressive, threatens to dissipate or neutralize it, eliminating the very force of its challenge. As I have intimated, one may recognize a tendency in modernity, perhaps accentuated in the recent past, for the sublimely ecstatic and the transgressive to be generalized and banalized without repeating and aggravating it to the point of hyperbole in one's own voice.

I have indicated that it is indeed important to reflect in a sustained manner on the extremely disconcerting phenomenon of the *Muselmann*, the living dead or hopeless being on the verge of extinction who was the object of disdain and avoidance among camp inmates themselves. But here one could maintain that the *Muselmann* should not be directly identified with, universalized, or spoken for—something that Levi, despite a reference Agamben quotes ("we speak in their stead, by proxy" [*RA*, 34]), at times resists doing, even as he presents the *Muselmann* as the true witness.[31] Rather, one might argue that the *Muselmann*, an actuality in Auschwitz, represents a potential that may become a real possibility for anyone in certain conditions, and the possibility may be related (as Agamben indicates) to split subjectivity and the "real" as analyzed by Lacan. This may be why the *Muselmann* provoked anxiety and avoidance, not simply indifference or curiosity, in the camps. One might also see Beckett as having had the daring to stage, in an incredible series of radically disempowered beings, the—or at least something close to the—*Muselmann*'s experience of disempowerment and living death. This is a view that would give a different perspective on Adorno's paradoxical attempt to present Beckett as more politically relevant and radical in his seemingly autonomous art than was Sartre in his defense of committed literature. Here something Žižek writes of the *Muselmann* as paradoxically beneath or beyond tragedy and comedy is apposite: "Although the Muslim is in a way 'comic,' although he acts in a way that is usually the stuff of comedy and laughter (his automatic, mindless, repetitive gestures, his impassive pursuit of food), the utter misery of his condition thwarts any attempt to present and/or perceive him as a 'comic character'—again, if we try to present him as comic, the effect will be precisely tragic."[32]

One should certainly acknowledge the importance of Levi's gray zone and recognize that it often presents the most difficult cases for analysis and understanding. But (following Levi rather than Agamben) one need not construe it as all-encompassing even in the camps, much less in present societies figured as the covert, postapocalyptic embodiment of the concentrationary universe. Although one may mention still other cases without utterly blurring the distinction between perpetrator and victim, Levi restricts his discussion of the gray zone to the Sonderkommando and the Jewish Council, notably the case of Chaim Rumkowski of the Lodz ghetto. The Auschwitz-now-everywhere hyperbole is itself provocative only as a prelude to a differential analysis of how and to what extent, in Benjamin's phrase, "the exception is the rule" in contemporary societies— an analysis Agamben does not provide. While Levi certainly did, in trying circumstances, get carried away and returned at least verbal blows in a manner that brought him close to his sometime adversary, Jean Amery,[33] I have noted that the gap between Levi and Agamben is marked by the distance between typically careful reserve or even cautious understatement and prevalent, at times histrionic, hyperbole. There is even a paradoxical sense in which the Auschwitz-now-everywhere hyperbole eventuates in a banalizing rhetoric (or a rhetoric of banalizing hyperbole in which almost every sentence seems to be followed by a virtual exclamation point) bizarrely reminiscent of Ernst Nolte's normalization of the Holocaust, during the 1986 *Historikerstreit*, through an appeal to the prevalence of genocide in modern times.[34] Indeed, one finds the Auschwitz-now-everywhere hyperbole in surprising quarters. It is, for example, invoked by radical anti-abortionists in the self-styled "Army of God" that even contains a "White Rose" faction. For those in the "Army of God," abortion is tantamount to the Holocaust, and they are resisters and rescuers for whom violence, including the murder of supposedly SS-like doctors practicing abortion, is justified. Of course Agamben would not seem to mean "that," but what he means—and how one stops the putatively omnipresent soccer match—is often unclear.

I would simply note in passing that the fact that perpetrators may be traumatized by what they do does not make them victims in the relevant sense. The very term "trauma victim" may invite confusion, and there is still much to be done in perpetrator history and theory. Hence Levi's gray zone should not be made into an oil slick or radically deregulated and generalized threshold of indistinction that covers everyone indiscriminately. It is inaccurate and perhaps projective to write of Levi, as Agamben does: "The only thing that interests him is what makes judgment impossible: the gray zone in which victims become executioners and executioners victims"

(*RA*, 70). With respect to the Shoah, the gray zone for Levi exists between relatively clear-cut "zones" of perpetrators and victims, and as Levi himself writes in his very chapter on "The Gray Zone":

I do not know, and it does not much interest me to know, whether in my depths there lurks a murderer, but I do know that I was a guiltless victim and I was not a murderer. I know that the murderers existed, not only in Germany, and still exist, retired or on active duty, and that to confuse them with their victims is a moral disease or an aesthetic affectation or a sinister sign of complicity; above all, it is precious service rendered (intentionally or not) to the negators of truth. I know that in the Lager, and more generally on the human stage, everything happens, and that therefore the single example proves little.[35]

Levi goes on to qualify but not to retract these emphatic comments made with some degree of exasperation.

Without fully agreeing with all of its aspects, one may also quote another passage from Levi that Agamben himself quotes without engaging its critical implications for aspects of his own approach. It concerns the poetry of Celan:

This darkness that grows from page to page until the last inarticulate babble fills one with consternation like the gasps of a dying man; indeed, it is just that. It enthralls us as whirlpools enthrall us, but at the same time it robs us of what was supposed to be said but was not said, thus frustrating and distancing us. I think that Celan the poet must be considered and mourned rather than imitated. If his is a message, it is lost in the "background noise." It is not communication; it is not a language, or at most it is a dark and maimed language, precisely that of someone who is about to die and is alone, as we will all be at the moment of death. (*RA*, 37)

A crucial reason Agamben believes the *Muselmann* invalidates all previous ethics and notions of dignity and decency is that the latter prove not to be universal since they do not apply to the *Muselmann*. He is also at points alert to the danger that his own views may approximate those of the SS, although he does not seem effectively to counter or perhaps even mitigate that possibility. He even asserts that "the SS were right to call the corpses *Figuren*" (*RA*, 70). He also writes:

Simply to deny the *Muselmann*'s humanity would be to accept the verdict of the SS and to repeat their gesture. The *Muselmann* has, instead, moved into a zone of the human where not only help but also dignity and self-respect have become useless. But if there is a zone of the human in which these concepts make no sense, then they are not genuine ethical concepts, for no ethics can claim to exclude a part of humanity, no matter how unpleasant or difficult that humanity is to see. (*RA*, 63–64)

The logic of this paragraph is dubious. One does not counteract the danger of transferential repetition with respect to the SS by claiming that it is the *Muselmann* himself or herself who "moved into a zone of the human where not only help but also dignity and self-respect have become useless." Indeed, this view would seem once again to avoid the role of the perpetrators as agents (not simply spectators, commentators, gesticulators, or judges) in creating the conditions Agamben tries to understand. It might seem to involve blaming the victim in a manner not that different from "gestures" of the SS. The *Muselmänner* did not simply "move" into a zone of abjection; they were kicked, whipped, and beaten into it. And the SS and their affiliates were the ones who conducted the "experiment" that Agamben seeks to replicate in his own way.

Moreover, one may claim that certain values are general or even universal in their relevance while nonetheless maintaining that in certain extreme situations, such as that of the *Muselmann* as well as other inmates of concentration and death camps, they are not applicable. Being placed in such a genuinely paradoxical position with respect to relevant, at times pressingly insistent, but inapplicable values or norms may be a reason why survivors felt "shame"—a reason Agamben does not entertain. Instead, the dominant note he strikes in his chapter on shame is the largely asocial idea that shame is ontological and constitutive of subjectivity. Shame is presumably the way, according to Heidegger, "we find ourselves exposed in the face of Being" (*RA*, 106), or, in a quotation from Levinas, "what is shameful is our intimacy, that is, our presence to ourselves" (*RA*, 105). However one may respond to this understanding of shame as Agamben employs it (I think it diverts attention from social interaction and ethicopolitical issues), one may insist that the nonapplicability of values or norms with respect to the *Muselmann* would be primarily the responsibility of the perpetrators, and it is only from a questionably skewed perspective that the *Muselmann* could be invoked to invalidate them.

The nature of this perspective is indirectly illuminated by a comment Agamben makes about philosophy: "Philosophy can be defined as the world seen from an extreme situation that has become the rule (according to some philosophers, the name of this extreme situation is 'God')" (*RA*, 50).[36] Here philosophy itself becomes a postapocalyptic, post-Auschwitz perspective of conceptual and ethical meltdown, or radical blurring of distinctions, wherein the threshold of indistinction, the gray zone, and the rampant state of exception seem fully to meld. And, in Agamben's understanding, this perspective, at least "according to some philosophers," is a God's-eye view— a god who is decidedly astigmatic if not cockeyed. But does anyone have the right to speak on behalf of, or as proxy for, this god?

Put in less polemical terms, one might say that writing from within the limit situation or the state of exception in which the *Muselmann* is everyman, Auschwitz is now everywhere, and the exception becomes the rule is in a sense to write *in extremis* as if each moment were the moment of death. One question is how general this exceptional writing should be and whether it should function to provide the perspective from which all else is approached "after Auschwitz." In what I would see as its most general form of pertinence, Agamben's threshold of indistinction might be related to transference and one's transferential implication in the object of study with the tendency to repeat symptomatically the forces active in it and, as well, to react to the formulations of others in a highly "cathected" or charged manner. My own response to Agamben has not escaped this pattern. As Agamben himself at times intimates, the challenge is not how to escape it but how to come to terms with it—how to work it through and acquire some critical perspective on it and some enlarged sense of possibility without ever entirely transcending its at times compulsive force. A question Agamben leaves one with is how to understand the historical and transhistorical, as well as the empirical and normative, relations between and among the threshold of indistinction, the gray zone, and the state of exception (and emergency), as well as the possibilities of a rethought (but not entirely new or sublimely postapocalyptic) ethics and politics. Another crucial question is whether utter abjection can be construed as both the end of all previous ethics and the beginning of a radically new ethics ecstatically linked to the sublime. I have tried to argue that utter abjection is the end or limit point of ethics, in that ethical norms do not apply to the behavior of the utterly abject and disempowered but, paradoxically, still remain relevant to it. I have also argued that the sublime does not suspend, or configure a radically new, ethics for sublunar beings such as humans for whom the specific conditions of possibility of ethics are not ontological but instead concrete social, economic, and political conditions. And I have resisted the attempt to conjoin abjection with, or transfigure it into, sublimity, particularly on the part of those who have not experienced the abjection in question, those who "were not there," except perhaps in their imagination and in their rhetoric.

One may be in a better position to come to terms critically with Agamben's own perspective on these questions, as well as my response to it, if I gather together and make explicit what I have represented as basic aspects of his orientation or framework that I find both problematic and worthy of further thought:

1. Modernity, especially after Auschwitz, is bereft, bankrupt, and within the age of accomplished nihilism.

2. Thought is to push this putative condition to the limit and make its vacuousness evident. In other words, thought is to engage in unyielding, radical critique of the present in its relation to the past. Hence the key role for aporia, paradox, and hyperbole as "in-your-face" strategies of provocation.

3. Especially in the present, one has only two real choices: a mystified view of full identity, rights, essence, and telos or a vision of the human as pure potentiality related to the bankruptcy of the past and all preexisting values with the reduction of life to naked, bare, or mere life.

4. The consequence of Agamben's choice of the latter option is an elimination or downplaying of a view of the human being as a compromise formation (in a sense even a "threshold of indistinction") between body (not reducible to naked or mere life) and signifying practices that are social, political, and ethical in various ways.

5. The further consequence is the unavailability of immanent critique with respect to the past or the present. Rather, one is in a position of *Stunde Null* (point zero) requiring creation ex nihilo.

6. The only true "ethics"—in contrast to a derided "morality" of responsibility, guilt, repentance, and perhaps normativity and normative limits in general—is an ethics of pure potentiality, openness, and exposure.

7. The only true "politics" is a form of blank, utopian, messianic (post)apocalypticism that combines Heidegger and a certain Benjamin.

In this intellectual context, the ultimate in traumatized abjection, the *Muselmann* becomes a figure of sublimity and Auschwitz emerges as a transhistorical *leçon de philosophie*. The formula here—whether paradox or one of the oldest of Christian *doxa*—seems to be that only by descending to the depths can one ascend to the paradisiacal heights of revelatory language.

Jamming the Anthropological Machine

Matthew Calarco

The Politics of Anthropocentrism

In a recent discussion with Judith Butler and Ernesto Laclau, Slavoj
Žižek voices a number of concerns in regard to the conciliatory and reformist tendencies of contemporary leftist and postmodernist politics that are
worth considering. Žižek's worry is that today's postmodern left, despite its
commitment to "radicalizing" democracy, has renounced the aim of seeking any *genuinely* radical change in the political and economic structure of
society. In effect, the left has, from Žižek's perspective, accepted global capitalism and liberal democracy as "the only game in town." In outlining the
limitations of this approach, Žižek asks rhetorically: "Who still seriously
questions capitalism, state and political democracy?"[1]

The work of Giorgio Agamben certainly constitutes one possible
affirmative response to this question. Agamben's texts, from the earliest
to the most recent, have provided some of the most persuasive, uncom-
promising, and rigorous arguments to be found in contemporary political
theory in favor of a non-capitalist, non-Statal, non-juridical, and non-
sovereign politics. This thought of the political has been worked out in
elaborate detail over the course of the past two decades by way of a series

of critical confrontations with a number of key theorists (Heidegger, Benjamin, Schmitt, Kojève, Foucault, Arendt, Derrida), and the creation and development of a series of political paradigms and concepts (infancy, exposure, potentiality, whatever singularity, bare life, *homo sacer*, form-of-life). It is not my intention in this chapter to enter into the debate over the merits of Agamben's larger project for a reinvigorated leftist politics, although I should acknowledge at the outset that I take his arguments concerning the limits of democracy, the State, and sovereignty to be decisive in many respects. Instead, and in line with Žižek's concerns about the future orientation of radical leftist politics, my concern here is to examine Agamben's thought from a somewhat oblique perspective: the perspective of the question of the animal.[2] How do non-human animals figure in Agamben's thought? Do animals have a place within a post-essentialist politics? And how do the limits of the humanist philosophical and political project (limits which Agamben has done much to uncover) allow us to rethink the ontology and politics of the human-animal distinction, as well as our ethical relations to human and non-human life? Such questions concerning non-human animals, as I shall attempt to argue in this chapter, help to highlight a key advance and limit in Agamben's recent writings, and, at the same time, provide additional reasons for adopting the kind of critical and skeptical perspective toward dominant trends in leftist politics put forward by Agamben and other radical political theorists.

These questions concerning animal life could in a certain sense be seen as misplaced, even violent, impositions on Agamben's texts—a demand to answer questions he has never claimed any particular competence or desire to address. Indeed, the main focus of nearly all of Agamben's published writings thus far has been avowedly anthropocentric. Despite his unflinching and far-reaching criticisms of metaphysical humanism, it is clear that he has never shown a sustained interest in exploring the anthropocentric dimensions and consequences of this metaphysical project. To the contrary, much of his work (especially those texts published prior to and including *The Coming Community*) can be read as a contribution to and deepening of the anthropocentrism underlying the metaphysical tradition. Where one might expect a radically post-humanist thinker such as Agamben to challenge the oppositional and reductionistic determinations of animal life characteristic of Western metaphysics, he has (in line with the majority of Continental philosophers) remained largely content to occupy the human side of the human/animal binary in order to complicate and rethink the political consequences of essentialist definitions of the human.

It is from this perspective that we can begin better to understand the narrowly anthropocentric approach of a number of Agamben's writings, including, for example: the distinction between human infancy and animal codes in *Infancy and History* and *The Idea of Prose*; the outlining of a non-essentialist notion of human finitude and the dogmatic endorsing of the Hegelian conception of animal death in *Language and Death*; and the neo-Heideggerian denial of exposure (and related concepts such as exposition and potentiality) among animals in *Means Without End, The Coming Community*, and "On Potentiality." What these texts demonstrate is a certain wariness on Agamben's part toward the neo-humanist project of trying to determine a more precise or enlarged conception of human essence; they do not, however, exhibit the same vigilance toward reductionistic determinations of animal life, wherein the multiplicity and singularity of those beings called "animal" are summarily brought under the rubric of "The animal."

And yet, as his work has shifted to the task of thinking through the links tying sovereignty, law, and the State to the isolation of bare life within human beings, the question of the animal has increasingly begun to impose itself on Agamben's thought from within. Thus, in the first volume of *Homo Sacer* we find the logic of the sovereign ban illustrated with the literary motif of the werewolf, a being that is neither human nor animal but rather situated at the margins of the human and the animal, and thus marking the constitutive outside of sovereign protection; and in the third volume of *Homo Sacer*, *Remnants of Auschwitz*, we are confronted with the image of the *Muselmann* (the singular human being at stake in Agamben's post-Auschwitz ethics) who wanders through the Nazi concentration camps like a "stray dog," simultaneously captured inside and outside the force of law. Although these texts fall far short of providing a full analysis of the place of animals within biopolitics, or the functioning of the human-animal distinction within the logic of sovereignty, the *necessity* for developing such an account is surely recognized here.

One of Agamben's more recent works, *The Open: Man and Animal*—a book which will serve as the primary focus for the remainder of this chapter—partially remedies these deficiencies by exploring the question of the animal at more length. In fact, in this text the issue of the human-animal distinction is granted a preeminent status among the problems facing contemporary political thought. Early in this text, Agamben writes:

What is man, if he is always the place—and, at the same time, the result—of ceaseless divisions and caesurae? It is more urgent to work on these divisions, to ask in what way—within man—has man been separated from non-man, and the animal from the human, than it is to take positions on the great issues, on so-called human rights and values. (*O*, 16)

Such remarks are indicative of the steadfast commitment to anti-humanism that characterizes all of Agamben's writings. For him there is little point in pursuing a politics and ethics based on human rights, when the full impact of the critique of humanism has not been measured and been allowed to transform our ideas of community and being-with others. Inasmuch as humanism is founded on a separation of the *humanitas* and *animalitas* within the human, no genuinely post-humanist politics can emerge without grappling with the logic and consequences of this division.

I will return momentarily and at more length to Agamben's discussion of the human-animal distinction, but before doing so, it is important to note that addressing this question—namely, the question of how the human/animal distinction functions in determining what it means to be human—alone will not suffice to call anthropocentrism into question. This is especially true where, as is the case in much of Agamben's writings, one limits the analysis to the manner in which this distinction is played out "within man." If this were all Agamben sought to do in *The Open*, there would be little to distinguish this book from the previous volumes in the *Homo Sacer* series, which analyze the separation of *zoē* and *bios* within human life only to leave suspended the question of animal life and politics. It seems, then, that if one is to address the philosophical and political question of the animal in any meaningful way, it will be necessary at the very least to work through both (a) the ontology of animal life *on its own terms*, and (b) the ethico-political relations that obtain between those beings called "human" and "animal."

Although Agamben, like much of anti- and post-humanist philosophy, has been slow to address the question of the animal from this broader perspective, there are at least two reasons why the question must inevitably be engaged in this enlarged form by thinkers who wish to formulate a genuinely post-humanist approach to politics. In the most general terms, the post-humanist critique of humanism is to be understood not as a misanthropic or dismissive rejection of the accomplishments of Enlightenment modernism, but as a critical investigation of human *subjectivity*, of the material (e.g., economic, historical, linguistic, and social) forces at work in the formation of human subjects. Specific to the post-Nietzschean and post-Heideggerian critique of humanism (a lineage to which Agamben clearly belongs) is a probing of the conditions of possibility that render subjects open to material forces as such. What does it mean to say that one comes to be a subject only in and through language or history? And how must a subject be structured such that it can be affected and transformed by material forces outside of itself? In offering answers to such questions, it quickly becomes clear that the pre-subjective conditions that give rise to human subjectivity (these conditions go by various names in different thinkers, for example, Heidegger's *Da-sein*, Nancy's and Levinas's exposure, Derrida's ex-appropriation, Agamben's exposition) cannot easily be restricted to human beings. And this is the first reason why anti-humanism ultimately opens onto the larger issue of non-human animals—for the subjective being of many non-human animals, too, is constituted by differential structures of exposure that render standard accounts of the human/animal distinction suspect. At this level of pre-subjective and pre-personal singularities, there are no clear-cut criteria for distinguishing animal modes of exposure from human modes; what we encounter, rather, are complex networks of relations, affects, and becomings into which both human beings and animals are thrown. As such, post-humanism is confronted with the necessity of returning to first philosophy with the task of creating a non-anthropocentric ontology of life, something like the ethology we find in Jakob von Uexküll or Deleuze and Guattari.

The second chief reason that post-humanists must account for the place of animals within their project arises at the ethico-political level. While it is clear that post-humanist philosophers do not accept *in toto* standard philosophical theories of value, there can be little doubt that the critique of humanism is motivated by a kind of ethical and political imperative. The assumption by many post-humanists is that nihilism and the major political catastrophes of our age are linked in a profound way with the very humanism typically offered by neo-humanists as a solution to these issues. For post-humanists, then, overcoming these problems would require something other than a humanist politics based on a naïve account of human subjectivity. The shared intuition and hope of most post-humanist philosophers seems to be that a less destructive and more sustainable form of politics can be developed beginning from a thought of the relational ontology mentioned above. Here we might take Levinas's project as an example of this approach. Although Levinas is usually approached as a purely ethical thinker, it is perhaps more appropriate to view his work in *political* terms, that is, as a response to a political problem. The great danger for Levinas arises when politics becomes unmoored from its ethical grounding and forgets its justification and calling as a response to the face of the Other. By recalling politics to its ethical foundations—which Levinas locates at the level of "sensibility" in a pre-subjective exposure to the Other human—he hopes to re-invigorate and radicalize existing forms of politics (such as liberal democracy) that take general human welfare into account but often forget the irreducibly singular human beings who constitute a political body. Of course, the problem here is that the ethical obligations and responsibilities incurred in exposure do not necessarily arise from the Other human alone, for non-human animals and other non-human beings also have the potential to interrupt and oblige. Consequently, a post-humanist politics that begins from a thought of exposure must come to terms with responsibilities potentially arising from beyond the sphere of the human.

It is only in recent years that philosophers in the Continental tradition have begun to think through the question of the animal in this more inclusive manner. I would suggest that Agamben's early work was unable to take such issues into account primarily because, following thinkers such as Heidegger and Benveniste, he was working with an overly narrow inter-human and proto-linguistic theory of the grounds of human subjectivity. At the same time, although his work was never explicitly *opposed* to an expanded notion of ethics and politics that would encompass non-human life, he failed to outline in a sufficient manner what form such an ethics and politics might take.

In a certain sense, then, Agamben's *The Open* marks a rupture in the itinerary of his thought. If his thinking began primarily as a response to the nihilistic tendencies of humanism and human-based politics, his most recent work indicates that these concerns lead necessarily to addressing directly the larger issue of anthropocentrism which had been held previously in abeyance. And this direction is explicitly announced at the very outset of *The Open*, in the section entitled "Theriomorphous" (meaning, literally, having the form of an animal). Taking his point of departure from an illustration found in a thirteenth-century Hebrew Bible in the Ambrosian Library in Milan, which depicts the messianic banquet of the righteous on the last day, Agamben pauses to consider a curious detail about the portrait. The righteous represented in the illustration—who are enjoying their feast on the meat of the Leviathan and Behemoth with no concern for whether the slaughter was kosher, since they inhabit a space and time that is outside the law—are depicted as having *human* bodies and *animal* heads. "Why," Agamben wonders, "are the representatives of concluded humanity depicted with animal heads?" (*O*, 2).

Following certain interpretations of both the rabbinic and Talmudic traditions, Agamben suggests that the illustration can be read as announcing a double consequence encountered on the "last day" of humanity. He writes:

It is not impossible . . . that in attributing an animal head to the remnant of Israel [i.e., those who are remaining, the righteous who remain alive during the time of the Messiah's coming], the artist of the manuscript in the Ambrosian intended to suggest that on the last day, the relations between animals and men will take on a new form, and that man himself will be reconciled with his animal nature. (*O*, 3)

What we have here, then, is an illustration representing two moments realized in the post-apocalyptic time of the "end of man" and the "end of history." On the one hand—and this theme will be familiar to readers of Agamben's other writings—we encounter human beings who are reconciled with their animal natures and who consequently no longer suffer the effects of the biopolitical separation of bare life and political life. To think through a human form-of-life that does not divide *zoē* from *bios*—such would be the task of the politics of the coming community, a task and a politics that, as Agamben tells us, remain "largely to be invented" (*HS*, 11). On the other hand—and this is where a certain rupture can be marked in Agamben's own thought—we are given to think a transmutation in the relations between human beings and animals, where this difference is understood, not simply as a division that occurs within human beings, but rather as a differential relation *between* human beings and so-called non-human animals. Although Agamben does not specify the precise dimensions of this transformed relation (any more than he specifies the exact form of the politics of the coming community), it is clear, given the context, that his reading of the illustration is pointing us toward a less violent conception of human-animal relations.

Thus, just as Agamben's thought of the coming community is an effort to come to grips with and avert the political failures of our age, his reworking of the human-animal distinction appears to be aimed at creating a space in which human interactions with non-human life can take on a new form and economy that avoids similar disastrous consequences for non-human life. It will be useful to keep both of these prongs of Agamben's argument in mind as we turn to an investigation of the political and ontological obstacles blocking access to the realization of this kind of alternative mode of being-with other animals.

Humanism and the Anthropological Machine

Agamben gives the name of "anthropological machine" (a concept he borrows from Furio Jesi, an Italian scholar of myth) to the mechanism underlying our current means of determining the human-animal distinction. This machine can best be understood as the symbolic and material mechanisms at work in various scientific and philosophical discourses that classify and distinguish humans and animals through a dual process of inclusion and exclusion. The opening chapters of *The Open* provide the reader with a fascinating overview of some of the historical variations on the anthropological machine at work in a variety of authors and discourses, ranging from the philosophy of Bataille and Kojève, to the taxonomic studies of Linnaeus and post-Darwinian paleontology. For the purposes of the argument I am developing here, it will suffice to recall the general structure of the machine and why Agamben argues that it is necessary to stop its functioning.

Agamben makes a distinction between two key variations on the anthropological machine: the modern and pre-modern. The modern anthropological machine is post-Darwinian. It seeks to understand, following the principles of natural science, the emergence of the fully constituted human being from out of the order of the human animal (the latter, of course, is in many ways indistinguishable from certain non-human animals, especially so-called "higher primates"). In order to mark this transition, it is necessary to determine and isolate the animal aspects of the human animal and exclude them from humanity proper. Agamben describes this process as involving an "animalization" of certain modes of human life, an attempt to separate out—within human beings themselves—what precisely is animal on the one hand and human on the other. This variation on the anthropological machine gives rise to the search by nineteenth-century paleontologists for the "missing link" that provides the biological transition from speechless ape to speaking human. But it also opens the way for the totalitarian and democratic experiments on and around human nature that function by excluding animal life from human life within human beings. Agamben suggests that "it is enough to move our field of research ahead a few decades, and instead of this innocuous paleontological find we will have the Jew, that is, the non-man produced within the man, or the *néomort* and the overcomatose person, that is, the animal separated within the human body itself" (*O*, 37).

The pre-modern form of the anthropological machine, which runs from Aristotle up through Linnaeus, functions in a similar but inverted form. Rather than animalizing certain aspects of the human, animal life is itself humanized. Human beings who take an essentially animal form are used to mark the constitutive outside of humanity proper: the infant savage, the wolf-man, the werewolf, the slave or barbarian, and so on. Here, the beings situated at the limits of humanity suffer similar consequences to those "animalized" beings caught within the working of the modern anthropological machine.

As Agamben suggests, the structure or machine that delimits the contours of the human is perfectly ironic and empty. It does not function by uncovering a uniquely human trait that demarcates a clean ontological break between human and non-human animals—for, as Agamben himself acknowledges, no such trait or group of traits is to be found. This much we know from current debates in evolutionary biology and animal ethics. And here it is not so much a matter of subscribing to a watered-down, quasi-Darwinian continuism that would blur any and all distinctions one might wish to make between and among human and non-human animals, but rather recognizing that deciding what constitutes "the human" and "the animal" is simply a scientific or ontological matter. The locus and stakes of the human-animal distinction are also deeply *political and ethical*. For not only does the distinction create the opening for the exploitation of non-human animals and others considered not fully human (this is the point that is forcefully made by animal ethicists), but it also creates the conditions for contemporary biopolitics, in which more and more of the so-called "biological" and "animal" aspects of human life are brought under the purview of the State and the juridical order.

As Agamben has argued in *Homo Sacer* and elsewhere, biopolitics, whether it manifests itself in totalitarian or democratic form, contains within it the virtual possibility of concentration camps and other violent and nihilistic means of producing and controlling bare life. It comes as no surprise, then, that Agamben does not seek to articulate a more precise, more empirical, or less dogmatic determination of the human-animal distinction; rather, he insists that *the distinction must be abolished altogether*, and along with it the anthropological machine that produces the distinction. Recalling the political consequences that have followed from the modern and pre-modern separation of "human" and "animal" within human existence, Agamben characterizes the task for thought in the following terms: "it is not so much a matter of asking which of the two machines [i.e., the modern or pre-modern anthropological machine] . . . is better or more effective—or, rather, less lethal and bloody—as it is of understanding how they work so that we might, eventually, be able to stop them" (*O*, 38).

Now, the critic of Agamben's argument is likely to see a slippery-slope fallacy here. Why is it a *necessary* or even virtual possibility that every time a human-animal distinction is made that there will be negative ("lethal and bloody") political consequences for certain human beings? Isn't the promise of democratic humanism and Enlightenment modernism (the very traditions Agamben would have us leave behind) their foundational commitment to reform, their perfectibility and inclusiveness? Isn't it precisely humanism that guards against the worst excesses of totalitarianism and human rights abuses?

The reader who takes up a careful study of Agamben's work from this angle, seeking answers to such questions, will be well positioned to grasp its novelty. The overarching thesis of Agamben's work since the 1990s is that there is in fact an "inner solidarity" between democracy and totalitarianism, not at an empirical level, but at a historical and philosophical level (*HS*, 10). Despite the enormous differences between these two political systems, they are nevertheless united in their investment in the politics of the anthropological machine, and in seeking to separate bare life from properly political life. Even if democratic regimes maintain safeguards designed to prevent many of the totalitarian excesses perpetrated against bare life (and Agamben's references to Karen Quinlan and others make it clear that democracies are actually far from successful in such matters), they continue unwittingly to create the conditions of possibility for such consequences. This hidden implication of democracy comes to the fore especially in those instances where the rule of law is suspended, for example, in the declarations of sovereign exception to the law or in the refugee crisis that accompanies the decline of nation-States. Such states of exception are, Agamben argues (following Benjamin), becoming more and more the rule in contemporary political life—and the examples one might adduce in support of this thesis are indeed becoming increasingly and troublingly commonplace. Considerations of this kind are what lead Agamben to the conclusion that the genuine political task facing us today is not the reform, radicalization, or expansion of humanism and democracy, but the creation of an altogether different form of political life.

Agamben's work faces two important challenges at this level. On the one hand, neo-humanists will (justifiably) wonder whether Agamben's "coming community" and rejection of the humanist tradition in favor of a non-sovereign and non-juridical politics will be better able than current democracies to guard against the injustices he condemns. On the other hand, theorists of a more deconstructionist and Levinasian orientation will likely see Agamben's project as being constituted by a false dilemma between humanist democracy and a non-essentialist thought of community. Although such theorists would share Agamben's concerns about the problematic virtual possibilities of democratic politics and its ontology, they would be less sanguine about completely rejecting the democratic heritage. For them, the chief political task would consist in filtering through our democratic inheritance to unlock its radical possibilities, insisting on democracy's commitment to perfectibility so as to expand democracy's scope and to open democratic politics to its Other. This would bring democracy and its humanist commitments into relation with another thought of being-with-Others that is similar to Agamben's coming community.

As I noted at the outset of this chapter, I believe Agamben offers us some of the most persuasive accounts of the limits of these forms of current political thinking. And throughout his work there are moments when he illustrates how his alternative thought of politics *can* be actualized in concrete circumstances. But even the most charitable reading of Agamben's work must acknowledge that, should Agamben wish to debate the kinds of questions posed by neo-humanists or deconstructionists, much remains to be worked out at both the theoretical and concrete political level. And if the scope of this discussion were limited to an anthropocentric politics, I would argue that the questions and criticisms raised by neo-humanists and deconstructionists are impossible to circumvent. Humanism, democracy, and human rights are complicated and rich historical constructs, with the intrinsic potential for extensive and remarkably progressive reforms.

And yet, if the question of the animal were taken seriously, and the political discussion were moved to that level as well, the stakes of the debate would change considerably. Who among those activists and theorists working in defense of animals seriously believes that humanism, democracy, and human rights are the sine qua non of ethics and politics? Even those theorists who employ the logic of these discourses in an extensionist manner so as to bring animals within the sphere of moral and political considerability do not seem to believe that an ethics and politics that genuinely respect animal life can be accomplished within the confines of the traditions they use.

On this political terrain, neo-humanist arguments concerning the merits of the democratic tradition have little if any weight. Even if one were to inscribe animal rights within a democratic liberatory narrative of expansion and perfectibility, such gestures can only appear tragicomic in light of the massive institutionalized abuse of animals that contemporary democracies not only tolerate but encourage on a daily basis. And in many democracies, the support of animal abuse goes much further. Currently, militant animal activists in the United States who engage in economic sabotage and property destruction in the name of stopping the worst forms of animal abuse are not just criticized (and in many cases without sound justification), but are placed at the top of the list of "domestic terrorists" by the FBI and subjected to outrageously unjust penalties and prison sentences. In view of the magnitude of such problems, animal activists are currently embroiled in a protracted debate over the merits of a reformist (welfarist) approach versus a stricter and more radical rightist (incrementalist) approach to animal issues, and over which approach is more effective in the contemporary political and legal contexts. However, the real question lies elsewhere: in the choice between the project of radicalizing existing politics to accommodate non-human life (neo-humanism and deconstruction) and that of working toward the kind of coming politics advocated by Agamben, which would allow for an entirely new economy of human/animal relations. While Agamben's thought is sometimes pejoratively labeled by critics as utopian, inasmuch as it seeks a complete change in our political thinking and practices without offering the concrete means of achieving such change, from the perspective of the question of the animal, the tables can easily be turned on the critics. Anyone who argues that existing forms of politics can be reformed or radicalized so as to do justice to the multiplicity of forms of non-human life is clearly the unrealistic and utopian thinker, for what signs or sources of hope do we have that human-ism and democracy (both of which are grounded in an agent-centered con-ception of subjectivity) can be radicalized or reformed so as to include and give direct consideration to beings beyond the human?[3]

Thus, when we consider the ethico-political status of animal life, the necessity for working toward a form of politics beyond the present human-ist, democratic, and juridical orders becomes clear beyond any shadow of a doubt. Even Jacques Derrida—who has always taken a nuanced and gen-erally respectful stance toward humanism and the law, refusing to either endorse them or reject them fully—has acknowledged the limits of legis-lation in this regard. Concerning political and ethical relations between human beings and animals, he argues:

A transformation is . . . necessary and inevitable, for reasons that are both con-scious and unconscious. Slow, laborious, sometimes gradual, sometimes accelerat-ed, the mutation of relations between humans and animals will not necessarily or solely take the form of a charter, a declaration of rights, or a tribunal governed by a legislator. I do not believe in the miracle of legislation. Besides, there is already a law, more or less empirical, and that's better than nothing. But it does not prevent the slaughtering, or the "techno-scientific" pathologies of the market or of indus-trial production.[4]

Were sufficient attention given to the question of the animal by Agamben his arguments aimed at the limitations of the logic of sovereignty and our current political and juridical models would become significantly more powerful and persuasive. That Agamben chooses to avoid this approach is indicative of what could be called a "performative anthropocentrism" in his texts. In the following section, I argue that if Agamben and other post-humanist approaches to politics are unable overcome this kind of anthro-pocentrism, the logic of the anthropological machine will reassert itself in places where we least expect it.

· · ·

Let us return, then, to Agamben's main question: how best to jam the anthropological machine and create a post-humanist politics that is no longer governed by its "lethal and bloody" logic?

One of the key theses of *The Open* is that Heidegger's thinking—despite its uncompromisingly critical relation to humanism—does little more than replicate the inner logic of the anthropological machine. The majority of the second half of *The Open* is taken up with a lengthy and intricate reading of Heidegger, in which Agamben attempts to demonstrate how Heidegger's scattered remarks on the difference between human Dasein and animal life implicitly obeys the inclusionary/exclusionary logic of the anthropological machine. Focusing primarily on Heidegger's *Fundamental Concepts of Metaphysics* and *Parmenides* lecture courses, Agamben's reading of these texts stresses the *proximity* of human Dasein with animal life, as well as the essential continuity that binds human and animal in their shared "captivation" by beings in their respective environments. As Agamben understands the matter, human Dasein differs from its animal other only by the very smallest of differences. What allows human Dasein to emerge in its singularity, along with the world relation and political possibilities concomitant with the emergence of Dasein, is simply that human animals have the unique capacity to grasp, or catch sight of, their being-captivated, a possibility that is (presumably) blocked off for animal life:

Man, in the experience of profound boredom, has risked himself in the suspension of his relationship with the environment as a living being. . . . [He is able] to remember captivation an instant before a world disclosed itself. . . . Dasein is simply an animal that has learned to become bored; it has awakened *from* its own captivation *to* its own captivation. This awakening of the living being to its own being-captivated, this anxious and resolute opening to a not-open, is the human. (*O*, 70)

In this "brief instant" before world opens, in the moment when the human animal awakens from its captivation *to* its captivation, human Dasein is thrust into the "space" or opening of the ontological difference. This is a topos that usually is hidden but that surfaces in certain moods such as anxiety and boredom, moods in which the tight grip of captivation that binds human beings to other beings in the world gives way to the malaise and uncanniness of the indifference of other beings.

Inasmuch as Heidegger's account of the emergence of human Dasein is predicated on the capture and exclusion of the animal's particular mode of relation (namely, *Benommenheit*, captivation) to other beings, Agamben suggests that his thinking follows in lockstep with the logic of the anthropological machine. And Heidegger's political thought—especially that of the early to mid-1930s—provides an even clearer example of how the anthropological machine is at play throughout his writings, as Heidegger seeks in these writings to "ground" political life in the unique world relation of human Dasein, which, in *An Introduction to Metaphysics*, is explicitly contrasted with the "worldless" realm of animal life.

It is arguable whether Heidegger ever gave up the aim of uncovering a new political or historical task for human beings. *If* he did in fact recognize the error of doing so along nationalistic lines, it is unclear whether he gave up hope in uncovering some other "ground" for reorienting human existence. At the very least, we *can* be certain that Heidegger's thinking remains beholden to the logic of the anthropological machine from beginning to end. Heidegger never renounces the task of determining the proper of the human (as Da-sein, ek-sistence, etc.), and of thinking through the redemption of nature (i.e., the letting be of beings in their Being) that would occur were this human propriety to be assumed as such.

Heidegger's inability to think the relation between human and nonhuman life beyond or outside the logic of anthropological machine is what leads Agamben to look elsewhere for an alternative thought of the political. Not surprisingly—for this is a common gesture in Agamben's texts—he finds his inspiration in Walter Benjamin's writings. Agamben is particularly interested in Benjamin's notions of the "saved night" and the "dialectic at a standstill," inasmuch as both notions offer us an alternative image of the relation between nature and the human that does not rely on a rigid conceptual separation of the two realms. Such notions seem to offer a thought of the human and the animal that places the anthropological machine "completely out of play" (*O*, 81). For Benjamin, the "saved night" refers to a natural world that is sufficient in itself, a world that has value independently of the role it might play as a dwelling place for human beings or as the stage where human history is acted out. When the natural world is granted inherent value as it is in itself—as irreparable and unsavable, as not in need of being redeemed by human beings or of serving human ends—it is at this point that the dialectic between human and animal comes to a "standstill." On Agamben's reading, Benjamin seeks this standstill, not because he is concerned with articulating another, more refined instance of the human/animal distinction, but because he seeks to abandon such conceptual work altogether. In the final analysis, Benjamin's texts leave the so-called "human" and "non-human" to be *as they are*, that is, in their singular, irreparable manner. Such letting-be has no need, as it does in Heidegger, of passing through human *logos* or history in order to come to presence. Rather, Benjamin's thought proposes for us the possibility of letting beings be *outside of being*.

It should come as no surprise to the reader that these Benjaminian themes provide the impetus and telos for Agamben's reading of Western history as the unfolding and vicissitudes of the anthropological machine. Benjamin's thought provides Agamben with the possibility of thinking about human beings and the non-human world beyond the dominant logic and terms provided by the Western metaphysical tradition. And the overarching task of *The Open*, at least as I understand it, is precisely to open up this possibility. In brief, Agamben's aim in this book is to provide readers with a philosophical concept, that is, with a conceptual monkey wrench that can be used to jam the anthropological machine—a machine that serves as the seemingly unsurpassable political and ontological horizon of our time. Agamben's notions of life as "unsavable" or "irreparable" are meant to provide readers with a glimpse of a world not subject to strictly anthropocentric aims or the "hyperbolic naïveté" of modern humanity and its human chauvinism.[5] As Agamben suggests in *The Coming Community*, affirming life in its irreparableness and profanity is a form of Nietzschean life-affirmation. In this sense, the concept of unsavable life is offered as one way among others of assuming Zarathustra's task of remaining "true to the earth" and its inhabitants.

Agamben himself admits that trying to think about a humanity that is absolutely exposed and irreparable is not an easy task (*O*, 90). Indeed, one could read the whole of Agamben's writings as a series of efforts to articulate this one thought: what form such an irreparable humanity, and a politics befitting such a humanity, might take. Reading Agamben from this perspective would also provide insight into the critical texts in which he probes the dangers and limitations of existing models of biopolitics and sovereignty. Our current models of politics are all, in one way or another, beholden to an image of humanity that is predicated on excluding our irreparableness. The task for thought, then, would be to highlight this limitation, and to offer another, more affirmative and compelling concept and practice in its place.

With regard to human politics, Agamben seems to realize that such a thought is not to be achieved "all in one go." Given the ubiquity of the anthropological machine in both symbolic and material structures, the critical and deconstructive gesture of jamming the anthropological machine is just as important as the positive project of articulating another non-binary and non-hierarchical concept of the human. With regard to rethinking *animal* life, the task is fraught with *far more severe difficulties*, if only for the simple fact that most of the theorists and philosophers working in this area have paid scant attention to the question of the animal. As I argued above, Agamben's writings are no exception here, as they focus entirely and exclusively on the effects of the anthropological machine *on human beings*, and never explore the impact the machine has on various forms of animal life. Surely the latter type of analysis is needed if we are to begin to develop another mode of relation and community with non-human life. Such a project, as humble and painstaking as it is, perhaps lacks the pathos characteristic of Agamben's messianic politics; but it is every bit as necessary if we wish to develop a notion of community that truly avoids the "lethal and bloody" logic of the anthropological machine.

For, after all, what *will* the righteous eat at the banquet on the "last day"? Will post-humanity dine on the flesh of animals whose lives have become irreparable and unsavable?

Biopolitics, Liberal Eugenics, and Nihilism

Catherine Mills

As Paolo Virno notes, the "equivocal concept" of biopolitics has recently become fashionable, and is "often and enthusiastically invoked in every kind of context."[1] For Virno, the solution to this "automatic and unreflexive" usage of the term is to shift focus to the more complex concept of labor-power. Yet while it is true that the notion of biopolitics, or biopower, is frequently invoked in a confused way, this is not reason to give up on the concept, but only an indication that the philosophical problems it raises have not yet been plumbed. What is required then is more, not less, philosophical focus on the concept. To this end, a clarification of the ways in which two of its principal theorists, Michel Foucault and Giorgio Agamben, elaborate it highlights a number of conceptual divergences in their accounts of biopower. The apparent irreconcilability in their accounts has not gone unnoticed within critical literature, such that it has even been suggested that a dialogue between Foucault and Agamben is impossible.[2] Whether that is accurate or not, the most striking difference between these theorists is undoubtedly the fact that Foucault's methodological approach to the concept of biopower is genealogical and historical, while Agamben strives for an ontologization of the political, evident, for instance, in

his insistence on an analytic connection between the metaphysical problem of potentiality and political problem of sovereignty.[3] While the broad
differences in their approaches to political analysis are thus clear, what is
less clear are the implications of this quasi-methodological difference for
an understanding of normativity: while both engage seriously with problems of law and normativity, little has been said to explicate the conceptual
divergences in their approaches to these issues, and the ways in which these
are related to divergences in their understandings of biopower.

In this chapter, then, I examine the philosophical critiques of law
and normativity that Foucault and Agamben develop in their accounts of
biopower, with particular focus on two themes. The first of these is how
each posits the relation between law and life, which is directly bound to
the differing roles that each gives to sovereignty in biopower. The second
thematic is that of the norm and the exception. What is interesting in considering these two themes is that while both Foucault and Agamben argue
that biopower entails an increasingly tight integration of life and law, at
few other conceptual points do their accounts converge. For Foucault, the
integration of life and law is achieved through the process of "normalization," which is said to increasingly infect the operation of law, such that
law itself operates by virtue of the norm. For Agamben, the status of sovereignty as the limit of the juridical order means that the exception that
ambivalently founds sovereignty and the constitution of the normal is itself
the mechanism by which life is taken into law. Moreover, in the critical
approaches of each to normativity, Foucault develops a genealogical critique of the integration and mobilization of the norm as a particular form
of rule in operations of power, while Agamben diagnoses a generalized
normative crisis introduced by the coincidence of life and law. In the final
section of the chapter, I will begin to demonstrate the interpretive consequences of these different approaches to normativity by focusing on an
emerging debate in bioethics on the notion of a "liberal eugenics." I argue
that while the technologies discussed in the debate entail the biopolitical
normalization of life processes identified by Foucault, the debate itself is
also indicative of the normative crisis identified by Agamben. Thus, the
chapter proceeds in three parts: the first two sections provide a discussion
of the conceptual differences in Foucault's and Agamben's understandings
of normativity and biopower, while the third seeks to mobilize and extend
their insights through a discussion of liberal eugenics.

Foucault on the Normativity of the Norm

In the final chapter of *History of Sexuality*, Foucault claims that politics in the West assumed a new form in the late eighteenth century, wherein the Aristotelian conception of "man" as an animal with the additional capacity for politics was definitively overturned, such that biological life itself became the object and target of political power. The transformation of politics rendered in this pithy comment was, Foucault argues, brought forth by a fundamental shift in the operative rationalities of technologies of power, from a power of deduction to one of production, indicated by two particular historical events. The first of these is the emergence of disciplinary techniques of power geared toward mastering the forces of the individual body. The second, which Foucault suggests developed somewhat later, is a "biopolitics" geared toward the regulation and management of the life of a new political subject, the population. Linked at the level of concrete arrangements, including the deployment of sexuality, these two axes or events lead to a technology of power aimed at life, which in turn leads to the emergence of a "normalizing society" that signals the demise or at least de-prioritization of sovereign power in favor of a regime of "biopower."[4] This power, which operates according to the maxim of "fostering life or disallowing it," signals for Foucault the threshold of our modernity, and entails new forms of government and social regulation as well as new forms of subjectivity. It also necessitates a wholly new relation between power and subjectivity. That is, power no longer operates through a violence imposed upon subjects from above, but through a normalizing regulation that administers and fosters the life of subjects. In this new regime of power, power incorporates itself into and takes hold of the body of the citizen not through violence, but through normative regulation or "the normalization of life processes."[5]

Foucault's considerable intellectual debt to Georges Canguilhem in the formulation of "normalization" is widely acknowledged, both in terms of his extension of the methodology of a "history of concepts" and in terms of the conception of life and norms that Canguilhem proposes in *The Normal and the Pathological*.[6] In this now classic study of the concept of the normal in medicine, Canguilhem notes that in its Latin origin, the term *norma* indicates a T-square, used for measuring right angles, while *normalis* meant perpendicular.[7] This, he suggests, means that

a norm, or rule, is what can be used to right, to square, to straighten. To set a norm (*normer*), to normalize, is to impose a requirement on an existence, a given whose variety, disparity, with regard to the requirement present themselves as a hostile, even more than an unknown, indeterminant. It is, in effect, a polemical concept which negatively qualifies the sector of the given which does not enter into its extension while it depends on its comprehension.[8]

Hence, a polemicism internal to the concept of the normal is expressed in the fundamental polarity of life in relation to the environment in which an organism finds itself. Within this, variation threatens the norm, and, depending on the relation of the organism and its environment, either constitutes pathology or a new possibility for living. Within this, the relation of the abnormal and normal is not one of "contradiction and externality" but of "inversion and polarity,"[9] such that the abnormal does not exist outside the extension of the norm as such, but expresses a less preferable possibility in relation to the norm. The abnormal does not signify a permanent impossibility, but indicates that possible modes of living are not normatively equivalent. Or as François Ewald puts it, "if all possible forms are not normal, it is not because some forms are naturally impossible but because the various possible forms of existence are not all equivalent for those who must exist in them."[10]

Without underestimating the importance of Canguilhem's conception of norms within Foucault's work, it is also important to recognize a significant shift from it, wherein Foucault's concern is not with elaborating an internal normativity in natural life itself, but with the ways in which norms are themselves imposed upon the living body of the subject and are subsequently taken inside that body. That is, Canguilhem focuses on the elaboration of a concept of life that emphasizes the normativity internal to it, insofar as an organism cannot be indifferent to the environment in which it lives. He argues further that such an internal normativity is itself the embryonic possibility of the "normativity essential to human consciousness," though this is not to say that social norms can be immediately derived from vital norms.[11] In contrast, Foucault begins with the presumption of the regulatory effectiveness of power to describe the historical modes of incorporation and corporealization of the norm, while also insisting on the possibilities for dis-incorporating any particular norm or set of norms. That is, it is in becoming embedded within relations of power that the norm gains a certain normative force, and normalization amounts to a particular mode of the institutionalization of that force, though not one that is necessarily effective in its striving to regularize the forces of the body at the level of either the individual body or that of the population. In this

light, it can be said that Foucault was consistently concerned with examining the political fixation of the boundaries of the normal and abnormal through the operations of normalization—from his early analyses of
the clinic and of madness through to the genealogy of desiring man—
although it is true that the conceptual and methodological tools elaborated
for that analysis transform considerably throughout.

Foucault's politicization of the concept of the norm has a number
of implications worth noting here. First, despite the rather brief appearance of the concept itself, this suggests that at least the *thematic* of biopower has a deeper significance in Foucault's work than is often attributed
to it. Indeed, Foucault's claim in *History of Sexuality* that the threshold of
modernity is reached with the entrance of life into politics, that is, into the
orders of knowledge and power, also points toward the analysis of the epis-
temic status of "life" in *The Order of Things* and the early analyses of the
clinic and of madness. Congruent with this, in *Society Must Be Defended,*
Foucault links the emergence of a normalizing society with the historical
emergence of the discourses of the human sciences, as well as the extension
of medicine, which, he argues, entails a "perpetual exchange or confrontation between the mechanics of discipline and the principle of right."[12] It is
in this perpetual exchange and confrontation of discipline and right that
a biopolitical society is normalizing. Contrary to his remarks in *Discipline
and Punish,* in *Society Must Be Defended* Foucault suggests that the claim
that modern society is normalizing does not simply mean that the techniques of discipline have "swarmed" from their originating institutions,
such as the prison, to take over the entire social field. Rather, he writes
that "the normalizing society is a society in which the norm of discipline
and the norm of regulation intersect along an orthogonal articulation."[13]
By this, he means that discipline and regulation have been brought into
articulation through the operation of a "natural rule, or in other words a
norm,"[14] such that a power that "took possession of life . . . succeeded in
covering the whole surface that lies between the organic and the biological,
between the body and the population."[15]

Further, as Foucault consistently maintains in his various discussions
of normalization, from his comments in *Discipline and Punish* to the final
chapter in *History of Sexuality,* within a normalizing society legal apparatuses are increasingly incorporated into a continuum of institutions, the
function of which are "for the most part" regulatory, such that the mode

by which the law operates is that of the norm. This clearly does not mean that law itself is superseded; rather, Foucault argues that as a regulatory apparatus, the law continues to operate within the regime of biopower, but in a different mode than previously. That is, rather than operating through an historical link to sovereignty, the law now operates in accordance with the exchange and confrontation between right and discipline. As Ewald notes, this means that for Foucault, legality itself is not intrinsically tied to sovereignty. Ewald goes on to show that norms are themselves not opposed to the law in any way, though they are opposed to the "juridical" code that links law to sovereignty, in which the law is "armed with the sword."[16] In fact, not only are norms not opposed to the law, they are increasingly the mode in which law operates. Norms are the operative condition of law in a biopolitical society, since it is precisely the norm that allows the law to operate in conjunction with a series of increasingly regulatory apparatuses, such as medicine. In effect, the norm gives the law access to the body in an unprecedented way, that is, as a continuous regulatory force rather than as a spectacularly violent instrument of sovereignty.

This decoupling of law and sovereignty points to an important and frequently noted ambiguity in Foucault's portrayal of sovereignty, which he himself sees as something of a paradox within the regime of biopower. Foucault argues that the historical rise of biopower entails a transformation in rationalities of power from that of sovereignty, which was characterized by a "right over life and death," to a power focused on fostering life, which "makes live or lets die." Despite the ostensible clarity of this distinction, there is much ambiguity in the exact relation of sovereignty and biopower that Foucault wants to posit, and his terms for describing this vary across texts published in roughly the same period of his work. For instance, in *History of Sexuality*, he writes as if sovereignty is replaced by biopower, whereas elsewhere he insists that discipline, government, and sovereignty coincide historically in a tripartite arrangement.[17] The most convincing resolution of these contradictory statements has been to emphasize the integration of sovereignty and governmentality. However, even if priority is ceded to the latter of these claims, this does not fully resolve the ambiguity. For given such a tripartite arrangement, it is not clear what the effective relations between these technologies or regimes of power might be, that is, in what they conflict or converge with, or reinforce or undermine each other. Further, while this tripartite arrangement suggests a configuration of governmentality, discipline, and sovereignty, it does not wholly clarify the relation of sovereignty and biopower, since the relation between biopower, governmentality, and discipline is itself unclear within Foucault's various formulations.[18]

This ambiguity is reinforced rather than clarified by Foucault's distinction between biopower and sovereignty, on the basis that the former "fosters life and allows it to die," whereas the latter is characterized by a "right over life and death." Of this, he argues that while both forms of power thus address themselves to life and death, within sovereignty, the right over life and death is unbalanced, since "sovereign power's effect on life is exercized only when the sovereign can kill," such that the "essence of the right of life and death is actually the right to kill."[19] By contrast, biopower is invested in the regularization of life through the operation of the norm, the control of the "aleatory" elements of the life of the population, and seeks to "improve life by eliminating accidents, the random element, and deficiencies."[20] Thus it seems that biopower is entirely interested in fostering life, and when that fails, or when the form of life at stake is considered unlivable,[21] it is simply abandoned to its own resources and "allowed" to die. Biopower, does not, however, entail an internal right over death as such. Indeed, Foucault suggests that within biopower, death itself is relegated to the margins of political power: it is no longer a manifestation of the power of the sovereign, but precisely indicates the limits of power, the moment when life slips from the grasp of governance. Within biopower, death, Foucault suggests, "is outside the power relationship" such that "power literally ignores death."[22]

In contrast to these seemingly unequivocal statements on the status of death in biopower, Foucault also suggests that death is in fact incorporated into biopower through racism. Without exploring his account of racism in depth, racism, and especially State racism, "is precisely a way of introducing a break into the domain of life that is under power's control: the break between what *must* live and what *must* die."[23] This means that for the modern state, racism is an "indispensable precondition," for the deployment of the sovereign right of death within the matrix of a power that fosters life. Racism justifies and makes possible the otherwise paradoxical deployment of death within a regime of biopower, and it does so precisely through a normalizing regulation that fragments "the field of the biological that power controls," that is, by introducing "caesurae within the biological continuum addressed by biopower."[24] In this way, then, the normalizing forces of racism, which allow for the biological fracturing of a population and designation of some races as inferior, are the mechanisms by which a state is able to "exercise its sovereign power." Thus Foucault concludes that "once the State operates in [the mode of biopower], racism alone can justify the murderous function of the State."[25] Racism is the precondition for "the power of normalization" to exercise the sovereign right to kill, just as it is also the precondition for a power of sovereignty to exercise the "instruments, mechanisms and technology of normalization." Hence racism provides the point of articulation between sovereign power and biopower. It is worth noting here that in this discussion of the right of death in biopower, "killing" does not only refer to "murder as such," but also "every form of indirect murder: the fact of exposing someone to death, increasing the risk of death for some people, or quite simply, political death, expulsion, rejection and so on."[26]

Leaving aside for the moment the problem of the mobilization of a right over death in biopower, the final point I want to make of the norm in Foucault's genealogy is directed toward the internal operation of the norm in normalization. While normalization is often construed as homogenizing, it is important that for Foucault, the norm does not simply operate through the homogenization of the population or eradication of difference at a biological or anatomical level. Rather, as a counterpart to normalization, infractions of the norm are *produced* as an effect of the application of the norm, such that the phenomenal particularity of an individual is itself identified and calibrated only through the operation of the norm. Thus, Foucault argues that normalization is simultaneously totalizing and individualizing in its operation; it both establishes a common standard and forces those placed in relation to the norm to reveal their own irreducible particularity through the identification of individual divergences from that standard: in this, it establishes both homogeneity and diversity. This means, then, that it is only on the basis of the application of the norm that the individual emerges, and it is in that sense that the individual is "simultaneously" both an effect and vehicle of power.[27] Individuality ties the body to a normalizing common standard through the identification of its irreducible particularity and the identification of oneself as individual both rests on and reinstates the operation of the norm. Hence, when Foucault claims that the individual emerges as a material artifact of a particular technique of power, that is, of normalization, this can be understood to mean that power operates at the level of the biological rudiments of human existence to produce individuals as the necessary mode and counterpart of the operation of norms.

The simultaneity of individualization and totalization brings into relief a key point of Foucault's divergence from Canguilhem. Canguilhem's reflections on vital norms of health and physiology are based on the insight that infractions maintain a position of historical or temporal anteriority in relation to the norm. He writes that "it is the historical anteriority of the future abnormal which gives rise to the normative intention. The normal is the effect obtained by the execution of the normative project, it is the norm exhibited in the fact. . . . Consequently it is not paradoxical to say that the abnormal, while logically second, is existentially first." This is not to say, however, that the infraction gives rise to the rule as such though; instead, as Canguilhem insists, "the infraction is not the origin of the rule but the origin of regulation,"[28] that is, not of the norm but of normalization. However, in the context of shifting focus from a consideration of vital norms to an analysis of the politicization of the norm, Foucault's insistence on the simultaneity of individualization and totalization puts Canguilhem's prioritization of the infraction in question. For as Foucault's history of the emergence of the abnormal individual in his 1974–75 lectures makes apparent, the politicization of the norm entails that abnormality itself be seen as an historical contingency that is inseparable from the rise of the power of normalization. Thus it is not that the abnormal individual is antecedent to the application of the norm, but instead, that this individual only arises in conjunction with that application in a regime of normalization, and in fact confirms the normal as much as it negates it. Further, as Jacques Derrida points out, the designation of divergences as abnormal already requires an axiology that presupposes the legitimacy and application of the rule, which means that the abnormal cannot be strictly identified as either antecedent or logically dependent.[29] That is, the designation of that which diverges from the rule as "abnormal" requires a decision distinguishable from the rule or its application per se, which, for Derrida, means that the identification of the priority or dependence of the normal or abnormal is arbitrary. Not altogether dissimilarly, given the historical emergence of the abnormal in conjunction with a power of norms, Foucault's account of normalization means that the abnormal is inseparable from the normal, without being either existentially antecedent or logically negating.

Agamben on Sovereignty and Nihilism

From Foucault's portrayal of the role of the norm in biopower, I now want to turn to a discussion of Agamben's contrasting account, in order to bring out the depth of their conceptual divergence in relation to normativity. As was noted in the previous discussion, Foucault's account of norms derives from the Latin term *norma*, and thus is elaborated in relation to the dynamic of the rule—in the sense of both regulation and average—and its infraction. Agamben, however, takes his conception of norms from the Greek term *nomos*, and is more concerned with the law and the conditions of its application or suspension, that is, with the exception. This terminological heritage begins to bring into focus the conceptual differences in their accounts, which extend to their characterizations of the role of sovereignty in biopower and the relation between law and life, as well as to the critical approaches to normativity that they derive from these. While Foucault's conception of the integration of life and law in biopower maintains an ambivalence toward the role of sovereign power within the emergence of a normalizing society, tied as it is to a preoccupation with death as power over life, for Agamben, it is precisely the logic of sovereignty that binds law irremediably to life. This is because the logic of sovereignty constitutes the limit of the juridical, such that law only finds its force in "the very life of men." Thus, biopower does not entail a more or less radical transformation of the rationality of power from a right of death to fostering life, but instead is merely the ever clearer manifestation of the logic of sovereignty at the heart of the juridico-political order of liberal democracy. Importantly, for Agamben, while characteristic of the form of law operative in the modern West, the coincidence of life and law also indicates a fundamental nihilism at the heart of law, which is in turn indicative of a crisis in normative or regulative discourse. This is because the coincidence of life and law indicates that the law is in force without significance, emptied of all content and regulatory authority beyond a naked violence.

Even this brief summary of Agamben's theorization of sovereignty, life, and law brings to the fore several key conceptual shifts from Foucault's account, the first and most obvious of which is his treatment of sovereignty.

Agamben's strongest formulation of the role of sovereignty in biopower is presented in *Homo Sacer*, where he seeks to elaborate the "unitary center" where the "subjective techniques" and "objective power" identified by Foucault are said to coincide. Setting aside the question of whether Agamben's interpretation of Foucault is accurate, what is important at this point is the general thesis that Agamben poses, that "biopower is at least as old as the sovereign exception" and "the production of a biopolitical body is the original activity of sovereign power" (*HS*, 6). This means that biopower has operated in conjunction with sovereign power from the beginning, and modern politics is not characterized by the rise of biopower as such, but merely the coming to light of this "secret tie" of sovereignty and biopower in bare life. This coming to light of the tie of sovereignty and biopower amounts to the realization of the state of exception or state of emergency as the normal situation of politics today. While posed as an historical thesis throughout *Homo Sacer*—an impression that is reinforced by the "genealogy" of the political manifestation of the exception in *State of Exception*—this claim rests on a philosophical thesis concerning the nature of the exception, understood as *anomie*, and its relation to the law.[30] Hence the contiguity of sovereignty and biopower is primarily the theoretical consequence of the privileging of the exception as the constitutive origin of Western politics, strikingly posed in the dictum that "the rule lives off the exception alone," with which Agamben both begins and significantly complicates.

Agamben initiates his theorization of the constitutive role of the exception in Western politics in the first several chapters of *Homo Sacer* and extends it in the companion volume, *State of Exception*.[31] He argues that Carl Schmitt's identification of the paradox of sovereignty, in which the sovereign is both inside and outside the domain of the law, brings into relief a deeper relation between law and violence, in which sovereignty is revealed to be the limit—"in the double sense of end and principle" (*HS*, 15)—of the juridical order. Schmitt's paradox rests on the ambivalent status of the exception, determined to exist in the sovereign decision, which, by virtue of being outside the domain of the law, allows the normal situation of the law's operation to be constituted. However, as Agamben makes clear, to designate the exception as external to law is not strictly accurate, since theories of the exceptional foundation of law such as Schmitt's complicate the simple topographical distinction between inside and outside, such that these are not opposed but blur into one another in a threshold or zone of indifference. Agamben identifies the resulting relation as one of "inclusive exclusion" or "being-outside and yet belonging," whereby whatever is excluded from the domain of law is also included by virtue of its exclusion. Further, the relation of law to that which is excluded from it is not simply one of non-application; rather, Agamben suggests that it is best described in Jean-Luc Nancy's characterization of the "ban," in which the law applies to its object only in its own withdrawal and suspension.[32]

As Agamben makes clearer in *State of Exception*, the importance of the exception within this formulation is that it is precisely through its capacity to bring about the suspension of the law that the exception provides the conditions for the law's application. But, contrary to Schmitt, for Agamben the exception is not only an irruption in the torpidity of regulatory mechanisms, but instead, indicates the "inner nature" of law itself, or at least an irremediable condition of its application. In effect, the necessity of the exception as a condition of the law's application introduces a lacuna in law, though not in terms of a shortfall in the letter of the law that can be remedied by an extension of the legal code. Rather, the lacuna that strikes the law resides in the relation between law and reality, between the norm and the world, or *nomos* and *physis*. Contrary to Canguilhem's insistence upon the immediate realization and extension of the norm in the normal,[33] for Agamben this lacuna brings into focus the lack of an internal nexus between the norm and its application or realization, such that the normal sphere cannot be immediately derived from the norm. This lack of immediate realization can only be breached through the creation of an exception. Thus, "in order to apply a norm it is ultimately necessary to suspend its application, to produce an exception" (*SE*, 40). Agamben concludes, then, that "far from being a response to a normative lacuna, the state of exception appears as a fictitious lacuna in the order for the purpose of safeguarding the existence of the norm and its applicability to the normal situation. The lacuna is not within law . . . but concerns its relation to reality, the very possibility of its application" (*SE*, 40). This indicates that the juridical order contains "an essential fracture," which can only be remedied through the creation of a state of exception in which the law is suspended but nevertheless remains in force.

It is in the space of this lacuna that the sovereign decision takes on a particular significance and indicates the threshold position of the sovereign in the relation of life and law. For it is only in the decision that the non-coincidence between life and law is breached, and life is truly brought into the sphere of law; that is, the unfounded decision of the sovereign establishes a passage from law to life and is thus the "threshold" through which life is taken inside law. But since the inclusion of life in law is only possible through the exceptional structure that suspends law, life is only included through its own exclusion. This means that life "can in the last instance be implicated in the sphere of law only through the presupposition of its own inclusive exclusion, only as an *exceptio*. There is a limit-figure of life, a threshold in which life is both inside and outside the juridical order, and this threshold is the place of sovereignty" (*HS*, 27). As the threshold between life and law, then, it is clear that sovereignty is absolutely internal to biopolitics. It is only the internal dynamic of sovereignty and the exception that allows for the application of law, such that life can be captured within the law through its own exclusion. Thus, while Foucault found it necessary to specify the operation of normalization as the mechanism by which law takes hold of the life of the body, no such mediating device is required in Agamben's account. Or rather, the structure of the exception that grounds law is itself the means by which life is taken into law, since the state of exception allows for an immediate coincidence of life and law. As he writes, the "law is made of nothing but what it manages to capture inside itself through the inclusive exclusion," such that it finds its own existence in the "very life of men" (*HS*, 27).

The status of the law that finds its existence in the "life of men" brings us to the problem of how to interpret the status of life before law, where "before" does not mean a position of historical anteriority or lost innocence. Key to Agamben's understanding of the contiguity and coincidence of life and law is a disagreement between Walter Benjamin and Gershom Scholem over the writings of Franz Kafka.[34] The two readings of Kafka proposed by Benjamin and Scholem are, for Agamben, the extreme points that any inquiry into the relation between life and law must confront, and for his part, in taking up this disagreement, he proposes a kind of rapprochement of their seemingly opposed conceptions. Taking up the phrase of "being in force without significance" that Scholem proposed as a way of articulating the inscrutability of law in Kafka's writings, Agamben argues that this provides the most accurate conception of the status of law in the state of exception characteristic of the contemporary age. What he means by this phrase is that the law has effectively been emptied of any determinate content, such that the object upon which it might be applied is itself no longer in existence. This introduces a problem not dissimilar to the void of the exception identified by Schmitt, in that the application of the law is definitively detached from the form of law. Crediting Kant with introducing the law in force without significance to modernity in his attempt to isolate the pure form of law apart from any particular content, Agamben proposes that the reduction of law to a purely formal principle of universal applicability means not that the law is no longer in force, but that it appears only "in the form of its own unrealizability," that it "applies in no longer applying." However, this points to the Benjaminian side of the disagreement, wherein Benjamin proposes that a law in force without significance is itself indistinguishable from life. Benjamin's interpretation of Kafka emphasizes that the indecipherability or inaccessibility of law is equivalent to its nullity, such that law no longer maintains any transcendence over life but is wholly coincidental with it.

Several further points can be made of this understanding of law, life, and anomie. First, just as with Foucault, the rise of state racism and, in particular, German Nazism is a central empirical point of reference in this account of biopolitics. However, rather than operating as an indispensable condition for the exercise of sovereignty, for Agamben the state racism of Nazism is itself an expression of the capture of life within law made possible through the sovereign exception, and in fact fully realizes the logic of that capture. In keeping with the complication of the topography of inside and outside, he argues that the camp structure mobilized by Nazism does not indicate a simple *topographical* space of confinement, but is instead a *topological* figure of the logic of sovereignty that conjoins law and violence in the exception. This means that rather than providing a description of a particular locale, Agamben's point regarding the camps is that this literal space of exception reveals an abstract logic of abandonment, which is by no means limited to the geographical space of internment. In *The Human Condition*, Hannah Arendt notes that the etymology of *nomos* links it to territorialization,[35] a spatial metaphorics that is reinforced by the Latin etymology of *exception*, which meant to take out, or as it is rendered in *Homo Sacer*, to take *out-side* (*HS*, 170). However, as a topological figure, the logic revealed in the camp is that of the normalization of the exception: the camp materializes a "new juridico-political paradigm in which the norm becomes indistinguishable from the exception . . . in which the state of exception . . . is realized normally" (*HS*, 170). Deriving from Walter Benjamin's eighth thesis on the philosophy of history, where he writes that the exception has in fact become the rule, this thesis effectively posits the camp as a "dislocating localization," in which the territorial order of the *nomos* is broken apart by the exception internal to it.

It is in positing the normalization of the exception that Agamben fully complicates the primacy of the exception posed by Schmitt, for if the exception itself has become the rule, then it is literally impossible to designate one as prior to the other. In this way, then, Benjamin's thesis is said to put Schmitt's formulation of the sovereign decision in check. It is also in this light, Agamben argues, that Benjamin's use of the distinction between the virtual and real state of exception should be read, for it points toward a potential resolution of the violent aporias of biopolitical sovereignty. Significantly, this resolution is not a return to a lost innocence, but can only be brought about through a new condition that shows "law in its nonrelation to life and life in its nonrelation to law," thereby opening a space for politics understood as human action (*SE*, 88). In the closing paragraphs of *Homo Sacer*, Agamben suggests that the resolution of the nexus of law and life is only possible through bringing about a new "form-of-life," which does not permit of the separation between *bios* and *zoē*. In either formulation, what is at stake is nothing less than the resolution of modern nihilism. Accepting the correlation between nihilism and messianism posited by Scholem and Benjamin, Agamben claims elsewhere that two forms of messianism or nihilism must be distinguished.[36] The first, which he calls "imperfect nihilism," nullifies the law but maintains "the Nothing [that is, the emptiness of the law] in a perpetual and infinitely deferred state of validity." The second form, called "perfect nihilism," nullifies even the Nothing, and does not permit the survival of validity beyond meaning; perfect nihilism, as Benjamin states, "succeeds in finding redemption in the overturning of the Nothing."[37] The task that contemporary thought is faced with, then, is the thought of perfect nihilism, which fulfills and thereby overturns the law in force without significance that characterizes the virtual state of exception of Western politics.

The final point I want to make here is that the crucial implication to be drawn from the normalization of the exception is that the contemporary condition entails an absolute confusion of law and fact, such that law truly coincides with life and life is indistinguishable from law. As Agamben sees it, the destruction of all political status within the camps entails that the biopolitical body or bare life thus produced becomes "a threshold in which law constantly passes over into fact and fact into law, and in which the two planes become indistinguishable" (*HS*, 171). However, just as the logic of the exception becoming the rule is not limited to the camp, but indicates a topological feature of Western political and juridical conditions more generally, nor is the collapse of fact and value that attends it limited to the camp. Rather, the collapse of fact and value is said to encompass not only the positive law of states, but "the entire text of tradition in its regulative form, whether the Jewish Torah or the Islamic Shariah, Christian dogma or the profane *nomos*" (*HS*, 51). Moreover, as Agamben's comments on Kant's formalization of moral law indicate, no distinction is made in this critique of normative discourse between legality and morality, not least because Western moral thought is itself fundamentally indebted to the juridical form. As indicated in *Remnants of Auschwitz*, categories such as guilt and responsibility rest on a more or less tacit confusion of ethical and juridical categories, and as such are also "irremediably contaminated" by the nihilism that infects law. Ethics then, Agamben suggests, "recognizes neither guilt nor responsibility; it is . . . the doctrine of happy life" (*RA*, 24). This is not the place to engage the question of whether the breadth of Agamben's critique is defensible, nor is it the place to take up his formulation of ethics as happy life. Instead, I simply want to emphasize the general point that Agamben's critique of normative discourse is directed, not only at the institutionalized apparatuses of law, but also at the juridification of ethics, and identifies a fundamental nihilism at the heart of the contemporary biopolitical condition, in which life and law have become indistinguishable.

Biopower and Liberal Eugenics

We have seen so far that the accounts of biopower offered by Foucault and Agamben diverge in their treatments of sovereignty, as well as of the thematic of the norm and the exception. Further, in terms of the critiques of normativity that each derives from these accounts, Agamben's is clearly much more vehement. While both emphasize the increasing coincidence of life and law, Foucault rests the case against the normativity of the norm on a genealogical critique of normalization. Agamben, however, suggests that the coincidence of life and law indicates nothing short of a nihilistic crisis, in which the distinction between fact and value has definitively collapsed. Given these critiques, I want now to briefly demonstrate the interpretive consequences of these diverse accounts of biopolitics, and to do this, I want to focus on an emerging debate within bioethics around the notion of a "liberal eugenics." This debate has developed around technologies such as certain uses of pre-implantation genetic diagnosis (PGD), reproductive cloning, and at its most speculative, the possibility of genetic enhancements.[38] Each of these technological developments obviously involves its own specific ethical and political problems, which I cannot address in detail here. This discussion is necessarily schematic, and I will simply pick out several features of the broader debate around these technologies and suggest ways in which the critiques of normativity developed by Foucault and Agamben bear upon these. For the most part, bioethical discussion has been limited to ascertaining the moral acceptability or otherwise of these practices. Drawing on Foucault and Agamben, I suggest here that not only do these technologies evidently entail biopolitical normalization in the Foucauldian sense, but the debate itself also reveals a deeper crisis in normative discourse.

Formulated in 1883 by Francis Galton, the term *eugenics* has an inglorious history. First associated with the movements for population health established in the United Kingdom and the United States in the late nineteenth century, its most potent referent is German National Socialism and the policies of enforced sterilization and "euthanasia" adopted by the Third Reich. As historians have shown, many of the techniques adopted by the Reich were in fact first utilized within the United Kingdom and United States—particularly, for instance, the use of population information, discourses of degeneracy, and the doctrine of hereditary health that underpinned practices such as enforced sterilization. While the notion of eugenics fell out of favor following revelations from World War II, such that the attribution of the term itself is often used as a form of moral condemnation, interest in eugenics has again been revived by advances in genetic knowledge and associated reproductive technologies, with some commentators adopting the term in a positive light. This has led to the formulation of the notion of a "liberal eugenics" to describe the project of improving human well-being, primarily at the level of individuals but also implicitly at that of populations, through the use of genetic technology.[39] While it is true that previous eugenics practices do not determine the acceptability or otherwise of this recent revival of interest in eugenics, they do nevertheless provide an important background to it. Aware of this historical background, those arguing for a liberal eugenics attempt to distinguish themselves from previous generations of eugenicists by insisting upon several important points of difference.

The first of these is the insistence on the necessity of state neutrality.[40] It is frequently argued that the principle difference of eugenics projects associated with totalitarian regimes and the project of new eugenics is that while the former entailed a restriction upon reproductive freedoms, the latter actively seeks to enhance reproductive freedoms by enlarging the scope of choices available to prospective parents with regard to the child that will be born to them, and by minimizing state intervention in and regulation of those choices. This entails two dimensions, in that libertarian advocates of technological enhancements emphasize the restrictions on state intervention per se, such that parental choice is the final arbiter of moral acceptability. A second, more complex, claim is the idea that the liberal state maintains a neutral stance in relation to conceptions of the good to be sought through genetic interventions. Thus, even if the state plays a regulatory function in relation to reproductive technology, it should not positively intervene to enforce a particular conception of biological or population health, since it is constrained by the liberal commitment to value pluralism. If the state does maintain neutrality in this way, then rather than reinvigorating the specter of Nazism, it is argued that new eugenics or liberal eugenics will in fact reinforce and enhance the liberal freedoms associated with reproduction and parenting, by giving parents more choice in and control over the genetic profile of the child that is born to them, and by reinforcing reproductive rights, such as the right to found a family, established in the UN Declaration of Human Rights.[41]

The second perceived point of difference is that while totalitarian eugenics tended to rely on unsophisticated and reductionist understandings of the interactions of biological, environmental, and social factors in child development, liberal eugenicists are not biological determinists. This allows liberal eugenicists ostensibly to avoid the charge of incorrectly presupposing a biological "ideal type" against which each future child is to be measured. Indeed, liberal eugenicists use the point that there is no essential or fixed norm against which to classify and evaluate each individual to argue that the distinction between negative and positive eugenics, or genetic manipulations for therapeutic purposes versus purposes of enhancement, is erroneous and unsustainable.[42] Advocates point out that this distinction is inherently unstable, since there is no such thing as a normal human, and the lack of essential normativity makes it difficult to specify what counts as a "disease" or "defect," leaving these open to the vagaries of judgment rather than simply being established on the basis of empirically given data. Ultimately, then, any effort to reduce suffering or potential suffering through genetic intervention amounts to a form of eugenics and this distinction does not provide ground to reject one form of intervention while allowing the other. Moreover, since eugenics does not aim simply at the avoidance of disease, but seeks to enhance the overall well-being of a person or population, eugenics should not be solely concerned with limiting negative effects but should also seek to enhance positive effects. This argument is given further strength by Buchanan and others, where, in an interesting twist on Rawls, it is argued that one consequence of the increasing technological control over the biological resources of humans is the "colonization of the natural by the just." This entails that not only are genetic manipulations permissible, but may well be required by the principles of justice, insofar as justice requires equality of resources.[43]

Against these claims, opponents of liberal eugenics have emphasized the ways in which such a project conflicts with the fundamental principles of liberalism. For instance, Jürgen Habermas claims that such technologies threaten to transform our "ethical self-understanding" by undermining the distinction between the "given" and the "made."[44] His opposition to the perceived threat of liberal eugenics rests on two particular arguments, the first of which is that, in undermining the distinction between the given and the made, genetic intervention has the capacity to undermine the individual's capacity to "be oneself" in the strong ethical sense of living one's own freely chosen life. Biotechnological intervention increasingly contributes to the "dedifferentiation" of the categories of the inorganic and organic, yet this intuitive distinction is "constitutive of our self-understanding as species members," and hence, the de-differentiation of these categories threatens our ethical self-understanding as autonomous persons.[45] The second point of opposition follows from this, in that he argues that genetic intervention establishes an unprecedented interpersonal relation, in which the programmed subject of genetic intervention never has the opportunity to reverse the relation that obtains between themselves and their "designer." As Habermas writes, "eugenic programming establishes a permanent dependence between persons who know that one of them is principally barred from changing social places with the other," since "the product cannot . . . draw up a design for its designer."[46] Such relations, he argues, are foreign to the reciprocal relations of dependence and mutual recognition otherwise established in the liberal social world of "free and equal persons," and effectively undermine the principle of universal egalitarianism that contemporary political liberalism holds to be of central importance.[47]

Without engaging in an analysis of the sustainability or otherwise of these arguments, it is clear that the core of this debate is a matter of ascertaining the extent to which eugenic applications of genetic technologies concur with or contradict the central principles of contemporary liberalism. The importance of establishing this is that concurrence with such principles is taken to be the necessary condition of the moral acceptability of such a project; as one defender of genetic enhancement, Nicholas Agar, strikingly puts the problem, "the addition of the word 'liberal' to 'eugenics' transforms an evil doctrine into a morally acceptable one."[48] Additionally, it involves the question of whether these principles apply at all. For what is interesting in this debate is the way in which the principle of moral consistency, of treating like cases alike, operates in dividing up the advocates and critics of liberal eugenics. That is, those in favor of such genetic interventions tend to emphasize the degree of similarity between new technologies, such as reproductive cloning, and already existent practices, or indeed, naturally occurring processes. For instance, John Harris argues that reproductive cloning is little different from naturally developing identical twins.[49] Similarly, other advocates of liberal eugenics argue that while genetic intervention by parents upon the genetic profile of their future child differs from totalitarian eugenics in a number of ways, it is not in itself radically different from other choices and influences that parents have over the lives of their children. While interventions in the genetic profile of an embryo may well be novel, this kind of influence is not qualitatively different from the manipulation of environmental factors in order to enhance a child's natural skill, talent, or ability. Thus, genetic enhancement is little different from private education, additional tutoring, or experimental diets.[50] By contrast, those opposed to liberal eugenics tend to emphasize the non-comparability of new genetic technologies, which they see as auguring the destruction of our current conceptions of the person through an unprecedented control over the biological foundations of our existence.

However, despite the apparent distance between the positions outlined above, both sides fail to grasp a key biopolitical point. For what this debate makes evident is an emerging condition in which certain potential forms of life are wholly dependent on the often conflict-ridden interaction of legal regulation and technological capacity. There is of course much to be said about the implications of technological dependency, but here I want to focus most particularly on the notion of life as dependent on legality for its existence. Certainly, this dependency is not complete, in the sense that regardless of the ultimate legal resolution on reproductive cloning, for instance, if the technological capacity is attained, there may be those who may proceed with it regardless of the legislative context. This suggests that the reach of the law is not without limitation—any given articulation of law is subject to contravention by the very fact that it does not entirely determine or fix the world in its formulation and implementation. Nevertheless, there is something important in the particular relation of life to law established by the technology and its contested regulation, in that the possible existence of certain forms of biological life appears to coincide with their designation as legal or illegal. That is, one might say, life is literally becoming indistinguishable from law.

Drawing upon the discussion in the previous sections, several points can be made about this relation here. First, in his lectures published under the title *Abnormal*, Foucault concludes on the provocative note that the nineteenth-century eugenics movements were linked to the rise of psychiatry, through the development of the doctrine of "degeneration." Through this notion, psychiatry gave rise to a new racism against the abnormal, the function of which "is not so much the prejudice or defense of one group against another as the detection of all those within a group who may be carriers of a danger to it. It is a racism that permits the screening of every individual within a given society," in the interests of population health and well-being.[51] Certainly, the language of degeneracy does not have a place in the contemporary debates on liberal eugenics. Nevertheless, it is not hard to see, in Foucault's account of normalization as giving rise to an internal racism that seeks to "improve life by eliminating accidents, the random

element, and deficiencies," the relevance for an analysis of liberal eugenics.[52] This is not to say that genetic technologies and the liberal eugenics
that they have given rise to undercut or eliminate individuality—quite the
contrary, in fact. But it is to suggest that such a project necessarily entails
normalization and the regularization of life through the elimination of the
errancy internal to it. Further, the danger of liberal eugenics is the capacity it entails for the mobilization of a sovereign right of death within the
power of normalization, where that power does not entail murder as such,
but the fact of an absolute exposure to death, "expulsion, rejection and so
on" for some embryonic manifestations of life.[53]

But more can be said here. Rather than engaging in a discussion of
whether liberal eugenics is morally acceptable or not, Agamben's analysis
of biopolitics suggests that the debate itself is in fact indicative of a normative crisis. As I have characterized it, the central concern in this debate is
the extent to which new genetic technologies concur with or contradict the
normative principles of liberalism. But there is also an additional problem
of whether those principles can rightly be said to apply at all, since it may
be that they are undermined by the very practices that they are supposed to
morally guide. In the light of Agamben's critique of law, one might suggest
that what is at issue here is not merely a question of the verifiable extension
of those principles and the capacity of them to incorporate more or less
unprecedented technological possibilities. Rather, what is at issue is a more
fundamental lacuna, in which such principles can only apply through their
suspension, that is, apply in no longer applying. Moreover, if, as Agamben suggests, "one of the paradoxes of the state of exception lies in the fact
that . . . it is impossible to distinguish transgression of the law from execution of the law, such that what violates a rule and what conforms to it coincide without any remainder" (*HS*, 57), then one might suggest that this is
precisely the predicament encountered in this debate. For it appears that
it is in fact impossible to disassociate perceived threats to liberalism from
liberalism itself, to distinguish between that which transgresses its fundamental principles from that which fulfills them.

Even if it is the case that this indicates a normative crisis, it is important to insist that this does not amount to a crisis of ethics per se. What it
does suggest is the necessity of rethinking ethics beyond the juridical form
to which normative thought is currently beholden. In this, both Foucault
and Agamben suggest ways in which a non-juridical conception of ethical

responsibility might be developed. In an interview toward the end of his life, Foucault suggested that a non-juridical form of ethics tied neither to discipline nor to sovereignty might be enacted through a non-normalizing aesthetics of the self, in which the key task is not obedience to a rule but taking care of oneself.[54] Given that Agamben sees the camps as the "*nomos of the modern*," that is, as the topological figure of the collapse of fact and value, it is not surprising that he also seeks some indication of a non-juridical ethics in these spaces of abandonment. Through an analysis of the aporetic structure of testimony, he suggests the notion of an unassumable responsibility, or responsibility before or beyond the law, which the subject cannot turn away from but simultaneously cannot take on as its own.[55] Interestingly, it may be in these disparate formulations of an ethics beyond or before the juridical form that Foucault's thought and Agamben's thought begin to converge more thoroughly. Agamben suggests in *State of Exception* that "one day humanity will play with law as children play with disused objects, not in order to restore them to their canonical use but to free them from it for good. What is found after the law is not a more proper and original use value that precedes law, but a new use that is born only after it" (*SE*, 64). But is this not precisely what is at stake in an aesthetics of the self, where the subject puts into play moral principles, not for the sake of restoring transcendental, universal value, but to give value to them only in a life understood as art? This is not the place to take up this question, but either way, what remains to be seen is whether these conceptions of playing with the rule can yield an ethics that allows engagement with the conundrums presented by emerging biotechnologies and opens possibilities for living beyond the integration of life and law.

Agamben and Foucault on Biopower and Biopolitics

Paul Patton

Giorgio Agamben argues in *Homo Sacer* that the key to understanding modern political phenomena lies in their biopolitical character: not only National Socialism's concentration camps, its genocidal "final solution" and programs designed to eliminate incurably ill and genetically unfit members of the non-Jewish population, but also the manner in which democratic states have used prisoners and other marginal populations for medical experimentation, along with the increasingly political character of biomedical interventions into the human organism. These and other events can only be understood against the background of the "biopolitical vocation" of the modern nation-state. Both the totalitarianism that flourished during the twentieth century and its democratic liberal counterpart remain trapped within a political horizon circumscribed by the convergence of biological and political life. Modern political government of whatever persuasion is both founded upon and preoccupied with the "bare life" of its citizens. In this condition, "once their fundamental referent becomes bare life, traditional political distinctions (such as those between Right and Left, liberalism and totalitarianism, private and public) lose their clarity and intelligibility and enter into a zone of indistinction" (*HS*, 122).

The famous declarations of the rights of man that inaugurated the modern political era announced the "bare natural life" of the subjects as the foundation of the sovereign nation-state, while at the same time ensuring that the boundaries and the quality of that life become objects of political concern: "It is not possible to understand the 'national' and biopolitical development and vocation of the modern state in the nineteenth and twentieth centuries if one forgets that what lies at its basis is not man as a free and conscious political subject but, above all, man's bare life, the simple birth that as such is, in the passage from subject to citizen, invested with the principle of sovereignty" (*HS*, 128). At the same time, if this passage from subject to citizen, from classical sovereignty to modern nation-state, marks the emergence of recognizably modern government, Agamben argues that in an important sense, Western politics has been a biopolitics "from the very beginning" (*HS*, 181), so that the transition from classical sovereignty to modern democratic politics is not so much a liberation of the former subjects as their more profound entrapment in the very biopolitical power from which they sought to escape.

Agamben's thesis concerning the biopolitical character of Western politics in turn rests upon one of the provisional conclusions of the inquiry undertaken in this book, namely the thesis that the "fundamental activity of sovereign power is the production of bare life as the originary political element and as threshold of articulation between nature and culture, *zoē* and *bios*" (*HS*, 181). He presents this thesis concerning the relationship between bare life and political sovereignty as a "correction" or at least a "completion" (*HS*, 9) of Michel Foucault's account of the emergence of biopolitics as a key moment in the development of modern techniques of state power. Agamben represents Foucault as asserting that a crucial threshold was crossed when the bare natural life of the governed first began to figure in the calculations of state power and became an object of specific techniques of government. "Bare life" is Agamben's term rather than Foucault's, and it is introduced here with reference to Aristotle's distinction between *zoē*, that is the simple fact of life in a biological sense, and *bios*, meaning a way of life shared among a particular group. In these terms, Foucault's thesis about the emergence of biopower amounts to "the entry of *zoē* into the sphere of the *polis*—the politicization of bare life as such" (*HS*, 4). Whether or not this reformulation corresponds to Foucault's thesis depends on precisely what is meant here by "politicization" and what is meant by "bare life." I return to these questions below after examining Foucault's concept of biopower.

Agamben's reformulation of Foucault's thesis continues by attributing to him the suggestion that the politicization of bare life constituted "the decisive event of modernity," and the further suggestion that this signaled "a radical transformation of the categories of classical thought" (*HS*, 4). His "correction" of Foucault consists of the claim that the entry of bare life into the sphere of political calculation and the exercise of sovereign power involved no radical transformation of political-philosophical categories. On the contrary, he argues, "the inclusion of bare life in the political realm constitutes the original—if concealed—nucleus of sovereign power. *It can even be said that the production of a biopolitical body is the original activity of sovereign power*" (*HS*, 6). His "completion" of Foucault draws upon his own account of the manner in which bare life was originally included in the political realm, namely in the form of an "inclusive exclusion," in order to suggest that the decisive feature of modernity is not so much the emergence of biopolitics as the manner in which a phenomenon originally situated at the margins of political order "gradually begins to coincide with the political realm" (*HS*, 9). It is on this basis that he draws wide-ranging conclusions with regard to the biopolitical character of modern politics, including the aporia embedded in the attempt of modern democracy to ground the liberties of citizens in their natural rights and the zone of indistinction which links liberal democracy with the modern forms of totalitarianism.

These large claims concerning the biopolitical character of modern politics rest upon the intelligibility of this thesis about the relationship between sovereign power and bare life. Since the concept of bare life is therefore a fundamental support of the argument as a whole, we are obliged to examine more closely this concept and the manner in which it is deployed by Agamben. And since this concept is introduced with primary reference to Foucault's remarks about biopower and biopolitics, we are entitled to explore both the fate of these concepts in Foucault's work and Agamben's use of Foucault in the elaboration of his concept of bare life. My aim in this chapter is to raise questions by way of Foucault, in order to problematize Agamben's concept of biopower and all that rests upon it.

Biopower in Foucault

Given how much has been written about it, it may come as a surprise to many to learn that the concept of biopower does not play a major role in Foucault's work. Nonetheless, with the publication of Foucault's lectures in which this concept was first announced and those that followed,[1] we are now in a position to see that, far from spending the last years of his life directing his enquiries "with increasing insistence towards the study of what he defined as biopolitics" (*HS*, 119), Foucault mentions it only a few times before moving on to other things. *Biopower* first appeared in a lecture on March 17, 1976, then again in a few pages at the end of *The History of Sexuality, Volume I* published later that year. Thereafter it largely disappears, in favor of other objects of analysis such as mechanisms of security, pastoral power, liberalism and neo-liberalism, before turning to the ancient forms of self-government and *parrhousia*. The fact that "biopolitics" never became the object of sustained enquiry by Foucault suggests that it may not have been, as Agamben suggests, only Foucault's death that "kept him from showing how he would have developed the concept and the study of biopolitics" (*HS*, 4). Rather, as I will argue below, it may have been problems internal to the concept of biopolitics itself that prevented its further development.

Foucault's 1977–78 course, *Sécurité territoire, population*, began with the statement that he would undertake a further study of the mechanisms by which the biological existence of the human species became the object of political intervention and strategy. Accordingly, the first three lectures addressed mechanisms of security, by contrast with disciplinary mechanisms, in relation to a series of examples such as the management of urban spaces and epidemics. By the fourth lecture, however, the focus shifted to the arts of government and the problematic of governmentality which occupied center stage for the remainder of this course and for the entire course the following year. After tracing the emergence of government as a problem in the sixteenth and seventeenth centuries, Foucault examined a series of distinct modes of governmental rationality: *pastoral government* and its application to individual conduct, *reason of state* as it emerged in the seventeenth century, and its relation to the art and science of police as this developed in the eighteenth century. The doctrine of *reason of state* played an especially important role in the emergence of modern forms of state government, since it gave expression, for the first time, to an autonomous art of political government that was no longer subject to the requirements of a divine order or to the particular interests of a monarch. Henceforth, the practice of state government acquired its own proper rationality, distinct from that of the government of households or the interests of princes in maintaining their own power. The science of government was now fully liberated from the constraints of sovereign rule. The rationale and purpose of government was not simply the maintenance of its own power but the welfare of the population, the improvement of its condition, the increase of its wealth, and so on. According to the seventeenth-century and eighteenth-century *science of police* spelled out in texts such as De Lamare's *Treatise on the Police* and von Justi's *Elements of Police*, the state must concern itself with all aspects of the lives of its citizens, not only roads, public safety, health, and supplies, but also religion, morals, and the liberal arts. The *science of police* concerned itself with the number of citizens, the means of procuring the necessities of life such as agriculture, the health and wellbeing of populations, as well as the circulation of persons and material goods. As such, it encompassed many of the domains and objectives associated with biopower. Foucault's interest in it, however, focused less on the ways in which it addressed the lives of citizens than the manner in which it amounted to a specific art of governing the activity of subjects, a detailed regulation of all aspects of social life with the overall aim of increasing the constitutive forces of the State.

Although Foucault's 1978–79 course was entitled Birth of Biopolitics, the focus was on particular forms of governmental reason, namely liberalism and post–World War II neo-liberal variants. At the end of the first lecture, Foucault justified his shift of focus by the suggestion that the liberal art of government provided the specific system of governmental reason and therefore the historical framework within which the techniques of biopower would be deployed.[2] Thereafter, "biopower" is only mentioned in passing in the course of the lectures themselves. From the outset, liberalism is presented as a distinct practice of government, defined above all by its acceptance of the idea that society and its economic processes follow laws of their own which government must understand and respect. Whereas police government operated on the principle that there could never be too much government regulation, liberalism operated on the converse principle that there is always too much government. Instead of supposing that the population was in need of detailed and constant regulation, liberalism relied upon a conception of society and the economy as naturally self-regulating systems that government should leave alone. At most, it should confine itself to setting in place mechanisms of security that sustain and facilitate natural regulation. Classical liberalism thus sought to limit government to mechanisms whose function was to assure the security of those natural economic processes.

The concept of biopower thus plays no role in Foucault's work after 1976. How did it function in the lecture in which it was introduced? The lecture on March 17, 1976, was the final lecture in a course devoted to the themes of war and race and the role that these played in seventeenth- and eighteenth-century history and political thought. Toward the end of this lecture, Foucault refers to the previous discussion of biopower as a "long digression" into which he had entered in order to provide an explanation of how it came about that racism became "inscribed as the basic mechanism of power, as it is exercised in modern states." In apparent anticipation of Agamben's thesis concerning the biopolitical character of politics today, he suggests that modern states "can scarcely function without becoming involved with racism at some point."[3] However, before we can properly compare Foucault's and Agamben's concepts of biopower, we need to be clear precisely what is meant by biopower in the context of this lecture.

Foucault's summary answer is that biopower refers to the manner in which, in the course of the eighteenth and nineteenth centuries, state power came to be exercised over human life, over "man in so far as he is a living being."[4] He contrasts this political technology with the mechanisms of discipline he had analyzed in *Discipline and Punish*. Whereas discipline worked on individual bodies, biopower was applied to subjects qua living beings. The period from the latter half of the eighteenth century onward saw the development of state policy in relation to birth control and rate of birth. It also saw the development of policies in relation to the problem of morbidity insofar as this was affected by endemic diseases within a given population. Concern with such phenomena gave rise to a medicine concerned with public hygiene. Other fields of intervention associated with biopolitics included the range of phenomena associated with old age, accidents, infirmities, and other anomalies. This lead to the introduction of insurance and other means of collective saving designed to preserve lives and improve the quality of lives. Finally, biopolitical government included various forms of control over the environment: water, swamps, and the conditions of urban life. These are the starting points and initial fields of knowledge and intervention of biopower: "the birth rate, the mortality rate, various biological disabilities, and the effects of the environment."[5]

A second distinguishing feature of this biopolitics was the scale at which it operated: populations rather than individual bodies. This period saw the emergence of populations as objects of political power: "Biopolitics deals with the population, with the population as political problem, as a problem that is at once scientific and political, as a biological problem and as power's problem."[6] The phenomena which affect populations and which power seeks to address are only predictable, measurable at the level of the collective. At the individual level, they are "aleatory and unpredictable."[7] Finally, not punctual phenomena but serial phenomena are what make themselves felt over time. In short, "the phenomena addressed by biopolitics are, essentially, aleatory events that occur within a population that exists over a period of time."[8]

Third, biopolitics employs very different mechanisms from those employed in the exercise of disciplinary power: forecasts, statistical measures, and so on, the purpose of which is to intervene not at the level of individuals but at the level of generality associated with a population: "The mortality rate has to be modified or lowered; life expectancy has to be increased; the birth rate has to be stimulated. And most important of all, regulatory mechanisms must be established to establish an equilibrium, maintain an average. . . . In a word, security mechanisms have to be installed around the random element inherent in a population of living beings so as to optimize a state of life."[9]

In comparison with the techniques of disciplinary power, biopower required the development of new mechanisms and new forms of knowledge to identify its objects and to facilitate its exercise. However, it remained a technology of power exercised by the state over people insofar as they are living beings and insofar as they belong to populations. In this sense, it enabled effective government by the sovereign of the biological life of the subjects. In the context of Foucault's definition of the concept, this is how Agamben's phrase "the entry of *zoē* into the sphere of the *polis*" must be understood. How then does this phenomenon relate to the other element of Agamben's redescription, namely his suggestion that, according to Foucault, "the politicization of bare life as such" would have constituted "the decisive event of modernity" (*HS*, 4).

Bare Life: Biology or Status?

The first issue, as we noted above, is what is meant here by "bare life." Agamben introduces this term in the context of his comments about Foucault and with reference to Aristotle's distinction between *zoē* and *bios*. As such, it appears that bare life here refers to the natural or biological life of human beings and that there is no reason not to identify Foucault's thesis concerning the emergence of biopolitics with the entry of *zoē* into the political domain. However, Agamben immediately confuses the issue by pointing out that the protagonist of this book is "bare life, that is, the life of *homo sacer* (sacred man), who *may be killed and yet not sacrificed*" (*HS*, 8).

Homo sacer is not the same as simple natural life, since it is, as Agamben later notes, the natural life of an individual caught in a particular relation with the power that has cast him out from both the religious and the political community. The sacred man in ancient Roman law is defined as one who may be killed with impunity by anyone, and as such is excluded from the political realm in which, subject to certain exceptions, killing is forbidden, but also as one who cannot be sacrificed, and as such is excluded from the realm of the sacred. The *homo sacer* is therefore caught in "a continuous relationship with the power that banished him precisely insofar as he is at every instant exposed to an unconditional threat of death" (*HS*, 183).

In this sense, *homo sacer* is not simply pure *zoē* but *zoē* caught up in a particular "status." This status is defined by "the particular character of the double exclusion into which he is taken" (*HS*, 82). The double exclusion in terms of which this figure is defined mirrors the exceptional status of the sovereign; hence Agamben's hypothesis that the figure of the sovereign and the figure of *homo sacer* are inextricably linked: "The sovereign sphere is the sphere in which it is permitted to kill without committing homicide and without celebrating a sacrifice, and sacred life—that is, life that may be killed but not sacrificed—is the life that has been captured in this sphere" (*HS*, 83). It is in this sense, given that bare life and sacred life are equivalent terms, that Agamben argues that "the production of bare life is the originary activity of sovereignty" (*HS*, 83, 181).

It follows that, for the purposes of the argument with Foucault, bare life is not simple natural life but rather natural life endowed with a peculiar status that is achieved by the subjection of an individual life to sovereign power, albeit in the form of an exclusion from the protection otherwise afforded by the sovereign. It is biological existence that is, in addition, subjected to a particular form of inclusive exclusion from the political domain. Because bare life in this sense is the originary activity of sovereignty, when Agamben turns to the biological life of individuals and the manner in which this became politicized in the course of the twentieth century he refers to biological life, sexuality, and so on, as the "modern avatars" of bare life (*HS*, 120). But since it is precisely these "avatars" that Foucault takes to be the objects of biopolitics, it seems that a gap has opened between Foucault's thesis concerning the emergence of biopolitics and Agamben's restatement of that thesis as "the politicization of bare life."

In effect, Agamben's argument relies on an equivocation with regard to the two senses of the term *bare life*. While in the context of his analysis of sovereignty, "bare life" is identified with the sacred life or status of *homo sacer*, in the context of his critical remarks about modern democratic politics he identifies it with the natural life of *zoē*. The decadence of democratic societies, he suggests, lies in the fact that their politics "knows no value (and, consequently, no non-value) other than life" (*HS*, 10). What life is Agamben referring to? This is not sacred life but the life of "mass hedonism and consumerism" (*HS*, 11). Modern democracy, he asserts, presents itself "from the beginning as a vindication and liberation of *zoē*" (*HS*, 9), but in doing so it only succeeds in reinforcing the subordination to sovereign power associated with *homo sacer*: "modern democracy does not abolish sacred life but rather shatters it and disseminates it into every individual body, making it what is at stake in political conflict" (*HS*, 124).

This ambiguity in the concept of bare life sustains Agamben's pessimistic conclusion that "every attempt to found political liberties in the rights of the citizen is, therefore, in vain" (*HS*, 181). He sees no merit in the prospect of a concept of human rights "separated from and used outside the context of citizenship" (*HS*, 133). What then would he make of the Draft Declaration of the Rights of Indigenous Peoples currently (in 2006) under review by the UN Commission on Human Rights? This document was drafted over a long period in explicit challenge to the authority of nation-states over colonized Indigenous Peoples. It is not founded on an appeal to their bare natural life (although in many cases this is also at stake), but on their commitment to a distinctive *bios* or way of life that is all too often not recognized in the conditions of citizenship in the colonial societies in which they now find themselves. Perhaps a more contextual and historical analysis is needed in order to appreciate what is at stake in contemporary debates over human rights and minority rights.

Biopower and Sovereign Power

Agamben rightly points out that one of "the most persistent features of Foucault's work is its decisive abandonment of the traditional approach to the problem of power," by which he means the juridico-political representation of sovereign power (*HS*, 5). Foucault made a point of contrasting his own approach to the techniques and technology of power, with its focus upon the "how" rather than the "why" of power, to the juridico-political theory of state power focused upon the figure of the sovereign and the question of legitimation. In these terms, the definition of biopower in his lecture of March 17, 1976, and in *The History of Sexuality, Volume I* refers to the manner in which state power was exercised rather than its representation in theories of sovereignty. Just as he earlier distinguished this juridico-political discourse on sovereignty from the disciplinary techniques deployed in the seventeenth, eighteenth, and nineteenth centuries, so Foucault points here to the emergence of a new "biopolitical" technology of power that operates on different objects, at a different level and different scale, and with different instruments or mechanisms.

Foucault contrasts this biopower with the earlier form of sovereign power that took and granted life: by contrast, this new form of power "consists in making live and letting die."[10] The reference to sovereign power draws us back to the primary contrast that frames the concept of biopower, namely, the contrast between a power that intervened on the conditions that sustain life and one that intervened on life only by imposing death, between a power that could make live or let die and one that could only take life or let live. Curiously, however, Foucault presents this contrast initially, not with reference to techniques or mechanisms of power, but with reference to the representation of state power in the classical theory of sovereignty. He describes the basic attribute of classical sovereign power as "the right of life and death."[11] Sovereign power is here described in terms of right, that is, in terms of the juridical and political representation of sovereign power rather than in terms of its effective exercise or technology. Foucault goes on to analyze this sovereign right, which is, he suggests, a strange right "even at the theoretical level."[12]

This right is strange because, to the extent that the sovereign really does have the right to decide whether subjects live or die, the subject is, as it were, suspended between life and death. Qua subject, he or she has no right to live or die independently of the will of the sovereign: "in terms of his relationship with the sovereign, the subject is, by rights, neither dead nor alive. From the point of view of life and death, the subject is neutral, and it is thanks to the sovereign that the subject has the right to be alive or, possibly, the right to be dead."[13] In this sense, since the life of the subject is entirely encompassed within the sphere of the sovereign's power, it is biopolitical power in Agamben's other sense of the term (*homo sacer*). Foucault calls this a paradoxical outcome, presumably because of the manner in which the material life or death of the subject is doubled in the sovereign right of life and death. At the level of the theory of sovereignty, "the lives and deaths of subjects become rights only as a result of the will of the sovereign."[14] The physical body of the subject is therefore doubled in his relation to the will of the sovereign, in the same way that, according to Kantorowitz's analysis in *The King's Two Bodies*,[15] the body of the sovereign is doubled by virtue of his legal status as the pinnacle and foundation of the kingdom.[16]

However, while in theory the sovereign has power over the life and death of the subject, in practice this power or right "is always exercised in an unbalanced way: the balance is always tipped in favor of death."[17] In other words, as Foucault already argued in *Discipline and Punish*, the exercise of sovereign power in the pre-modern period was primarily negative. It took life, or threatened to do so, just as it extracted tributes or taxes on the basis of a creation of wealth that lay largely outside its understanding or control. In terms of the contrast that frames all of Foucault's analyses of power between theory or representation and practice or techniques, the asymmetry that he points to here in relation to classical sovereign power applies at the level of practice and of the exercise of power, rather than at the level of representation. It is at this level that the ensuing discussion of the emergence of biopower takes place: new objects, a different scale of application, and different techniques and mechanisms are deployed.[18]

Agamben insists, in apparent "correction" of Foucault, that the bare life of subjects has always been at the heart of sovereign power. However, it is apparent that Foucault's analysis of classical sovereignty in this lecture already anticipates Agamben's thesis that the biological life of subjects (*zoē* as opposed to *bios*) was always included within the scope of sovereign power. Although his analysis is restricted to the classical theory of sovereign right, and although he does not discuss the figure of the sacred man (*homo sacer*) who is at once excluded from the protection of both the political and the divine order, Foucault's suggestion that the subject of sovereign power is neutral with respect to his right to live or die implies the possibility of the withdrawal of that status, and along with it the exclusion of the subject from the sphere of sovereign power, thereby exposing the exiled figure to the loss of protection of his life as much as to the freedom from the threat of death at the hands of the sovereign. The life of the subject in the terms of the classical theory of sovereignty, as Foucault defines it, is structurally identical to the bare life of the *homo sacer*: it is biological existence doubled by its exclusive inclusion within the political sphere. In this sense, Foucault's analysis of classical sovereign right removes the need for any correction on this point. If we take "bare life" to mean simple biological life, or *zoē*, then his analysis is already consistent with Agamben's claim that bare life and the possibility of its ban or exclusion has always constituted the essential structure of sovereign power (*HS*, 111).

Foucault's concept of biopower therefore sits uneasily astride the methodological divide that opposes his analyses of the techniques through which power is exercised to the juridico-political representation of power. At the level of representation, classical sovereignty was already biopower. At the level of political technology, it only became biopower in the course of the nineteenth century. In an apparent attempt to restore a materialist temporality to these two dimensions of the biopower hypothesis, he then suggests that political right was also transformed in the course of the nineteenth century, when the old right of sovereignty "to take life or let live" was complemented by the addition of its opposite, namely "the right to make live and let die."[19] The manner in which he uses the terms *right* and *power* interchangeably here creates confusion over whether the transformation he is talking about involves the actual exercise of sovereign power or its representation. In the light of what he goes on to say in this lecture about the emergence of new objects, instruments, and techniques of biopower during the nineteenth century, we would expect him to be suggesting a change in the manner in which sovereign power is exercised. In fact, he suggests that there was also a transformation in the representation of sovereign power, that is, in political right proper. Moreover, he suggests that this transformation can be traced in the theory of right, and goes on to offer an "extraordinarily rapid" account of how this might be done.

Surprisingly, the example offered comes not from nineteenth-century political thought but from the classical theorists of sovereignty in the seventeenth and eighteenth centuries. Foucault points to the debate within political philosophy over the extent of the rights of the sovereign as these are understood in the terms of social contract theory. To the extent that individuals only enter into the contract on the basis of the desire to protect their own lives, does it make sense to suppose that they would grant a right over their life to the sovereign? "Isn't life the foundation of the sovereign's right, and can the sovereign actually demand that his subjects grant him the right to exercise the power of life and death over them, or in other words, simply the power to kill them? Mustn't life remain outside the contract to the extent that it was the first, initial and foundational reason for the contract itself?"[20]

Foucault doesn't provide details of this argument, but we can readily find examples among the classical social contract theorists. Hobbes and Locke both believed that individuals had rights in the pre-political state of nature, although they gave different accounts of the basis of such natural rights. For both, however, the right to life was foremost among these natural rights, where this included the right to pursue the objects of their desires. For Locke, for example, everyone is entitled to "the necessities and conveniences of life." It is because this fundamental right is threatened in the state of nature that rational individuals will choose to enter into political society under sovereign rule. Again, Hobbes and Locke give different accounts of the reasons for insecurity in the pre-political state, and of the reasoning behind the decision to contract to establish a sovereign power. In both cases, however, the preservation of individual life is the fundamental reason for the establishment of government. And in both cases, the natural right to life sets limits to the extent of sovereign power. In the case of Hobbes, for whom the sovereign is accountable to subjects only via the performance of the ends for which the commonwealth was established in the first place, "the obligation of subjects to the Sovereign is understood to last as long, and no longer, than the power lasteth by which he is able to protect them."[21] Locke also defended a natural right of rebellion when the sovereign failed in its obligation to protect the lives and property of subjects.

Taken at face value, Foucault's elaboration of the concept of biopower is bizarre. Having suggested that there was in the course of the nineteenth century a transformation in the representation of sovereign power alongside the emergence of biopolitical techniques for the exercise of state power, he provides examples from approximately two centuries before the period in which this transformation was supposed to have taken place. While he provides extensive detail on the changes in the techniques, modes of exercise, and objects of political power in the modern period, in this lecture at least he provides no evidence or examples of any corresponding transformation in the representation of state power. The question naturally arises when, where, and how this transformation in the theory of political right took place. Where do we find evidence of the emergence of a new conception of sovereign political right that corresponds to the emergence of biopower? Perhaps no such transformation took place in nineteenth-century political thought. Or perhaps this is where Foucault's concept of biopower falls apart, torn between the recognition that the life of subjects had long been included with the scope of sovereign right and the observation that only from the turn of the nineteenth century onward was state power effectively exercised over the conditions that sustain the lives of its subjects. In any event, as we have already seen, the concept of biopower plays no further role in Foucault's lectures or published works after 1976. With one or two exceptions, his analyses of governmentality were entirely concerned with the mechanisms and techniques of government.

Where Foucault pursues a historical inquiry into the different conceptions of the purpose, objects, methods, and instruments that have informed the exercise of political government since the seventeenth century, Agamben prefers to subsume all under a single amorphous concept of biopolitics. Thus, where Foucault carefully distinguishes liberalism and the science of police as distinct forms of reflection on the practice of government, or what he called "governmental rationalities," and both of these from the post-war neo-liberalism of the German *Ordoliberalen* and the American Chicago school, Agamben condenses bodies of thought separated by a century or more into a single sweeping sentence: "From the end of the nineteenth century, Francis Galton's work functions as the theoretical background for the work of *the science of police, which has now become biopolitics"* (*HS*, 145; emphasis added). Phenomena as disparate as Hobbes's account of the pre-political life of man subject to the omnipresent threat of death, the 1679 writ of habeas corpus, the 1789 rights of man and citizen, the brain-dead body of Karen Quinlan, and the "imploring eyes" of a Rwandan child all bear witness to the biopolitical vocation of modern politics. In every case, it is the ambiguous concept of bare life and the shadowy figure of *homo sacer* that reappear in new guises.

Foucault's failure to pursue the question of transformation in the form of representation of sovereign power might be explained by the fact that he was not especially interested in political theory. However, at one point in the second lecture of his 1978–79 course he does address the question of the intersection of traditional juridical theory of sovereign power with liberalism.[22] He returns to the question of the nature and justification of state power, in the form of the question of the limits of public law (*droit public*). Within the context of liberalism understood as an internally limited mode of government, a question arose: how should this limitation be presented in juridical terms? Foucault suggests that, in the eighteenth and nineteenth centuries, two ways of answering this question were followed.[23] The first, which he calls the revolutionary, "juridico-deductive" path, sought to set limits to the legitimate functions of government on the basis of a theory of the imprescriptible, natural rights of individuals. This was the path followed by the American Declaration of Independence (1776), which declared the existence of certain inalienable rights, including the right to life, liberty, and the pursuit of happiness. Governments are established in order to secure these rights. It was also the path followed by Rousseau and by the French revolutionaries, who declared that men were born with certain rights. Foucault summarizes this approach as the attempt to delimit the powers of government on the basis of a conception of the rights of man, by way of an understanding of the constitution of sovereign power.

The second path was the one followed by English radicalism at the turn of the nineteenth century. It consisted in seeking to determine the limits of legitimate government by reference to what was useful to government, given its aim of increasing the forces of the state and the well-being of its citizens, and useful to the citizens themselves, given their overriding interest in being governed as little as possible. In other words, the limits of government are set by the principle of utility. In practice, this turns into a calculus of interests, since it is the concept of interest that links the liberal concern with self-regulating markets and the utility of public policy. Government was undertaken both in the interests of the governed and as a means to ensure that individual interests would be satisfied through the market. Both of these two forms of legitimation of liberal democratic government—the revolutionary theory of natural rights and the radical theory of human interests—are still active, although Foucault suggests that the utilitarian conception of government has long been the dominant one. However, it remains an open question as to what other forms of legitimation have been and may yet be employed and, as his intervention in support of the creation of an international committee to act in support of Vietnamese refugees makes clear, Foucault does not think that the reliance on the calculus of interests by governments means that citizens cannot rely on the same principles in order to claim new rights. The fact that governments believe and would have others believe that they are concerned for the welfare of their citizens is one of the conditions that enables governments to be held responsible for the suffering of citizens, and that allows the emergence of a duty on the part of the international citizenry to speak out against abuses or derelictions of power.[24]

By contrast, Agamben's analysis of the biopolitical foundations of modern democratic government mentions only the revolutionary theory of natural rights and draws conclusions which foreclose the possibility of a reinterpretation of human rights. On his account, such rights are indelibly marked as the founding fiction of the modern nation-state, representing only "the originary figure of the inscription of natural life in the juridico-political order of the nation-state" (*HS*, 127). This analysis relies on a conceptual fundamentalism according to which the meaning of concepts is irrevocably determined by their origin. Agamben settles for nothing less than a conceptual revolution that takes us beyond the terms in which Western politics has been played out and that lead to "the constitution and installation of a form of life that is wholly exhausted in bare life and a *bios* that is only its own *zoē*" (*HS*, 188). In the end, the difference between his approach and that of Foucault is not so much a matter of correction and completion as a choice between epochal concepts of biopolitics and bare life and a more fine-grained, contextual, and historical analysis intended to enable specific and local forms of escape from the past.

The Ontology and Politics of Exception

Reflections on the Work of Giorgio Agamben

Bruno Gullì

Asked to give a definition of our age, we might say that it is the age of the actual or potential suspension of the law. The law has been suspended in all actuality with respect to the Guantanamo Bay detainees and in many ways in the futile and unfinished conflict that has destroyed Iraq—a conflict that has not, of course, been humanitarian in character, nor merely motivated by oil, but has rather been a demonstration of global sovereignty and an attack against the law. Thus, with respect to the abuses at the Abu Ghraib prison, George W. Bush claimed the right to suspend the Geneva Convention laws and order torture, but he also said that he declined to exercise that right. Whether the suspension of the law is actual or potential does not affect the discourse on its significance. That the law can be suspended is not a novelty in politics and history. What is novel is that the specter of the suspension of the law becomes a measure of global dominance and control, the ground for repressive policies and the surest way to turn everyday life, everybody's life, into naked life; that, particularly, the state of exception which defines this suspension becomes the rule. What is also novel, particularly with the concept of pre-emptive war, is that the law is suspended, not because there is a state of emergency requiring exceptional measures, but because such a state of emergency could arise. Thus we have recently witnessed the passage from a justification of the war based on the factual evidence of Iraqi possession of weapons of mass destruction to a justification based on Iraqi *capacity* for a development of those weapons. The actual suspension of the law enters now, and acts within, the realm of the potential; it is within potentiality (and *of* potentiality) that repression and control become most efficient and powerful. When the law is thus suspended, that is, reaching into the sphere of potentiality, we enter the paradox of a regime of a *permanent* state of exception.

. . .

It is perhaps Agamben's greatest merit that he has provided a clear philosophical focus, as well as a forum, for an understanding of the political and ontological structure of the suspension of the law. He does that by going back to the work of Walter Benjamin and Carl Schmitt, who have treated the question in apparently similar, but ultimately different, ways. The concept of the suspension of the law occupies a central place in Agamben's recent work, and it will also be the center of our discussion in this chapter. Understanding it requires that we show the twofold manner of its unfolding, according to the conceptual figures of neither/nor and of exception.

In a way that at times seems obsessive, Giorgio Agamben emphasizes in his recent works two conceptual figures: the structure of neither/nor and the concept of exception. These two figures are intimately related, and the former is certainly more fundamental, from a philosophical point of view, than the latter: the structure of neither/nor grounds the concept of exception. Neither/nor names the concept of potentiality, which for Agamben, according to a careful reading of Aristotle, is also always impotentiality, that is, the potentiality not to. In this sense, neither/nor always pertains to the sphere of ontology. However, what makes Agamben's thought particularly interesting is his ability, much needed in our time, to constantly and indissolubly link ontology with politics—a link which is not the result of the mere juxtaposition of two different spheres of thought, but rather a powerful and compelling showing of their intimate and essential connection. Only by looking at the structure that makes the factual possible (but could make it impossible as well)—only by looking at the ontological structure of contingency—can a new and radically different way of understanding and living the political be found and founded. This is, I think,

Agamben's main contribution to philosophy and the world—an invaluable contribution in our dark times.

Potentiality and the Potentiality Not To

What is potentiality? For Agamben, an adequate grasp of this concept will not be attained if one does not also consider impotentiality, or the potentiality not to, which at first sight seems to be potentiality's negative counterpart but in truth is something altogether different. It is not potentiality's negative counterpart because impotentiality is not the absence of potentiality, but that without which the essence of potentiality itself cannot be thought. The potentiality not to is still a potentiality; it indicates the possibility of a positive withdrawal from the act, as in "Bartleby, the Scrivener," to which Agamben's dedicates an essay on contingency (*P*, 243–71).

It is then necessary to begin with a definition of the concepts of potentiality and of the potentiality not to. In "Potentiality and the Law," which is, philosophically speaking, the strongest and most interesting chapter of *Homo Sacer*, Agamben calls attention to the necessity of adequately thinking the existence and autonomy of potentiality, which is essential if one wishes to understand the relation between constituent power and constituted power, under discussion therein. He says that Aristotle "always takes great care to affirm the autonomous existence of potentiality" (*HS*, 44–45). This does not mean that the potential is divided from the factual in the sense of being outside reality. Rather, the opposite is the case: the autonomous existence of potentiality makes potentiality absolutely real, an integral part of reality. Reality is usually reduced to the factual, the empirically given; the truth is, the potential grounds what is thus given. However, it does not ground it in a mechanical and deterministic fashion. The most important thing to keep in mind here is that what is grounded could also not have been grounded. Yet, this could and could-not modality of the grounding element is not ideal, it does not need actuality to become real, but it is what, ontologically speaking, is the most real. Agamben says that, for Aristotle, "if potentiality is to have its own consistency and not always disappear immediately into actuality, it is necessary that potentiality be able *not* to pass over into actuality, that potentiality constitutively be the *potentiality not to* (do or be), or, as Aristotle says, that potentiality be also im-potentiality (*adynamia*)" (*HS*, 45).

In a short essay entitled "On Potentiality," Agamben explains that Aristotle distinguishes between two kinds of potentiality. One is *generic*—for instance, the potentiality of the child to learn or to become the head of State; the other is *existing*—for instance, the potentiality of the poet to write a poem. The difference is that in the former case an alteration must be suffered for the potentiality to become actual, while in the latter the potentiality is already there. Precisely because of this, however, whoever has existing potentiality can also choose not to bring it into actuality (*P*, 179). It is this second form of potentiality that interests both Aristotle and Agamben: "It is a potentiality that is not simply the potential to do this or that thing but potential to not-do, potential not to pass into actuality" (*P*, 179–80). Quoting Aristotle from book 9 of the *Metaphysics*, Agamben says that the essence of potentiality is the relation that potentiality has with its own privation, its own non-being. In a manner that recalls Sartre's categories of *Being and Nothingness*, Agamben says: "To be potential means: to be one's own lack, *to be in relation to one's own incapacity*" (*P*, 182).[1] Being capable of one's own impotentiality, capable of choosing between doing and not doing, is the very form of freedom. This is the way in which Aristotle also defines freedom in the *Nicomachean Ethics*. And Agamben says: "To be free is . . . *to be capable of one's own impotentiality*, to be in relation to one's own privation" (*P*, 183). Yet, the paradox of freedom—that one is not free not to be free, as enunciated by Sartre—surpasses the modality of potentiality/impotentiality, giving to the latter, precisely, the function of choosing between this or that thing, or the power to refuse to do this or that thing, which Agamben feels has been left behind. A better definition of potentiality is given by Aristotle himself in the *Metaphysics*, a definition quoted here by Agamben: "A thing is said to be potential if, when the act of which it is said to be potential is realized, there will be nothing impotential" (*P*, 183; *Metaphysics* 1047a, 24–26). Agamben is correct in criticizing the usual interpretation of this sentence, according to which Aristotle meant to say: "What is possible (or potential) is that with respect to which nothing is impossible (or impotential). If there is no impossibility, then there is possibility" (*P*, 183); to which Agamben replies, "Aristotle would then have uttered a banality or a tautology" (*P*, 183). His own interpretation of Aristotle's difficult definition reads as follows: "if a potentiality to not-be originally belongs to all potentiality, then there is truly potentiality only where the potentiality to not-be does not lag behind actuality but passes fully into it as such" (*P*, 183; emphasis removed). And he continues: "This does not mean that it disappears in actuality; on the contrary, it *preserves itself* as such in actuality. What is truly potential is thus what has exhausted all its impotentiality in bringing it wholly into the act as such" (*P*, 183).

I do not disagree with this interpretation, but I think it needs to be qualified and developed. What Agamben is here pointing to is the modality of the *could*, but he does not name it, for he begins this essay by asking: "What do I mean when I say: 'I can, I cannot'?" (*P*, 177), and he remains within the framing of this question, within the *can* modality. Yet, as both Duns Scotus and Deleuze show, it is from the perspective of the *could*, the open series of disjunctions (or . . . or . . . or . . . or . . .), the plurality of possibilities, that true potentiality can become evident. The *could* allows for a *could have*, a perfective, which is logically and ontologically forbidden to the *can*. This *could have*, which neutralizes itself in determination, is what shows forth in Agamben's interesting interpretation of Aristotle's definition: this *could have* is the impotentiality that "does not lag behind actuality but passes fully into it as such." In fact, the *could have* does not belong to a theory of the act, but rather to a theory of potency, of a potency which has imploded as one instance of the *could* has passed over into actuality; but as this one instance passes over as determined and actual, all the others "do not lag behind"; rather, they also pass over, constituting the undetermined ground of all determinations, a reminder of the fact of their contingency. The essential relation between potentiality and the potentiality not to is not a relation between two elements of an absolute constitution—it is not an either/or—but rather, it is the open indeterminacy that precedes the act, that can even neutralize the act. We are here within the realm of contingency, a structure closely linked to that of potentiality, rather than to the structure of actuality as is often thought. In fact, contingency is most clearly grasped at the level of the potential (if one looks deep enough), and it is there, within potentiality, that contingency also renders graspable the concept of the potentiality not to. Thus, Duns Scotus says: "let me say that by 'contingent' I do not mean something that is not necessary or which was not always in existence, but something whose opposite *could have* occurred [*posset fieri*] at the time that this actually did. That is why I do not say that something is contingent, but that something is *caused contingently*."[2] Duns Scotus is here arguing against Aristotle's idea that the first cause does not cause contingently. He regrets the fact that Aristotle "places contingency in

the lower beings and not in the fact that God wills things contingently."[3]
If contingency is taken away at any level of the chain of beings and necessity is introduced, then contingency can never be found again, for, even
if one considers the argument from motion, which is Aristotle's argument
in this respect, one cannot reintroduce contingency at any point once one
starts with necessity. This is so, "because if the motion as a whole proceeds
from its cause in a necessary manner, every single part of it is caused necessarily at the time it occurs."[4] Thus, Duns Scotus says that "either nothing
ever happens unavoidably or contingently, or the first cause immediately
causes *what it was also able not to cause*."[5] In Duns Scotus, this necessarily
follows from the structure of univocity, which makes no substantial distinctions, from this point of view, among different beings, and from the
primacy of the will.

As Ernst Bloch notes: "Scotus taught that the good is not good
because God willed and commanded it, because God could just as well
have ordained murder, thievery, and adultery in the commandments and
then not murdering, not stealing, and not committing adultery would be
sins."[6] To cause what one is also able not to cause is certainly a definition,
not only of contingency, but also of what Agamben calls the "essence of
potentiality," that is, the relation between potentiality and the potentiality not to. Once the causing is accomplished and potentiality passes over
into actuality, the "I can and I cannot" of now becomes an "I did and I
could have not"; it is in this latter form that impotentiality also passes fully
into actuality and is preserved as such. In the same way, the not causing
of what could be caused changes the "I can and I cannot" into an "I did
not and I could have"; here, too, the essential relation between potentiality and impotentiality is preserved—especially preserved in the refusal of
the act. All that this says is that we act in the midst of absolute indeterminacy, in the neutrality or neither/nor of the potential; and this is also
what Spinoza's famous dictum means: *omnia determinatio est negatio*. The
negatio, which always passes fully into the act and is thus preserved, is the
"I could have not," which always accompanies the "I did," or the "I could
have," which always accompanies the "I did not," for even the decision not
to act is a determination. This does not mean, of course, that the open possibilities of the moment of decision remain open: they close forever, and, as
Aristotle says discussing the principle of agency, once the stone is thrown,
it cannot be taken back (*Nicomachean Ethics* 1114a, 20). However, what

gives the throwing its true meaning is precisely the fact that at the moment of its occurrence it could also not have occurred. This is what makes something tragic, as we see, for instance, in Milton's *Paradise Lost*: "But past who can recall, or done undo?" (9.926). As Aristotle says in his *Nicomachean Ethics*, "we do not decide to do what is already past," but in deliberating about the future, we deal with what "admits of being or not being," that is potentiality and the potentiality not to (1139b, 7–9).[7] However, the fact that "the past does not admit of not having happened" (1139b, 9) does not imply—and Scotus shows this well—that at the time of its happening it did not admit of being or not being.

It is the structure of potentiality thus understood that makes it possible to grasp the double figure of exception: sovereign power and bare, or naked, life. In the chapter "Potentiality and Law" in *Homo Sacer*, Agamben says that existing potentiality "maintains itself in relation to actuality in the form of its suspension; it *is capable* of the act in not realizing it, it is sovereignly capable of its own im-potentiality" (*HS*, 45). Existing potentiality founds the figure of the sovereign: "Potentiality (in its double appearance as potentiality to and potentiality not to) is that through which Being founds itself *sovereignly*, which is to say, without anything preceding or determining it . . . other than its own ability to be" (*HS*, 46). An act is then defined as sovereign when it "realizes itself by simply taking away its own potentiality not to be, letting itself be, giving itself to itself" (*HS*, 46). The passage from potentiality to sovereignty is accomplished through the structure of exception.

. . .

The concept of double negation or neither/nor is perhaps the most central concept in Agamben's discourse on the relationship between ontology and politics. I will, accordingly, deal particularly with the neither/nor that founds, at the ontological level, the figure of exception, as well as the symmetrical figures that this exception characterizes: sovereign power and naked life. As Agamben says in *Homo Sacer*: "The exception is an element in law that transcends positive law in the form of its suspension" (*HS*, 17). He says that the exception is to positive law what negative theology is to positive theology: a "neither . . . nor" of all attributes and predicates of God. The exception made possible by the neither/nor is, Agamben says, a form of exclusion, which is at the same time also an inclusion.

The Time That Remains

In his splendid comment on Paul's letter to the Romans, *Il tempo che resta* (*The Time That Remains*)[8]—a study of Paul's messianic thinking—the concept of exception, already present in *Homo Sacer*, appears as *separation*. Paul calls himself "separate, set apart"; this separation is the condition of his messianic calling. The concept of separation, linked to the doings of the law (the law that posits and suspends the law) is related to those of exception and sovereignty. In this sense, Paul prefers the messianic and apostolic modality to the prophetic one. In the latter, we hear the announcement of a future time, but the former speaks of *this* time, the *now*; not the apocalyptic end of time, but the messianic time of the end. And that is the same as the time of the beginning: ontology of time, that is, the contraction of all time in the beginning of its end. In fact, the messiah comes to restore a law that precedes creation. What the law accomplishes is its own transgression; or rather, it is no longer possible to distinguish between accomplishment and transgression of the law. "What remains" after the messianic rupture is a double negation, a neither/nor, which also indicates the impossibility of a people to coincide with itself.

The time that remains, the *rest*, messianic time, is the contraction of time itself, "the only real time" (*TcR*, 13), the present time, "the time of now [*il tempo di ora*]." The comment is centered on the ten initial words of Paul's letter, which in the English Revised Standard Version read as follows: "Paul, a servant of Jesus Christ, called to be an apostle, set apart for the gospel of God." The Greek text is: *Paulos doulos Christoú Iēsoú, Klētós Apóstolos Aphōrisménos Eis Euaggélion Theoú.* Here the concept of exception figures as *separation*. Paul is separated, "set apart," and in this separation there is, for Agamben, Paul's alleged universalism. This same concept, exception as separation, is what sheds light on the ontological structure of neither/nor.

The seminar, and thus the book, is divided into six days and a threshold (or *tornada*). The first day, Agamben analyzes the words *Paulos doulos Christoú Iēsoú*; the second day he analyzes the word *Klētós*; the third day, the word *Aphōrisménos*; then, on the fourth day, the word *Apóstolos*; the fifth and sixth days, are centered on the words *Eis euaggélion theoú*. I will not deal with the threshold.

On the first day, the question is posed as to what messianic time is

(*TcR*, 24). This is done after having established that *christós* is not a proper name, but the equivalent of the Hebrew *mašiah*, that is, messiah. As Agamben says, "Paul does not know Jesus Christ, but Jesus the messiah, or the messiah Jesus, as he interchangeably writes" (*TcR*, 22).

Then, on the second day, a more important, or at least more complex concept is considered with the word *klētós*, from the verb *kaléo*, which means "to call." Agamben says that all related words, particularly *klēsis* (vocation, call), acquire a technical meaning in Paul's vocabulary. He quotes a passage from the first letter to the Corinthians (1 Cor. 7:17–22)—which I will not reproduce in its entirety—where Paul says, "Every one should remain in the call [*klēsis*] in which he was called."[9] And the passage continues: "Were you a slave when called? Never mind. But [even] if you can gain your freedom, make use of your present condition instead."[10] At this point, Agamben considers critically the modern German translation of *klēsis*, "messianic vocation," with *Beruf*, "vocation," but also as "worldly profession," as in Luther's translation of this passage and as accepted and elaborated by Max Weber in his *Protestant Ethic and the Spirit of Capitalism*. For Agamben, Paul's messianic vocation is the mutation and, ultimately, the nullification of all juridical status and worldly condition. To remain in the call in which one was called is a first step toward the structure of neither/nor, the structure of neutrality, which makes possible the exception of the separation. In other words, it does not matter whether one is a free person or a slave, or whether one is circumcised or uncircumcised: this sense of the vocation is neutralized by the messianic vocation, a *call of the call* (*una chiamata della chiamata*) (*TcR*, 28; Agamben's emphasis). Agamben says: "*The messianic vocation is a revocation of all vocation*" (*TcR*, 29). Yet, precisely because of this, it "can coincide with the factual condition in which every one happens to be called" (*TcR*, 29).

In this sense, Agamben quotes another passage from the first letter to the Corinthians, which he calls an "extraordinary passage" and the "most rigorous definition that [Paul] gave us of messianic life" (*TcR*, 29). This passage is very important because it introduces the concept of *as not* (*hōs mē*; *come non*), which has a very special function in Agamben's comment to the letter. In the Revised Standard Edition of the Bible, the *hōs mē* is translated with *as though . . . not* and the passage reads: "I mean, brethren, the appointed time has grown very short; from now on, let those who have wives live as though they had none, and those who mourn as though they

were not mourning, and those who rejoice as though they were not rejoicing, and those who buy as though they had no goods, and those who deal
with the world as though they had no dealings with it. For the form of this
world is passing away. I want you to be free from anxiety" (1 Cor. 7:29–32).
A translation of Agamben's Italian rendering of this passage would read:
"This then I say, brothers, time has contracted; for the rest, let those having wives be as not having wives, and the mourning ones as not mourning,
and those who rejoice as not rejoicing, and those who buy as not owning
goods, and those who use the world as not abusing. For the figure of this
world is passing away. I want you to be without care" (*TcR*, 29). The *hōs
mē* is the revocation of all vocation, which happens not as an abolition of
all activity but rather as its suspension: "doing *as not* doing," or "being *as
not* being," can be taken as its general form. Agamben explains that the
comparative form of the *as* (*hōs*) (and thus the negative *as not* [*hōs mē*])
introduces a *tension*—a tension of any condition, or activity, toward itself.
He says that "by putting each thing in tension toward itself in the *as not*,
the messianic does not simply cancel it, but it makes it pass, it prepares its
end" (*TcR*, 30). He also calls the messianic vocation an "immanent movement" and a "zone of absolute indiscernibility between immanence and
transcendence, between this world and the future world" (*TcR*, 30), and
says how the messianic life entails the *depropriation* of any property. This is
the meaning of the lines "those who buy as not owning goods, and those
who use the world as not abusing." The messianic call (*klēsis*) recognizes
only the category of use, not of property (*TcR*, 31). After making a reference to the Franciscan category of use against that of property, which for
him acquires full meaning if looked at from the perspective of Paul's letter, Agamben also explains the Marxian concept of class in terms of *klēsis*.
He calls attention to the relevance of Benjamin's thesis according to which
Marx's concept of the classless society is a secularization of messianic time.
He says: "In the same way in which the class represents the dissolution of
all ranks and the emergence of the split between the individual and his
social condition, the messianic *klēsis* means the emptying and the nullification, in the form of the *as not*, of all juridical-factual divisions" (*TcR*, 35).
In pointing out the similarity between those who follow the messianic call
according to the form of the *as not* and the Marxian proletariat, whose
total loss of humanity is the condition for its total liberation, Agamben
says something very important, and usually overlooked, with respect to the

concept of the proletariat itself. In a parenthetical remark he says:

The fact that, in the course of time, the proletariat has been identified with a determinate social class—the working class, which demanded prerogatives and rights—is, from this point of view, the worst misunderstanding of Marxian thinking. What was in Marx a strategic identification—the working class as *klēsis* and as a contingent historical figure of the proletariat—becomes a true and substantial social identity, which necessarily loses its revolutionary vocation. (*TcR*, 35)

This is absolutely evident when one considers the distinction Marx draws between the proletariat and the working class at the outset of his *Economic and Philosophical Manuscripts*, and it is particularly important today, when a redefinition of the proletariat has become necessary at the level of both theory and practice.

The third day of the comment is dedicated to the analysis of the word *aphōrisménos*, which means "separated, set apart." The problem here, first of all, is understanding why Paul, "who preaches universalism and announces the messianic end of all separation between Jews and pagans, refers to himself as 'set apart'" (*TcR*, 47). The answer to the question is that *aphōrisménos* indicates a "separation of separateness itself [*una separazione della stessa separatezza*]" (*TcR*, 49), which, in turn, indicates *the rest*, that which remains in the overcoming of the division between Jews and non-Jews, which would be the category of the non-non-Jews. This category is arrived at by a new division created by Paul, that between those who are Jews outwardly or according to the flesh and those who are Jews inwardly or according to the breath. Agamben says that this further division also applies to the non-Jews. This is a very important way of reasoning at present, because it challenges in a substantial way one of the most superficial and pernicious, yet dominant, ideologies of our times: identity politics. As Agamben says, this "division of the division" compels us to "think in a completely new way the question of the universal and the particular, not simply in logic, but also in ontology and politics" (*TcR*, 53–54). Thus he reinterprets what he calls Paul's "alleged" universalism. He rejects Alain Badiou's interpretation of the universal as "production of the same" and sees in Paul's messianic thinking, not a search for the universal, but the isolation of a rest, an identity which is unable to coincide with itself:

At the bottom of the Jew and the Greek, there is not the universal man, neither as principle nor as end: there is only a rest, there is only the impossibility of the Jew and the Greek to coincide with themselves. The messianic vocation separates each *klēsis* from itself, it puts the latter in tension with itself, without giving it a further identity: Jew *as not* Jew, Greek *as not* Greek. (*TcR*, 55)

Yet, this should not exclude the possibility that this rest is a universal. In fact, as Agamben says, this rest can in no way be identified with the chosen people, the people of Israel—its identification with that which remains in the breaking up of all identity, the ground of neutrality, can indeed be conceived of as the universal as such. Renouncing the notion of universality today only plays into the politics of identity one needs to defeat. Indeed, the concept of the people, with which Agamben concludes this third day, has a universal aspiration. For Agamben, the people, which is neither the whole nor the part, but rather that which can never coincide with itself, is today "the only real political subject" (*TcR*, 59). There is here, probably, a veiled critique of the concept of multitude, rendered popular today particularly by Hardt and Negri. But more important is the totalizing aspect of the dialectic of what cannot coincide with itself, which can be understood if one keeps in mind Sartre's concept of the open dialectic—a totalizing movement, always also detotalizing; never a finished totality.

On the fourth day, Agamben analyzes the word *apóstolos*, which means "messenger." Agamben says that Paul describes himself as an apostle rather than as a prophet because in messianic time the apostle takes the place of the prophet. The latter speaks of a future time, the former of this time, the present time, the time that remains. The time of the apostle, messianic time, is not that of the prophet and the visionary, apocalyptic time; it is not the end of time, but *the time of the end*: "What interests the apostle is not the last day, it is not the instant in which time ends, but the time which contracts and begins to end . . . —or . . . the time which remains between time and its end" (*TcR*, 63). It is "*the time time takes to end* [il tempo che il tempo ci mette per finire]" (*TcR*, 67). This time, "the time of now," the present, whose representation is almost impossible to attain, can only be conceived as the neither/nor of time. It is the time of a transition between the profane aeon and the future one of eternity. Agamben says:

Apparently, things are simple: there is, first of all, profane time—to which Paul usually refers with the term *chronos*—which goes from creation to the messianic event (which, for Paul, is not the birth of Jesus, but his resurrection). Here time contracts and begins to end: but this contracted time—to which Paul refers with the expression *ho nyn kairós*, "the time of now"—lasts until the *parousia*, the full presence of the messiah, which coincides with the day of wrath and the end of time (which remains undetermined, though imminent). Here time explodes—or rather, it implodes, in the other aeon, into eternity. (*TcR*, 64)

It is neither simply the profane aeon, for it exceeds *chronos*; nor is it simply eternity, for it exceeds the future aeon: it is the inner passage of one into the other, "a time within time" (*TcR*, 67). Using a figure from the work of the linguist Gustave Guillaume, who looks at language starting from the Aristotelian distinction between potency and act, Agamben calls this time *operative time*, that is, the ulterior time always implied in any representation of time, a time that cannot be exhausted by any representation. This time is not ulterior in the sense of a supplement to be added to the chronological time; rather, it is interior: the time that operates the transformation from one aeon to the other but that is neither one of them—a sort of transhistoricality, where *trans-* is to be taken not as "beyond" but as "crossing through." To be sure, Agamben makes no use of the concept of transhistoricality, even so qualified, and his explanation of the time which remains is indeed different from what I am proposing. It is neither an additional time nor an ontological time that remains because it also precedes, ontologically speaking, all possible epochs. It is not "a third aeon between the two times, but, rather, a caesura which divides the very division between times, introducing a rest between them, a zone of indifference which cannot be assigned to either, in which the past is displaced in the present and the present is distended into the past" (*TcR*, 74). It is, Agamben says, "the time *which* we ourselves are" (*TcR*, 68). Yet, if this caesura is not to be a third aeon between the two times (a proposition with which I completely agree), it must be the apparition of a neither/nor which is "always already" there, and in this sense the use of the notion of transhistoricality here is completely justified.

On the fifth and sixth days, Agamben comments on the words *eis euaggélion theoú*, which mean "for the gospel of God." These sections of the book deal mainly with Paul's understanding and critique of the law. This is particularly interesting because it will introduce us to important questions developed by Agamben in other works, questions that have to do with the structure of neither/nor and the ontology of exception. The main initial concepts analyzed in these sections are those of faith (*pistis*), promise (*epaggelía*), and law (*nomos*). The promise relates to the announcement (the gospel, *euaggélion*), insofar as the announcement is the "form that the promise takes in the contraction of messianic time" (*TcR*, 91); faith, on the other hand, has to do with the conviction that the promise can also be realized. Promise and faith are seen by Paul in opposition to the law. However, what seems to be an antinomian stance is in reality a critique of mundane law and a redefinition of the law at a higher order, which is that of the unity of promise and faith: the messianic law. Agamben repeatedly quotes a passage from the letter to the Romans: "Do we then overthrow the law by this faith? By no means! On the contrary, we uphold the law" (Rom. 3:31). Agamben explains: "The messianic law is the law of faith, and not simply the negation of the law" (*TcR*, 91). The point, however, is not replacing one law with another, it is rather "opposing a non-normative figure of the law to the normative one" (*TcR*, 91). Agamben then asks what a non-normative aspect of the law is. To answer this question, he analyzes a new concept, that of *katargeín*, which will also come back in *State of Exception*, under the form of a different institution. This is a very important concept, and the analysis of it is, as is often the case with Agamben, fascinating. It is important because it reaches into the structure of neutrality, the structure of neither/nor, which is the focus of this chapter. Here the relation between potentiality and impotentiality, fundamental in Agamben's work, becomes evident; here it shows its relevance, not only philosophically but also politically.

Katargeín means "to disactivate" and is the negative of *energeín*, which means "to activate" (*TcR*, 92). Agamben says that Paul's use of the concept is based on the Aristotelian opposition between *dynamis* and *enérgeia*, potency and act, which he often mentions. Disactivation becomes a key concept in messianic thinking, because of the inversion whereby "potency passes over into act and reaches its telos not in the form of strength and *ergon*, but in that of *asthéneia*, of weakness" (*TcR*, 93). This is for instance shown in the second letter to the Corinthians, where God says: "my power is made perfect in weakness" (2 Cor. 12:9). The inversion of the relationship between potency and act also has an implication at the level of the law, which is thereby not simply abolished and nullified, but, precisely, disactivated: "The messianic is not the destruction, but the disactivation and the unfeasibility of the law" (*TcR*, 93). This is the meaning of the verb *katargéō*. We will find the same figure in *State of Exception*, with the concept of *iustitium*, which seems to be the Roman equivalent of *katárgēsis*, though *iustitium* is an institutional, rather than a messianic, figure (see below). What is at work here is the concept of impotentiality, the potentiality not to, which is a fundamental figure in Agamben's work. It indicates the neutrality of the act, or better the neutrality of potency with respect to the act, and thus the contingency of causality: that which has been let out of the act, and certainly also that which has not yet entered the act. With respect to Paul, this is the meaning of the messiah, "the completion of that which has been dis-activated," as Agamben translates the *telos tou katargouménou* of the second letter to the Corinthians (2 Cor. 3:12–13). Agamben says: "It is possible to bring the law to completion only if it has first been returned to the inoperative state [*inoperatività*] of its potency" (*TcR*, 94). He also says: "What is disactivated, let out of *enérgeia*, is not annulled thereby, but it is retained and held fast for its completion" (*TcR*, 94). Agamben then traces the genealogy of the concept of *Aufhebung*, with the double meaning of "abolishing" and "retaining"—a key concept in Hegel's dialectic—back to the concept of *katárgēsis*, disactivation.

Within this fifth day there is a subsection entitled "State of Exception." The question here, as in the book with the same title, has to do with the meaning of a law that is at the same time suspended and accomplished. Agamben refers to Carl Schmitt, for whom "the paradigm which defines the structure and the functioning proper to the law is not the norm, but the exception" (*TcR*, 98). For Schmitt this becomes evident in the paradox of the sovereign, who is at the same time inside and outside of the law. This is a central moment in Agamben's work, which comes back in *State of Exception* and is already present in *Homo Sacer*. For Agamben, "in the state of exception it is . . . impossible to distinguish between observance and transgression of the law" (*TcR*, 99). As a paradigmatic example of this, Agamben considers, here as elsewhere, the Decree for the Protection of the People and of the State, established in Germany on February 29, 1933. This decree, which remained in force for the whole period of the Nazi regime, only said: "The articles 114, 115, 117, 118, 123, 124 and 153 of the Constitution of the *Reich* are suspended until further orders." Agamben comments: "This laconic enunciation neither orders nor prohibits anything—yet, through the simple suspension of the articles of the Constitution concerning personal freedoms, it makes it impossible to know and say what is licit and what illicit" (*TcR*, 100). The result of this is the concentration camp, whose structure and meaning is studied by Agamben in *Homo Sacer*, where he defines it as the "hidden paradigm of the political space of modernity" (*HS*, 123). In Paul's messianic thinking, the state of exception takes on the form of the "law of the faith." It is a form of "justice without the law," which, Agamben says, "is not the negation, but the realization and completion . . . of the law" (*TcR*, 101). This is the concept of *anomía*, or absence of the law. The question is now to understand, Agamben says, what keeps the *anomía*, which is the suspension and completion of the law, from taking place. Thus he analyzes the concept of *katéchōn*, "that which holds back." It is the power that opposes and hides the disactivation and, ultimately, the absence of the law characterizing the messianic time; thus it "postpones the revealing of the 'mystery of *anomía*.'" What is important is that when the mystery is revealed and the law disactivated, the "substantial illegitimacy of any power in messianic time" becomes evident (*TcR*, 104). "Profane power—whether the Roman Empire or any other—is the appearance covering the substantial anomy of messianic power. With the undoing of the 'mystery,' this appearance is taken away, and the power takes on the figure of the *ánomos*, of the absolute outlaw" (*TcR*, 104). On the last day of the comment, Agamben clarifies this by saying that Paul plays "the plane of constituent power against that of constituted right" (*TcR*, 111). He continues: "The split between constituent power and constituted power, which in our own time shows itself with special evidence, has its theological foundation in Paul's split between the plane of faith and that of *nomos*" (*TcR*, 111). "From this point of view, messianic thinking appears as a struggle within the law, in which the element of the pact and of constituent power has the tendency to oppose and to emancipate itself from the element of the . . . norm in the strict sense" (*TcR*, 111).

State of Exception

In *State of Exception*, Agamben's project is to explore the "no-man's land between public right and political fact, as well as between the juridical order and life" (*SdE*, 10). Starting from Carl Schmitt's problematic analysis and definition of the concept (according to which the state of exception is the decision of the sovereign, who is at the same time inside and outside the juridical order), Agamben says that the state of exception "presents itself as the legal form of what cannot have any legal form" (*SdE*, 10). For Agamben, it is nothing neither more nor less than "the paradigm of dominant governance in contemporary politics" (*SdE*, 11). Thus the state of exception is no longer a state of exception, but a fact of everyday life as well as this fact's paradoxical definition: it is a "threshold of indeterminacy" that characterizes the "time of now." Agamben points out the biopolitical significance of the state of exception, "the original dispositif whereby the law refers back to life and includes it by means of its own suspension" (*SdE*, 10). He points out the biopolitical nature of this by making a reference to the Patriot Act of October 26, 2001, and to the subsequent "military order" authorizing the "indefinite detention" of aliens suspected of terrorist activities. With a reference to the detainees at Guantanamo Bay and an analogy with the Nazi concentration camps, Agamben says: "The novelty of President Bush's 'order' is that of radically erasing the juridical status of an individual, thereby producing a being that is juridically unnamable and unclassifiable" (*SdE*, 12). The similarity between this state of affairs and the situation which followed the Decree for the Protection of the People and of the State of 1933 in Germany, which Agamben also refers to in this work, cannot be stressed enough. In truth, it is not the sovereign who decides of the state of exception (as Schmitt holds), but the other way around: the violence that posits the state of exception also decides on sovereignty, on who is the sovereign—and in this sense Benjamin's critique of violence becomes fundamental here, especially his emphasis on the cruder form of violence represented by the police, where the separation between lawmaking and law-preserving is suspended. Particularly in democracies, the formless power and ghostly presence of the police bear "witness to the greatest conceivable degeneration of violence."[11] This is indeed what we are witnessing today at the global level, the polarization between sovereign power and naked life brought about by the politics of the new world order which gives the institution of the police a supra-national, alongside its national, character. Here, the violence which is inherent in lawmaking as "power making,"[12] because of its identity with law preserving, becomes immediately apparent. Thus, what the International Red Cross, speaking of the prisoners at the U.S. naval base at Guantanamo Bay, as well as of many others hidden "in lockups across the globe," has called "ghost detainees,"[13] clearly and painfully exemplifies the fact of naked life, or mere life, in our age; it proves Agamben's claim that the camp has become the paradigm of political modernity, a structure of everyday life.

What is important is that the state of exception surpasses the state of emergency, the state of war, and the state of siege in its indeterminacy and indefiniteness. With the temporary and progressive abolition of the distinction among legislative power, executive power, and juridical power, the state of exception tends toward "transforming itself into a lasting model of governance" (*SdE*, 17). Understanding the state of exception as a function of necessity implies aporetic conclusions, for it points toward a decision of what is ultimately undecidable, both from the point of view of life and of the law. The question of the *locus*, the "where," of the state of exception becomes important, given that the state of exception always presents itself as occupying a threshold and a zone of indifference between fact and right, life and the law—a movement of suspension, a neither/nor with respect to the juridical order. Agamben says: "In truth, the state of exception is neither external nor internal to the juridical order, and the question of its definition has in fact to do with a threshold, or a zone of indifference, in which inside and outside do not exclude each other, but rather determine each other" (*SdE*, 33–34). As he makes clear in the section on the Roman institution of *iustitium*, which literally means a "suspension of the law," "not simply a suspension of administrative justice, but of the law as such" (*SdE*, 56), the place of the state of exception, as such suspension, is really an "absolute non-place" (*SdE*, 67). It is only with modernity that the state of exception makes its appearance within the juridical order, that is, the "principle according to which necessity defines a peculiar situation whereby the law loses its *vis obligandi* . . . overturned into the principle according to which necessity constitutes, so to speak, the ultimate ground and the source of the law itself" (*SdE*, 37). This is, according to Agamben, the double meaning of the Latin saying *necessitas legem non habet*, "necessity does not recognize any law" and "necessity creates its own law," which, however, does not say that necessity creates or suspends the law as such; rather, it "limits itself to subtract one single case to the literal application of the norm" (*SdE*, 36). It is, then, what defines the state of exception proper, not its extension, within modernity and in the contemporary age, to the point that it becomes a general paradigm and thus no longer a state of exception. With a reference to the thought of the jurist Santi Romano, Agamben says: "Insofar as it is a figure of necessity, the state of exception thus presents itself—alongside the revolution and the de facto implementation of a constitutional ordinance—as a measure which is 'illegal,' yet perfectly 'juridical and constitutional,' which concretizes itself in the production of new norms (or of a new juridical order)" (*SdE*, 38). It is important to recall here how different the situation was in the case of the messianic law, where a non-normative figure of the law was opposed to the normative one (*TcR*, 91).

Speaking of the confusion between the state of exception and the dictatorship, Agamben says: "The state of exception is not a dictatorship . . . , but a space emptied of the law, a zone of anomy in which all juridical determinations . . . are disactivated" (*SdE*, 66). It is the neither/nor of the law. The disactivation of the law is what Agamben also considers in his comment on Paul, where it figures, as we have seen, as the concept of *katargeín*, proper to messianic law. The state of exception, which produces sovereign power as well as naked life, can be seen in a double sense. Exception can be a positive concept when it defines the messianic law (the anomic state: anomic with respect to all profane power) and the coming of a higher law, based on faith for Paul, ethical law in a more general sense. This is, of course, the state that also defines exception as the true revolution, which corresponds to its concept only insofar as it grounds itself in principles of universality, or, for Agamben, in the rest. But we have shown why there is really no need to renounce the concept of universality. Yet, exception is a negative concept when the disactivation of the law, brought about by decrees and ordinances that simply replace the law in virtue of their might (and it makes no difference whether the example considered is the Nazi decree of 1933 or Bush's "military order" of 2001), only engenders a no longer exceptional situation, one of systematic and systemic violence in the sense explained by Benjamin. It is at this point that Agamben deals with Benjamin's essay. He emphasizes the concept, central in Benjamin's work, of "pure" or "divine" violence, which is absolutely outside of and beyond the sphere of the law, and which becomes "revolutionary" violence within the human sphere (*SdE*, 69). For Agamben, proving the reality of this type of violence is the explicit task of Benjamin's critique. Here again we have the fundamental figure of the dis-activation of the law, for, as Agamben says, the "proper character of this violence is that it neither posits nor preserves the law, but rather deposes it, and thus inaugurates a new historical epoch" (*SdE*, 70). In this sense, Benjamin's pure violence corresponds to Schmitt's concept of sovereign violence as articulated in *Political Theology*. In *Homo Sacer*, Agamben distinguishes between sovereign violence and divine violence as follows: "Sovereign violence opens a zone of indistinction between law and nature, outside and inside, violence and law" (*HS*, 64). On the other hand, the "violence that Benjamin defines as divine is instead situated in a zone in which it is no longer possible to distinguish between exception and rule" (*HS*, 65). However, the fundamental difference between Schmitt and Benjamin lies in the fact that the latter sees in the institution of the police the degeneration of this form of violence: not indeed the distinction between lawmaking and law-preserving (i.e., the violence that poses the law and that which preserves it), but their blurring and identification in the suspension or deposition of the law brings to the fore the paradox of an exceptional situation which is no longer exceptional. For Benjamin, the revolutionary task is to oppose, to this form of degeneration, an "effective state of exception," in which the polarization between sovereign power and naked life is reduced and taken away. This is the meaning of the passage from Benjamin's eighth thesis on the philosophy of history, cited by Agamben at this point. Let me quote it: "The tradition of the oppressed teaches us that the 'state of emergency' in which we live is not the exception but the rule. We must attain to a conception of history that is in keeping with this insight. Then we shall clearly realize that it is our task to bring about a real state of emergency, and this will improve our position in the struggle against Fascism."[14] The meaning is clear: the violence that poses the state of exception, in which sovereign power reduces the richness and the potentiality of everyday life to mere or naked life, can only be countered by a real or effective state of exception that poses the revolution as the measure. Because this real, effective, or actual state of exception is the product of the *same type* of violence, an extremely important distinction must be made. The sameness of the violence that posits sovereign power, as it necessarily also posits naked life and revolutionary violence, is only ontological, not political. Ontological sameness means that the structure of potentiality and impotentiality is present in both manifestations—present as their source. However, the direction that each of them takes in actual history is what counts, from a political point of view, and this direction differs according to whether one and the same form of pure violence tends toward the particular and partial (as is the case with the regime of repression and control brought about by the polarization between sovereign power and naked life) or the universal and total (as is the case with real revolutionary violence). In the former case, we simply have a degeneration of the original, pure violence, which is no longer in touch with its ontological ground: a ridiculous duplicate, a caricature of what this original form was—but a dangerous one. To this form, which Benjamin calls "ignominious" (the form of the police), the entrance into history should be denied by all means necessary, as its eradication would only benefit the earth and, in Vico's phrase, this "world of nations." This is the form that produces the decree of 1933 and the military order of 2001. Yet, this is the form that wears the mask of progress and humanitarianism, and it is generally accepted as such. It is in this sense that Benjamin can continue his eighth thesis on the philosophy of history as follows: "One reason why Fascism has a chance is that in the name of progress its opponents treat it as a historical norm."[15] In the latter case, real revolutionary violence, we have a politics which is still informed by its ontological disposition, which cannot discriminate or establish the game of partiality, but is the motor of a coming totality, the image of "pure" law, as Agamben says, following Benjamin.[16] Politics is redefined, for Agamben, as the "action which cuts off the link between violence and the law" (*SdE*, 112). At the end of his book he says: "The state of exception has . . . today reached its utmost planetary unfolding. The normative aspect of the law can thus be obliterated with impunity and contradicted by a governmental violence which, while ignoring international law at the outside, and producing a permanent state of exception in its inside, still claims to be applying the law" (*SdE*, 111). This degeneration of the pure violence that posits and preserves the law, this institutionalization of violence by means of the systematic identification of the making of the law and its execution—a permanent state of exception which effectively cancels the law—is what calls forth an antagonistic state of exception, as Benjamin says, a movement of resistance, as well as of history formation and social change. That the state of exception has become the rule, that we live in the age of the suspension of the law, is what the work of Agamben constantly stresses. If what defines the state of exception is the impossibility to "distinguish transgression of the law from execution of the law" (*HS*, 57), then the transgression that appeals to a higher order of the law, the ethical order, the transgression that defines all instances of civil disobedience and anti-institutional practices, produces a passage from the empirically given (where the exception is the privilege of the police regime) into what-could-be, "the rest," to use Agamben's phrase in his study of Paul's letter; and this is the only meaningful movement, the only *philosophical* position (to end with Benjamin) in a world that has certainly lost meaning and which no longer sees the open.

. . .

By politicizing the whole history of Western metaphysics, Agamben shows how the paradigm of modern politics—namely, the state of exception in the specific reality of the concentration camp (a reality which, Agamben correctly stresses, is not limited to the Nazi episode and the totalitarian state)—has become the rule. This rule constitutes the biopolitical and thanatopolitical tendency of our age—a widespread reality, a sort of universal, certainly global, structure. Thus, in *Homo Sacer* Agamben says: "If today there is no longer any one clear figure of the sacred man [who can be killed but not sacrificed], it is perhaps because we are all virtually *homines sacri*" (*HS*, 115). However, what divides, but also unites in intimate relationship, sovereign power and naked life raises the question of what agency, within that relationship, might be able to find the principle of subversion of the relationship itself; in other words, what agency is capable of initiating, at the level of the neither/nor of the law, that is, the level of potentiality and freedom, a new directionality for "the time that remains," a new metaphysics, an ontology of liberation; or again, what agency will be able to bring about the "real state of exception" sought by Benjamin. The opposition between sovereign power and naked life brings to mind two other similar oppositions: between empire and the multitude and between capital and labor. In all of these oppositions, very similar in character, the question of what can subvert their order, at the ontological as well as practical level (an order which is defined by a fundamental antagonism), has to do with the question of the subject: where is the subject capable of exiting the ontology and politics of exception, the logic of subsumption and domination, typical of these relationships? At this point, we can give the name of *fictitious* state of exception to that to which Benjamin wishes to oppose a *real* state of exception. "Fictitious," not because it has no empirical reality, for it is beyond question that it does, but rather because it is no longer in touch with the ontological structure of neutrality from which it also originated. Having lost connection with the original ontological structure, it has in truth also lost ethical validity and legitimacy. The mere fact that it remains all-powerful gives it no validity or legitimacy. Acts of the crudest violence are possible, but this does not mean that they can be justified, for their existence depends exclusively on the temporary erasure of the twofold structure of potentiality and impotentiality, namely, on the erasure of true freedom. This type of state of exception, a fictitious or spurious one, is nothing but the imposition of a partial will on the totality of existence, of a particular interest on universality. Yet, the answer to our question must be looked for, precisely, in the direction of what is at the same time inside and outside, what grounds the exception itself, which in turn gives sovereignty, and that is the modality of neither/ nor, where potentiality is also impotentiality. The *real* state of exception is that which remains in touch with this fundamental structure, which does not erase freedom, and which does not, in accepting sovereignty, feel compelled to posit the opposite figure of naked life, for this real sovereignty does not depend on there being naked life. Instead, as a mode of universality and totality, every being becomes "sovereign"—and sovereignty as we understand it now cancels itself. Really, what cancels itself is sovereignty as domination, subsumption, and control: the sovereignty that is the product of what Nietzsche called *slave* morality, the morality of the last man, the sick man. In this sense, if all individuating differences are exceptional, then nothing really is. Moreover, whatever remains at the level of pure potentiality, that is, a potentiality which is at the same time impotentiality, is able to ground the contingent with a view to what, without descending into contingency, remains universally and univocally valid. We could call this the ethical moment, perhaps, in a Kantian sense. Yet this is also the sense that Agamben gives to ethics, notwithstanding his distance from the concept of universality (see, for instance, the discussion of scientific experiments on humans in part 3 of *Homo Sacer*).

The question of the subject calls forth the concept of the will, treated by Agamben in the section on *poiesis* and *praxis* in *The Man Without Content*. The will, the *rational* will in philosophers as different as Duns Scotus, Kant, and Gramsci, gives directionality to human action. For Agamben, the metaphysics of the will that characterizes Western thought is based on the blurring of the original Aristotelian distinction between *poiesis* (production) and *praxis* (action)—and the will is what initiates and sustains the movement of the latter (*MWC*, 68–93). The problem here, however, is that Aristotle's distinction, contrary to his own claim, can only have analytical, not ontological, value. In a different handling of the same problem, Etienne Balibar calls Marx's abolition of the distinction between *poiesis* and *praxis* "a revolutionary thesis," and I tend to agree with him.[17] In Western metaphysics, the unity of *poiesis* and *praxis* had already been accomplished by Vico—this is the meaning of his *poetic* metaphysics. This intentional unity, or abolition of the distinction, of *poiesis* and *praxis* is different from Agamben's thesis of a "blurring" of the original distinction. In recuperating, or originally establishing, the dialectical "passing over" (Balibar) of *poiesis* into *praxis* and of *praxis* into *poiesis*, a step forward is made in adequately addressing the question of the subject, of the revolutionary subject, of the agent of subversion of the modality of effective exception. What this would accomplish is the *diffusion* of exception itself, where the distinction between sovereign power and naked life is eliminated. The subject would be labor, principle of the good life—but, on the basis of the identity of *poiesis* and *praxis*, this would be a labor that has overcome the distinction between mere production and artistic production (that is, production as the exception and the extraordinary), as well as, of course, a labor which is no longer wage labor, having withdrawn into itself, returned to itself, and left the logic of capital spiraling in its own madness. Thus, according to a rigorous application, *in practice*, of the *principium individuationis* (treated by Agamben in *The Coming Community*),[18] each individuating difference, in its absolute self-identity, would find itself in a state of exception where sovereignty and naked life are both present, but not external to one another; or rather, a state in which if there is anything sovereign, it is precisely the fact of *this* naked life.

Selected Bibliography of Giorgio Agamben

1964

"Decadenza." *Futuro* 6 (May 27–June 27): 28–32.

1966

"La 121ª giornata di Sodoma e Gomorra." *Tempo presente* 11, nos. 3–4: 58–70.
"Favola e fato." *Tempo presente* 11, no. 6 (June): 18–21.
"Il pozzo di Babele." *Tempo presente* 11, no. 11 (November): 42–50.

1967

"Radure." *Tempo presente* 12, no. 6 (June): 53–54.

1968

"L'albero del linguaggio." *I problemi di Ulisse* 63 (September): 104–14.
"Ricerca della pietra e dell'ombra." *Nuovi argomenti* 11: 26–35.

1970

"Il Dio nuovo." *Nuovi argomenti* 20: 59–64.
"L'Sui limiti della violenza." *Nuovi argomenti* 17: 154–73.
"Tre poesie entre el alma y lo espodo." *Nuovi argomenti* 23–24: 166–70.
L'uomo senza contenuto. Milan: Rizzoli.

1972

"Il dandy e il feticcio." *I problemi di Ulisse* 71 (February): 9–23.
"José Bergamin." In *Decadenza dell'analfabetismo,* edited by José Bergamin,
    7–29. Milan: Rusconi.

1974

"I fantasmi di Eros: Interpretazione di un emblema psicologico." *Paragone: Rivista mensile di arte figurativa e letteratur* 25, no. 290 (April): 19–41.
"Risvegli." *Settanta* 5, no. 3 (May–June): 112–15.

1975

"Gli intellettuali e la menzogna." *Prospettive settanta* 1, no. 3 (October–December): 76–78.
"La poesia di Solmi e le 'epifanie.'" *Prospettive settanta* 1, no. 1 (April–June): 107–10.

1977

Stanze: La parola e il fantasma nella cultura occidentale. Turin: Einaudi.

1978

"Comedia: La svolta comica di Dante e la concezione della colpa." *Paragone: Rivista mensile di arte figurativa e letteratura* 29, no. 346 (December): 3–27.
Infanzia e storia: Distruzione dell'esperienza e origine della storia. Turin: Einaudi.
"Il principe e il ranocchio: Il problema del metodo in Adorno e in Benjamin." *Aut aut* 165–66 (May–August): 105–17.

1979

"Fiaba e figura." In *Fiaba di magia: Opere, 1962–1972; Novembre–dicembre 1979, Mantova Suzzara*, by Giosetta Fioroni, edited by Laura Baccaglioni, Edigio Del Canto, and Alberto Lui, 13–15. Mantua: Provincia di Mantova, Casa del Mantegna, and Suzzara: Galleria civica d'arte contemporanea.
"Gusto." In *Enciclopedia*, edited by Ruggero Romano, 6: 1019–38. Turin: Einaudi.

1980

"L'io, l'occhio, la voce." In *Monsieur teste*, by Paul Valéry, 9–24. Milan: Saggiatore.
"La parola e il sapere." *Aut aut* 179–80 (September–December): 155–66.
"La voce, la morte." *Alfabeta* 15–16 (July–August): 26.

1981

"Pascoli: Esperienza della lettera." *Alfabeta* 20 (January): 7–8.

1982

"Un importante ritrovamento di manoscritti di Walter Benjamin." *Aut aut* 189–90 (May–August): 4–6.

"Introduzione a Friedrich Heinle." *Aut aut* 189–90 (May–August): 26–29.

Il linguaggio e la morte: Un seminario sul luogo della negatività. Turin: Einaudi.

Opere. By Walter Benjamin. Edited by Giorgio Agamben. Turin: Einaudi, 1982–93.

"Pascoli e il pensiero della voce." In *Il fanciullino*, by Giovanni Pascoli, edited by Giorgio Agamben, 7–21. Milan: Feltrinelli.

"*Se. L'Assoluto e l''Ereignis.'" *Aut aut* 187–88 (January–April): 39–58.

"Il sogno della lingua: Per una lettura del Polifilo." *Lettere italiane* 34, no. 4 (October–December): 466–81.

"La trasparenza della lingua." *Alfabeta* 38–39 (July–August): 3–4.

"Walter Benjamin e il demonico: Felicità e redenzione storica nel pensiero di Benjamin." *Aut aut* 189–90 (May–August): 143–63.

1983

"La Glossolalie comme problème philosophique." *Discours psychanalytique* 6: 63–69.

"Lingua e storia: Categorie linguistiche e categorie storiche nel pensiero di Benjamin." In *Walter Benjamin: Tempo, storia, linguaggio*, edited by Lucio Belloi and Lorenzina Lotti, 65–82. Rome: Riuniti.

"L'origine e l'oblio: Su Victor Segalen." In *Risalire il Nilo: Mito, fiaba, allegoria*, edited by Ferruccio Masini and Giulio Schiavoni, 154–63. Palermo: Sellerio.

"Il silenzio del linguaggio." In *Margaritae*, edited by Paolo Bettiolo, 69–79. Venice: Arsenale.

1984

"Aby Warburg e la scienza senza nome." *Aut aut* 199–200 (January–April): 51–66.

"L'angelo della faccia: Per la pittura di Gianni Dessi." In *Gianni Dessi: Galleria Salvatore Ala, Milano, New York / Gianni Dessi: Salvatore Ala Gallery, New York, Milan*, translated by Suzanne Palermo. Milan and New York: Galleria Salvatore Ala.

"La cosa stessa." In *Di-segno: La giustizia nel discorso*, edited by Gianfranco Dalmasso, 1–12. Milan: Jaca.

"The Idea of Language: Some Difficulties in Speaking About Language." *Graduate Faculty Philosophy Journal* 10, no. 1: 141–49.

"L'idea del linguaggio." *Aut aut* 201 (May–June): 67–74.

1985

"Das Ende des Gedankens." *Akzente: Zeitschrift für Literatur* 32, no. 3 (June): 262–64.
"Hölderlin-Heidegger." *Alfabeta* 69 (February): 4–5.
"Idea del dettato." *Arsenale* 1 (January–March): 43–46.
"Idea della gloria." In *Dieter Kopp: Dipinti, acquarelli, disegni*, 5–7. Rome: De Luca.
"An Idea of Glory." *Flash Art* 124 (October–November): 80–81.
Idea della prosa. Milan: Feltrinelli.
"L'idée du langage." *Critique* 41, nos. 452–53 (January–February): 148–56.
"Le Philosophe et la muse." *Le Nouveau Commerce* 62–63 (Autumn): 73–90.
"Tradizione dell'immemorabile." *Il centauro* 13–14 (January–August): 3–12.

1986

"The Eternal Return and the Paradox of Passion." *Stanford Italian Review* 6, nos. 1–2: 9–17.
"Langue et histoire: Catégories historiques et catégories linguistiques dans la pensée de Benjamin." In *Walter Benjamin et Paris*, edited by Heinz Wismann, 793–807. Paris: du Cerf.
"Quattro glosse a Kafka." *Rivista di estetica* 26, no. 22: 37–44.
"Über die Schwerkraft." *Akzente: Zeitschrift für Literatur* 33, no. 1 (February): 79–81.

1987

"Bataille e Benjamin." *Lettera internazionale* 11 (January–March): 18–19.
"Bataille e il paradosso della sovranità." In *Georges Bataille: Il politico e il sacro*, edited by Jacqueline Risset, 115–19. Naples: Liguori.
"Los fantasmas de la melancholia." *Pasajes* 8: 5–22.
"Idée de la cesure et autres proses." *Poesie* 40, no. 1: 79–85.
"La passione dell'indifferenza." In *L'Indifferente*, by Marcel Proust, 7–22. Turin: Einaudi.
"Su *Le Livre du partage*." *Metaphorein* 9, no. 1: 43–47.
"The Thing Itself." *Sub-Stance* 162, no. 53: 18–28.

1988

"Bartelby non scrive più." *Il manifesto*, 3 March, 3.
"The Eternal Return and the Paradox of Passion." In *Nietzsche in Italy*, edited by Thomas Harrison, 9–17. Saratoga, CA: Anma Libri.

"Idee de la cesure et autres proses." *Poesie* 44: 79–84.

"Language and History in Benjamin." *Differentia: Review of Italian Thought* 2 (Spring): 169–83.

"La passion de la facticité." *Le Cahier* (du Collège international de philosophie): 63–84.

1989

"Guy Lardreau: *Fictions philosophiques et science-fiction; Récréation philosophique.*" In *L'Annuaire philosophique, 1988–1989*, edited by François Wahl, 185–98. Paris: Seuil.

"Il silenzio delle parole." In *In cerca di frasi vere*, by Ingeborg Bachmann, v–xv. Bari: Laterza.

"Sur Robert Walser." *Détail* (Autumn): 17–25.

"Violenza e speranza nell'ultimo spettacolo: Dal maggio francese a piazza Tian An Men." *Il manifesto*, 6 July, 1–2.

1990

"La caccia della lingua." *Il manifesto*, 23 January, 12.

"La comunitá che viene." In *Sentimenti dell'aldiqua: Opportunismo, paura, cinismo nell'etá del disincanto*, 67–88. Rome: Theoria.

La comunità che viene. Turin: Einaudi.

"Un enigma della Basca." *Marka* 27: 93–96.

"Glosse in margine ai *Commentari sulla società dello spettacolo.*" In *La società dello spettacolo: Commentari sulla società dello spettacolo*, by Guy Debord, 233–50. Milan: Sugarco.

"Jean-Claude Milner: Introduction à une science du langage." In *L'Annuaire philosophique, 1989–1990*, edited by François Wahl, 97–116. Paris: Seuil.

"Kommerell, o del gesto." In *Il poeta e l'indicibile: Saggi di letteratura tedesca*, by Max Kommerell, edited by Giorgio Agamben, vii–xv. Genoa: Marietti.

"'Pardes': L'Ecriture de la puissance." *Revue philosophique de la France et de l'étranger* 180, no. 2 (April–June): 131–45.

"Viaggio nell'Italia degli anni ottanta." *Marka* 28: 22–29.

1991

"Disappropriata maniera." In *Res amissa*, by Giorgio Caproni, edited by Giorgio Agamben. Milan: Garzanti.

Language and Death: The Place of Negativity. Translated by Karen E. Pinkus, with Michael Hardt. Minneapolis: University of Minnesota Press.

"Parole segrete del popolo senza luogo." *Luogo comune* 1: 40–42.

Rue Descartes: Collège international de philosophie. Edited by Giorgio Agamben et al. Paris: Albin Michel.

"Sovranità clandestine." *Luogo comune* 2 (January): 1.

"Violenza e speranza nell'ultimo spettacolo." In *I situazionisti*, 1–17. Rome: Manifestolibri.

1992

"L'Ange de l'apparence." In *Philosophes à vendre et autres écrits*, by Lucien de Samosate, 7–11. Paris: Rivages.

"Appunti sulla politica." *Derive approdi* (July): 10–11.

"La geste et la danse." *Revue d'esthétique* 22: 9–12.

"I giusti non si nutrono di luce." *Idra*: 5.

"Noten zur Geste." In *Postmoderne und Politik*, edited by Jutta Georg-Lauer, 97–107. Tübingen: Diskord.

"Pascoli e il pensiero della voce." In *Il fanciullino*, by Giovanni Pascoli, edited by Giorgio Agamben, 7–21. Milan: Feltrinelli.

"Polizia sovrana." *Luogo comune* 3: 1–2.

"Pour une éthique du cinema." *Trafic* 3: 49–52.

1993

The Coming Community. Translated by Michael Hardt. Minneapolis: University of Minnesota Press.

"La festa del tesoro nascosto." In *Per Elsa Morante*, 137–45. Milan: Linea d'ombra.

"Forma-di-vita." In *Politica*, 105–14. Naples: Cronopio.

Infancy and History: Essays on The Destruction of Experience. Translated by Liz Heron. London: Verso.

Stanzas: Word and Phantasm in Western Culture. Translated by Ronald L. Martinez. Minneapolis: University of Minnesota Press.

1994

"Dove inizia il nuovo esodo." *Derive approdi* 5–6 (Spring): 35–36.

"Felicità e redenzione storica nel pensiero di Walter Benjamin." In *Interiéurs*, by Pietro Finneli, 9–17. Piacenza: Tipleco.

"Lebens-Form." In *Gemeinschaften: Positionen zu einer Philosophie des Politischen*, edited by Joseph Vogl, 251–57. Frankfurt am Main: Suhrkamp.

"Maniere del nulla." In *Pezzi in prosa*, by Robert Walser, translated by Gino Giometti, 7–11. Macerata: Quodlibet.

"Le Philosophe et la muse." *Archives de philosophie* 57, no. 1 (January–March): 87–90.

"Soggetto e legame sociale nella contemporaneità." With Annalisa Davanzo, Massimo De Carolis, and Chiara Mangiarotti. *La psicoanalisi* 15: 185–204.

1995

"A propos de Jean-Luc Godard." *Le Monde*, 6 October, 11.
La città è nuda. Edited by Giorgio Agamben et al. Milan: Volontà.
"Il dettato della poesia." In *Poesie della fine del mondo; e, Poesie escluse*, by Antonio Delfini, edited by Daniele Garbuglia, ix–xx. Macerata: Quodlibet.
"Du noir." *Dédale* 1–2 (Autumn): 111–13.
Homo sacer: Il potere sovrano e la nuda vita. Turin: Einaudi.
Idea of Prose. Translated by Michael Sullivan and Sam Whitsitt. Albany: State University of New York Press.
"Politica." In *Segnalibro: Voci da un dizionario della contemporaneità.* Edited by Lucio Saviani. Naples: Liguori.
"Sauf les hommes et les chiens." *Libération*, 7 November, 37.
"Les Silence des mots." *Nouvelle Revue française* 508 (May): 1–10.
"Sovranità e biopolitica: Per una rifondazione dei concetti delle scienze umane." *Futuro anteriore* 1: 5–13.
"La vie nue." *Revue de littérature générale* 1: 410–11.
"We Refugees." *Symposium* 49, no. 2 (Summer): 114–19.

1996

"Bataille et le paradoxe de la souveraineté." *Liberté* 38, no. 3 (June): 87–95.
Categorie italiane: Studi di poetica. Venice: Marsilio.
"Corn: Dall'anatomia alla poetica." In *Le Moyen Âge dans la modernité: Mélanges offerts à Roger Dragonetti*, edited by Jean R. Scheidegger, Sabine Girardet, and Eric Hicks, 3–20. Paris: Champion.
"L'immaneza assoluta." *Aut aut* 276 (November–December): 39–57.
Introduction to *Alcune riflessioni sulla filosofia dell'hitlerismo*, by Emmanuel Levinas, translated by Andrea Cavalletti and Stefano Chiodi, 7–17. Macerata: Quodlibet.
Mezzi senza fine: Note sulla politica. Turin: Bollati Boringhieri.
"No amanece el cantor." In *En torno a la obra de José Ángel Valente*, edited by Amigos de la Residencia de Estudiantes, 47–57. Madrid: Alianza.
"The Passion of Facticity: Heidegger and the Problem of Love." In *The Ancients and the Moderns*, edited by Reginald Lilly, 211–29. Bloomington: Indiana University Press.
"Il talismano di Furio Jesi." In *Lettura del Bateau ivre di Rimbaud*, by Furio Jesi, 5–8. Macerata: Quodlibet.

"Violencia y esperanza en el último espectáculo / Violence and Hope in the Last Spectatcle." In *Situacionistas: Arte, política, urbanisme / Situationists: Art, Politics, Urbanism*, edited by Libero Andreotti and Xavier Costa, 73–81. Barcelona: Museu d'Art Contemporani de Barcelona/ACTAR.

1997

"The Camp as the Nomos of the Modern." In *Violence, Identity, and Self-Determination*, edited by Hent de Vries and Samuel Weber, 106–18. Stanford, CA: Stanford University Press.
"Cattive memorie." *Il manifesto*, 23 December.
"Les corps à venire." *Les Saisons de la danse* 292 (May): 6–8.
"Repetition and Stoppage: Guy Debord's Technique of Montage / Wiederholung und Stillstellung: Zur Kompositionstechnik der Filme Guy Debords." In *Documenta X: Documents*, edited by Jean-François Chevrier, 68–75. Ostfildern: Cantz.
"Gli uomini, i nomi . . . " *Derive Approdi* 14: 11.
"Vocation and Voice." *Qui Parle: Literature, Philosophy, Visual Arts, History* 10, no. 2 (Spring–Summer): 89–100.

1998

"Bartleby; o, Della contingenza." In *Bartleby: La formula della creazione*, by Giorgio Agamben and Gilles Deleuze, 47–92. Macerata: Quodlibet.
"Discorso sulla morte." In *Propilei: Diciasette pittori europei*, edited by Boris Brollo, 51. Naples: Lo Spazio.
"Du bon usage de la mémoire et de l'oubli." In *Exil*, edited by Antonio Negri, translated by François Rosso and Anne Querrien, 57–60. Paris: Mille et une nuits.
Homo Sacer: Sovereign Power and Bare Life. Translated by Daniel Heller-Roazen. Stanford, CA: Stanford University Press.
Image et mémoire. Translated by Marco Dell'Omodarme et al. Paris: Hoëbeke.
"Il Messia e il sovrano: Il problema della legge in Walter Benjamin." In *Anima e paura: Studi in onore di Michele Ranchetti*, edited by Bruna Bocchini Camaiani and Anna Scattigno, 11–22. Macerata: Quodlibet.
"Non più cittadini, ma solo nuda vita." Interview by Beppe Caccia. *Il manifesto*, 24 October.
"Politica dell'esilio." *Derive approdi* 16: 25–27.
Quel che resta di Auschwitz: L'archivio e il testimone; Homo sacer III. Turin: Bollati Boringhieri.
"Il testimone invisibile." Interview by Antonio Gnoli. *La repubblica*, 8 October, 38–39.

"Verità come erranza." In *Sulla verità*, edited by Massimo Dona, 13–17. Padua: Poligrafo.

1999

"Agamben, le chercheur d'homme." Interview by Jean-Baptiste Marongiu. *Libération*, 1 April, i–iii.
"Une Biopolitique mineure." Interview by Mathieu Potte-Bonneville and Stany Grelet. *Vacarme* 10 (Winter): 4–10.
The End of the Poem: Studies in Poetics. Translated by Daniel Heller-Roazen. Stanford, CA: Stanford University Press.
"La fin du poème." In *L'Orgueil de la littérature: Autour de Roger Dragonetti*, edited by Jacques Berchtold and Christopher Lucken-Christopher, 107–13. Geneva: Droz.
"La guerra e il dominio." *Aut aut* 293–94 (September–December): 22–23.
Introduction to *Contributo critico allo studio delle dottrine politiche del '600 italiano*, edited by Giorgio Manganelli, 7–18. Macerata: Quodlibet.
"El lenguaje y la muerte: Séptima jornada." In *Teorias sobre la lírica*, edited by Fernando Cabo Aseguinolaza, 105–26. Madrid: Arco/Libros.
The Man Without Content. Translated by Georgia Albert. Stanford, CA: Stanford University Press.
"Per un autoritratto di Furio Jesi." With Andrea Cavalleti. *Cultura tedesca* 12 (December): 9–10.
Potentialities: Collected Essays in Philosophy. Edited and translated, with an introduction, by Daniel Heller-Roazen. Stanford, CA: Stanford University Press.
Remnants of Auschwitz: The Witness and the Archive. Translated by Daniel Heller-Roazen. New York: Zone Books.

2000

"Una lettera alla modernità." Interview by Antonio Gnoli. *La repubblica*, 14 June, 51.
Means Without End: Notes on Politics. Translated by Vincenzo Binetti and Cesare Casarino. Minneapolis: University of Minnesota Press.
Il tempo che resta: Un commento alla Lettera ai Romani Turin: Bollati Boringhieri.

2001

Infanzia e storia: Distruzione dell'esperienza e origine della storia. Turin: Einaudi.
"Un possibile autoritratto di Gianni Carchia." *Il manifesto*, 7 July, 18.
"Stato e terrore: Un abbraccio funesto." *Il manifesto*, 27 October.

"Das unheilige Leben." Interview by Hanna Leitgeb and Cornelia Vismann. *Literaturen* 2, no. 1: 16–22.

2002

L'aperto. Turin: Bollati Boringhieri.
"L'Etat d'exception." *Le Monde,* 12 December.
"Europe des libertés ou Europe des polices?" *Le Monde,* 3 October, 16.
"The Time That Is Left." *Epoché* 7, no. 1 (Fall): 1–14.

2003

"Une guerre contre l'Europe." Interview by Tiziana Mian. *Le Figaro,* 7 April.
L'ombre de l'amour. With Valeria Piazza. Paris: Rivages.
Stato di eccezione. Turin: Bollati Boringhieri.

2004

"L'Elegie de Sokourov." Cahiers du cinema, no. 586 (January): 49–50.
"Friendship." *Contretemps,* no. 5 (December).
Introduction to *La linea e il circolo: Studio logico-filosofico sull'analogia,* by Enzo Melandri. Macerata: Quodlibet.
"Life, a Work of Art Without an Author: The State of Exception, the Administration of Disorder, and Private Life." Interview by Ulrich Raulff. *German Law Journal* 5, no. 5 (May): 609–14. www.germanlawjournal.com/article.php?id=437# ednref8 (accessed 12 October 2006).
"No to Bio-Political Tattooing." *Le Monde,* 10 January.
The Open: Man and Animal. Translated by Kevin Attell. Stanford, CA: Stanford University Press.

2005

Introduction to *La trasparenza delle immagini: Averroè e l'averroismo,* by Emanuele Coccia. Milan: Mondadori.
State of Exception. Translated by Kevin Attell. Chicago: Chicago University Press.
The Time That Remains: A Commentary on the Letter to the Romans. Translated by Patricia Dailey. Stanford, CA: Stanford University Press.

Notes

THE WORK OF MAN

1. Passages from Aristotle are based on the English translations in *The Complete Works of Aristotle*, edited by Jonathan Barnes (Princeton, NJ: Princeton University Press, 1984). They have been modified to reflect Agamben's own translations of the texts.

2. Passages from Dante are based on the English translation in *Monarchy*, edited and translated by Prue Shaw (Cambridge: Cambridge University Press, 1996). They have been modified to reflect Agamben's own translation of the text.

BARE LIFE OR SOCIAL INDETERMINACY?

1. Frantz Fanon, *The Wretched of the Earth* (New York: Grove Press, 1968), 130.

THE COMPLEXITIES OF SOVEREIGNTY

1. For two essays that are particularly pertinent on this point, see Bonnie Honig, "Declarations of Independence: Arendt and Derrida on the Problem of Founding a Republic," *American Political Science Review* (Winter 1991): 97–113; and Alan Keenan, "Promises, Promises: The Work of Arendt," *Political Theory* (May 1994): 297–322.

2. Rousseau, *On the Social Contract: With Geneva Manuscript and Political Economy*, translated by Judith Masters (New York: St. Martin's, 1978), bk. 1, 46. I discuss this paradox with respect to the relation between territory, global politics, and democracy in chapter 5 of *The Ethos of Pluralization* (Minneapolis: University of Minnesota Press, 1995). A thoughtful and detailed engagement with its effect on Rousseau's theory is developed by Steven Johnston in *Encountering Tragedy: Rousseau and the Project of the Democratic Order* (Ithaca, NY: Cornell University Press, 1999).

3. Rousseau, *On the Social Contract*, 69–70.

4. I explore an ethos of multidimensional pluralism as an alternative to the ethos of the nation in chapter 3 of *Why I Am Not a Secularist* (Minneapolis: University of Minnesota Press, 1999).

5. Alexis de Tocqueville, *Democracy in America*, translated by George Lawrence, 2 vols. (New York: Harper and Row, 1969), 58.

6. Ibid., 336. I explore Tocqueville's rendering of the relation between the Christian civilization of America and Amerindians who were excluded by it in *The Ethos of Pluralization*, chap. 6.

7. Tocqueville, *Democracy in America*, 294.

8. Gilles Deleuze and Félix Guattari, *A Thousand Plateaus*, translated by Brian Massumi (Minneapolis: University of Minnesota Press, 1987), 214.

9. *Empire* (Cambridge, MA: Harvard University Press, 2000). Pages for the quotations to follow are given in the text of the chapter.

10. For a thoughtful review of *Empire* that explores the meaning and role of the multitude, see Kam Shapiro, "From Dream to Desire: At the Threshold of Old and New Utopias," *Theory & Event*, http://muse.jhu.edu/journals/theory _and_ event/v004/4.4r_kam.html.

11. Even when the planet was crystallizing into the earth, a "decisive reason why it was able to hold on to these volatile layers of melted comets was the emergence of living organisms that regulated crucial climatic conditions and kept them constant." Tor Nørretranders, *The User Illusion*, translated by Jonathan Sydenham (New York: Viking Press, 1998), 340.

BOUNDARY STONES

1. Jean Bodin, *On Sovereignty*, translated by Julian H. Franklin (Cambridge: Cambridge University Press, 1992), 1.

2. R. P. Wolff, *The Conflict Between Authority and Autonomy* (Oxford: Basil Blackwell, 1990), 20.

3. Michael Hardt and Antonio Negri, *Multitude: War and Democracy in the Age of Empire* (New York: Penguin Press, 2004), 332.

4. Maurizio Lazzarato, "From Biopower to Biopolitics," *Pli* 13 (2002): 100–111.

5. Carl Schmitt, *Political Theology: Four Chapters on the Concept of Sovereignty*, translated by George Schwab (Cambridge, MA: MIT Press, 1985), quoted in *HS*, 16.

6. Schmitt, *Political Theology*, quoted in Agamben, *HS*, 15.

7. The Code of Hammurabi, line 154: "If a man be guilty of incest with his daughter, he shall be driven from the place (exiled)."

8. Aristotle, *Aristotle's Politics*, translated by Benjamin Jowett, edited by Stephen Everson (Cambridge: Cambridge University Press, 1988), 71–72.

9. Ibid., 72.

10. Ibid.

11. Thomas Hobbes, *Leviathan*, translated by Edwin Curley (Indianapolis: Hackett Publishing, 1994), 138–39; emphasis added.

12. Aristotle, *Aristotle's Politics*, 73.

13. A. H. J. Greenidge, *The Legal Procedure of Cicero's Time* (Oxford: Oxford University Press, 1901), 509.

14. Justinian, *The Institutes of Justinian*, translated by Thomas Collett Sanders (New York: Longmans, Green, 1910), bk. 1, chap. 16.

15. Ibid.

16. Marcus Tullius Cicero, "Orations for His House," in *The Orations of Marcus Tullius Cicero*, translated by and edited by Charles Duke Yonge (London: G. Bell, 1894–1903), XXIX.

17. Bearing in mind the conventional use of the interdiction, and the actions that typical triggered the state to take these punitive measures, Thomas Collett Sanders explains in his commentary in the 1910 edition of the *Institutes*:

> There was always something of a public character in the reasons which induced the praetor to grant an interdict. He adopted it as a speedy and sure remedy in cases where danger was threatened to an object which public policy is especially interested to preserve uninjured, such as public roads and waters, burial-grounds, or sacred places; and though interdicts were granted where the quarrel was entirely between private parties, it was originally, perhaps, only when the subject of dispute was such as to render a breach of the public peace.

Sanders, in Justinian, *The Institutes of Justinian*, bk. 1, chap. 16.

18. Cicero, "Orations for His House," in *The Orations of Marcus Tullius Cicero*, XXX.

19. On this point, it is perhaps instructive to call to mind the religious precedent which remains paradigmatic of all such punitive withdrawals, the *poena damni*. From the earliest times, Christianity has maintained that, for the souls of those who have been damned, punishment is not originally the fires of hell but the pain of loss, the *poena damni*, the loss of the beatific vision. Together with the loss of all supernatural gifts, including faith, it is the loss of the vision of God and the catastrophic withdrawal of God's concern that inflicts suffering. Damnation is a subtraction, an exclusion, an abandonment. No longer in the presence of God, and having been excluded from the protection of divine law, the damned seek in vain a place to rest. The Greek *Haides*, from the privative form of the root *fid*, "to see," denotes this unseen, dark place beyond the reach of God's sight. No longer in God's presence and excluded from the sovereign field of divine law, the souls of the damned, like bare life, suffer the exposure of exile.

20. Justinian, *The Institutes of Justinian*, bk. 1, chap. 12, 1–2.

21. Cesare Beccaria, *On Crimes and Punishments*, edited by Adolph Caso (Boston: International Pocket Library, 1992), 58–59. Note that in this passage we once again find that banishment is applied to those who "disturb the public tranquility," rather than merely to those who break laws. One can reference numerous similar cases, for instance, Montesquieu who, in *The Spirit of the Laws* (bk. 12, chap. 4), writes:

> There are four sorts of crimes. Those of the first kind run counter to religion; those of the second, to mores; those of the third, to tranquillity; those of the fourth, to the

security of the citizens. The penalties inflicted should derive from the nature of each of these kinds. The crimes of the third class are those that run counter to the citizen's tranquillity, and the penalties for them should be drawn from the nature of the thing and relate to that tranquillity, such as deprivation, exile, corrections, and other penalties that restore men's troubled spirits and return them to the established order.

Charles Louis de Secondat, Baron de Montesquieu, *The Spirit of Laws*, 4 vols. (London: T. Evans, 1777), 218.

22. Cassius Dio, *Roman History*, translated by Earnest Cary, 9 vols. (Cambridge, MA: Harvard University Press, 1914–27), bk. 38, chap. 17.

23. Hobbes, *Leviathan*, 112.

24. Bodin, *Six Books of the Commonwealth*, translated by M. J. Tooley (Oxford: Basil Blackwell, 1955), bk. 2, chap. 5.

25. Ibid.; emphasis added.

26. It is interesting to note that, according to the legend, Rome, under Romulus, was established as a place of refuge for exiles and outlaws.

27. Livy, *The History of Rome*, translated by Canon Roberts (New York: E. P. Dutton, 1912–24), bk. 1, chap. 45.

28. According to William Smith's lexicon, the custom of making a *pomoerium* was common to the Latins and Etruscans, and the manner in which it was done in the earliest times, when a town was to be founded, was as follows:

> A bullock and a heifer were yoked to a plough, and a furrow was drawn around the place which was to be occupied by the new town, in such a manner that all the clods fell inward. The little mound thus formed was the symbolical wall, and along it ran the *pomoerium*, within the compass of which alone the city-auspices could be taken. . . . This custom was also followed in the building of Rome, and the Romans afterwards observed it in the establishment of their colonies. The sacred line of the Roman *pomoerium* did not prevent the inhabitants from building upon or taking into use any place beyond it, but it was necessary to leave a certain space on each side of it unoccupied so as not to unhallow it by profane use.

William Smith, "Postliminium," in *A Dictionary of Greek and Roman Antiquities* (London: John Murray, 1875).

29. The mythological origins of this prohibition appear in the rituals accompanying the god Terminus, the god of boundaries and the protector of the limits both of private property and of the public territory of Rome, who was represented iconographically by a stone or post. According to the 1911 edition of the *Encyclopaedia Britannica*, the placement of new stones was accompanied by a ceremony: "a trench was dug, in which a fire was lighted; a victim was sacrificed, and its blood poured into the trench; the body, upon which incense and fruits, honey and wine were thrown, was then cast into the fire. When it was entirely consumed, the boundary stone, which had been previously anointed and crowned with garlands, was placed upon the hot ashes and fixed in the ground. . . . Any one who removed a boundary stone was accursed (*sacer*) and might be slain with impunity." The

importance of these boundaries is made even more apparent when we learn that the Sabine prince Titus Tatius had dedicated a stone to Terminus on the Capitoline Hill. When Tarquinius Superbus later wished to build a temple to Jupiter on the same spot, the auguries prohibited the removal of the stone—"an indication of the immovability of such stones and of the permanence of the Roman territory." *Encyclopaedia Britannica* (1911), s.v. "Terminus."

30. The reference is from "Of the Right of *postliminum*," in Hugo Grotius, *The Rights of War and Peace* (1625):

> Amidst a great variety of opinions, upon the meaning of the word, postliminium, that of Scaevola seems the most natural, who derives it from the word *post*, signifying a return after captivity, and *limen* the boundary or entrance of the house, or from *limes*, a public boundary. Thus the ancients called exile or banishment, *eliminium*, that is, sending any one out of the boundaries of the country. . . . Postliminium therefore, according to its original signification, means the right, accruing to any one in consequence of his return home from captivity. (bk. 3, chap. 9)

Hugo Grotius, *The Rights of War and Peace*, translated by A. C. Campbell (New York: M. Walter Dunne, 1901), bk. 3, chap. 9.

31. See also James Muirhead's *Law of Rome*:

> Take some of those offences whose recognized sanction was *sacratio capitis*. Breach of duty, resulting from the fiduciary relation between patron and client, maltreatment of a parent by his child, exposure or killing of a child by its father contrary to the Romulian rules, the ploughing up or removal of a boundary stone, the slaughter of a plough-ox,—all these were capital offences; the offender, by formula *sacer esto*, was devoted to the infernal gods. Festus says that although the rules of divine law did not allow that he should be offered as a sacrifice to the deity he had especially offended (*nec fas est eum immolari*), yet he was so utterly beyond the pale of the law and its protection that any one might kill him with impunity.

James Muirhead, *Law of Rome* (New York: Macmillan, 1985), 50.

32. I discuss this point further, and with respect to Johann Herder, in Steven DeCaroli, "Tarrying on the Threshold: Nationalism and the Exemplary," in *Defining Nations in Enlightenment Europe/Interfaces artistiques et littéraires dans l'Europe des Lumières*, edited by Allan Ingram and Elisabeth Détis (Montpellier: Université Paul Valéry, 2004), 145–58.

33. See Cicero, "Pro Caecina" (For Caecina).

34. Hobbes, *Leviathan*, 207.

35. Hobbes suggests the liberty of exile in *The Elements of Law Natural and Politic*, where a parallel is drawn between the release of a slave from bondage and the exile of a citizen from the commonwealth: "Servants immediate to the supreme master, are discharged of their servitude or subjection in the same manner that subjects are released of their allegiance in a commonwealth institutive. As first, by release; for he that captiveth (which is done by accepting what the captive transferreth to him) setteth again at liberty, by transferring back the same. And this kind

of release is called MANUMISSION. Secondly, by exile; for that is no more but manumission given to a servant, not in the way of benefit, but punishment" (pt. 1, chap. 22, para. 7). Thomas Hobbes, *The Elements of Law Natural and Politic* (1640).

36. Aristotle, *Politics*, 113.

37. I would like to thank Goucher College and the Beatrice Aitchison Faculty Professional Advancement Fund for generously supporting my research for this project. I would also like to express my appreciation to Jason Read and Fouad Kalouche, who read an earlier version of this chapter and provided helpful suggestions for revision.

WHATEVER POLITICS

This chapter builds on my earlier work with Véronique Pin-Fat, and I am very much in her debt for the stimulating conversations we have had on this topic and others over many years of collaboration in crime. Thanks are also due to Michael Dillon, Stuart Elden, Marie Suetsugu, Hidemi Suganami, Nick Vaughan-Williams, and Maja Zehfuss for their detailed comments on a first draft of this chapter, and Rens Van Munster for very helpful pointers. Mistakes no doubt remain, and are, of course, mine.

1. The tetralogy includes Agamben, *HS*, *SE*, and *RA*.

2. For example, Giorgio Agamben, "Über Sicherheit und Terror" (On Security and Terror), *Frankfurter Allgemeine Zeitung*, 20 September 2001; and Giorgio Agamben, "No to Bio-Political Tattooing," *Le Monde*, 10 January 2004.

3. See, for example, Carsten B. Laustsen and Bulent Diken, *Culture of Exception: Sociology Facing the Camp* (London: Routledge, 2005); Bulent Diken and Carsten Bagge Laustsen, "Zones of Indistinction: Security, Terror and Bare Life," *Space and Culture* 5, no. 3 (2002): 290–307; Jenny Edkins, Véronique Pin-Fat, and Michael J. Shapiro, eds., *Sovereign Lives: Power in Global Politics* (New York: Routledge, 2004); Jenny Edkins and R. B. J. Walker, eds., *Zones of Indistinction: Territories, Bodies, Politics* (Boulder, CO: Lynne Rienner, 2000); Jef Huysmans, "Minding Exceptions: The Politics of Insecurity and Liberal Democracy," *Contemporary Political Theory* 3, no. 3 (2004): 321–41; Rens Van Munster, "The War on Terrorism: When the Exception Becomes the Rule," *International Journal for the Semiotics of Law* 17, no. 2 (2004): 141–53; Andrew Neal, "Cutting Off the King's Head: Foucault's *'Society Must Be Defended'* and the Problem of Sovereignty," *Alternatives: Global, Local, Political* 29, no. 4 (2004): 373–98; Mika Ojakangas, "Impossible Dialogue on Bio-Power: Agamben and Foucault," *Foucault Studies*, no. 2 (2005): 5–28; Sergei Prozorov, "Three Theses on 'Governance' and the Political," *Journal of International Relations and Development* 7, no. 3 (2004): 267–93; Sergei Prozorov, "X/Xs: Toward a General Theory of the Exception," *Alternatives: Global, Local, Political* 30, no. 1 (2005): 81–112; Prem Kumar Rajaram and Carl Grundy-Warr, "The Irregular Migrant as Homo Sacer: Migration and Detention in Australia, Malaysia and Thailand," *International Migration* 42, no. 1 (2004): 33–64.

4. Antonio Negri, "The Ripe Fruit of Redemption," *Il manifesto*, 26 July 2003. For a discussion of the relationship between Negri and Agamben, see Brett Neilson, "*Potenza Nuda?* Sovereignty, Biopolitics, Capitalism," *Contretemps* 5 (2004): 63–78.

5. Stefano Franchi, "Passive Politics," *Contretemps* 5 (2004): 30–41; 30.

6. Jenny Edkins, "Sovereign Power, Zones of Indistinction and the Camp," *Alternatives* 25, no. 1 (2000): 3–25; 21. Most recently, see Michael Dillon, "Cared to Death: The Biopoliticised Time of Your Life," *Foucault Studies*, no. 2 (2005): 37–46.

7. R. B. J. Walker, "Sovereignties, Exceptions, Worlds," in *Sovereign Lives: Power in Global Politics*, ed. Edkins, Pin-Fat, and Shapiro, 239–49.

8. William E. Connolly, "The Complexities of Sovereignty," included in the present volume, also in *Sovereign Lives: Power in Global Politics*, 23–40; 29.

9. Michel Foucault, *Power: Essential Works of Foucault, 1954–1984*, vol. 3 (New York: New Press, 2000).

10. Ulrich Raulff, "Interview with Giorgio Agamben—Life, a Work of Art Without an Author: The State of Exception, the Administration of Disorder, and Private Life," *German Law Journal* 5, no. 5 (May 2004): 609–14, www.germanlaw-journal.com/article.php?id=437# ednref8 (accessed 12 October 2006).

11. Jean-Luc Nancy, *The Inoperative Community* (Minneapolis: Minnesota University Press, 1991); *Being Singular Plural*, translated by Robert D Richardson and Anne E. O'Byrne (Stanford, CA: Stanford University Press, 2000).

12. It is important to note that "sovereignty" here does not refer to the sovereign territorial state but to a form of authority, sovereign power, that operates through the sovereign ban or practices of inclusive exclusion. This is a more extensive use of the term "sovereignty" than is usual in many writings on politics and international politics. Though states exemplify sovereign power, so do other entities.

13. Jacques Derrida, "Remarks on Deconstruction and Pragmatism," in *Deconstruction and Pragmatism*, edited by Chantal Mouffe (London: Routledge, 1966), 77–88; 83.

14. This is reminiscent of Jacques Derrida's differentiation between the *qui* and the *quoi*, the who and the what, in his discussions of "love" and "forgiveness." It is interesting to note also at this point the notion of exposed singularity in Jean-Luc Nancy. See, for example, Derrida, *Politics of Friendship*; and Nancy, *The Inoperative Community; Being Singular Plural*.

15. See, among many others, Stuart Hall, "Religious Ideologies and Social Movements in Jamaica," in *Religion and Ideology: A Reader*, edited by Robert Bocock and Kenneth Thompson (Manchester: Manchester University Press, 1985), 269–96; bell hooks, *Ain't I a Woman: Black Women and Feminism* (London: Pluto Press, 1981); Aletta Norval, *Deconstructing Apartheid Discourse* (London: Verso, 1996); Ernesto Laclau, ed., *The Making of Political Identities* (London: Verso, 1994).

16. In *The Coming Community* Agamben uses the term "the state"; in later works he speaks more in terms of "sovereign power." The latter terminology is preferable; Agamben is concerned with a form of authority that is not dependent on the territorial state as an institution (Jenny Edkins and Véronique Pin-Fat, "Life, Power, Resistance," in *Sovereign Lives: Power in Global Politics*, 1–21).

17. Or, to expand a little here, with the production of "population" as a "problem" through or alongside the emergence of specific techniques of governance. Michel Foucault, "Governmentality," in *Power*, 3: 201–22; 215.

18. Clearly Foucault attaches importance to the emergence of the category of "population" as such, whereas Agamben, here at least, focuses on the biopolitical body.

19. Among many others see, for example, my discussion in Jenny Edkins, *Trauma and the Memory of Politics* (Cambridge: Cambridge University Press, 2003), 178–82. See also the account in Catherine Mills, "Agamben's Messianic Politics: Biopolitics, Abandonment and Happy Life," *Contretemps* 5 (2004): 42–62.

20. Or, rather, perhaps, the *attempted* or *claimed* distinction of *zoē* and *bios*. There are two points worth making briefly here. First, as subsequent sentences clarify, this distinction is one of inclusive exclusion rather than one that successfully and unproblematically (or metaphysically, perhaps) delineates two opposites; such an unproblematic distinction would be impossible. Second, Agamben is arguing that a particular passage in Aristotle which makes this distinction "became canonical for the political tradition of the West" and foundational for the operation of sovereign power in its initial historical phases (*HS*, 2). Later, the distinction no longer functioned in the same way. See also Jacques Derrida, *Rogues: Two Essays on Reason*, translated by Pascale-Anne Brault and Michael Naas (Stanford, CA: Stanford University Press, 2005), 24; and Stuart Elden, "Heidegger's Animals" (unpublished paper, 2005).

21. *Ban* is a term that Agamben takes from Jean-Luc Nancy. Nancy remarks that the law of abandonment applies to the abandoned being through its withdrawal ("Abandoned Being," in Jean-Luc Nancy, *The Birth to Presence* [Stanford, CA: Stanford University Press, 1993], 36–47; 44).

22. Whereas *inclusive exclusion* characterises the exception, the example, as the other way in which a set maintains its coherence, functions as an *exclusive inclusion* (*HS*, 21–22).

23. For a discussion of the refusal to draw lines or make distinctions between forms of life as a contestation of sovereign violence, see Jenny Edkins and Véronique Pin-Fat, "Through the Wire: Relations of Power and Relations of Violence," *Millennium: Journal of International Studies* 34, no. 1 (2005): 1–26; and "Life, Power, Resistance."

24. In other words the force that institutes the system of law and the force that enforces the law (Jacques Derrida, "Force of Law: The 'Mystical Foundation of Authority,'" in *Deconstruction and the Possibility of Justice*, edited by David Gray

Carlson, Drucilla Cornell, and Michel Rosenfeld (New York: Routledge, 1992), 3–67.

25. For an interesting discussion of the work of Paolo Virno and his engagement with the question of potentiality and labor power, see Neilson, "*Potenza Nuda?*" Neilson argues that, in contradistinction to Agamben, Virno rejects the notion of an indistinction between potentiality and actuality in favor of the view that "potential and act relate to each other as the general capacity to language (or what Saussure calls *langage*) relates to the enunciation of language (*parole*) or as the general capacity for labor (what Marx called *labor-power*) relates to the empirical act of labor itself" (Neilson, "*Potenza Nuda?*" 75). For Marx, labor-power is "the aggregate of all those mental and physical capabilities existing in a human being," or in other words "the *common name* of all potentials" (Neilson, "*Potenza Nuda?*" 77).

26. For Agamben's earlier work on potentiality see Giorgio Agamben, *P*, in particular the essays in parts 3 and 4.

27. As a constitutive outside in Derridean terms. Henry Staten, *Wittgenstein and Derrida* (Oxford: Basil Blackwell, 1984).

28. Daniel Heller-Roazen, "Editor's Introduction: 'To Read What Was Never Written,'" in *P*, 1–23; 16.

29. Ibid., 17.

30. The Italian *nuda vita* has been translated into English both as *bare life* and as *naked life* (see *MWE*, 143, translators' note 1).

31. Primo Levi, *The Drowned and the Saved*, translated by Raymond Rosenthal (London: Abacus, 1989), 23.

32. Primo Levi, *If This Is a Man and the Truce*, translated by Stuart Woolf (London: Abacus, 1979), 96.

33. Levi, *The Drowned and the Saved*, 63.

34. Ibid., 64.

35. Ibid.

36. Ibid.

37. Ibid., 62.

38. Ibid., 63.

39. Or rather, according to Alexander García Düttmann, not the witness but "testimony as that which consists of an always-already and a never-before, and which is but a call to testimony" ("Never Before, Always Already: Notes on Agamben and the Category of Relation"), *Angelaki: Journal of the Theoretical Humanities* 6, no. 3 (2001): 3–6.

40. The parallels here with Jacques Lacan's notion of the subject as a divided or split subject and the subject of a lack are interesting: "Once the subject himself comes into being, he owes it to a certain nonbeing upon which he raises up his being" (Lacan, quoted in Bruce Fink, *The Lacanian Subject: Between Language and Jouissance*) (Princeton, NJ: Princeton University Press, 1995), 33.

41. We must be careful, enjoins Agamben, of repeating the gesture "by which one thing . . . must be separated and effaced for human life to be assigned to subjects as property" (*RA*, 158).

42. The use of the term *man* is deeply problematic here, as in Agamben's other work (Jenny Edkins, "Sovereign Power, Bare Life, and the Camp," *Alternatives* 24, nos. 3–4 (2000): 3–25; 5; Dinesh Wadiwel, "Animal by Any Other Name? Patterson and Agamben Discuss Animal (and Human) Life," *Borderlands e-journal* 3, no. 1 (2004), www.borderlandsejournal.adelaide.edu.au/vol3no1_2004/wadiwel_animal. htm (accessed 12 October 2006); Adam Thurschwell, "Specters of Nietzsche: Potential Futures for the Concept of the Political in Agamben and Derrida," Cleveland State University, Cleveland-Marshall College of Law faculty Web pages, www.law. csuohio.edu/faculty/thurschwell/nietzsche.pdf (2002) (accessed 12 October 2006).

43. In *The Open* Agamben analyses in some detail Heidegger's view of Dasein as an animal that is aware of its own captivation: for Heidegger "this awakening of the living being to its own being-captivated, this anxious and resolute opening to a not-open, is the human" (*O*, 70).

44. For two excellent discussions that bring out some of the difficulties with this text, see Rens van Munster, "Review Essay: Girogio Agamben," *Leiden Journal of International Law* 17 (2004): 833–40; and Wadiwel, "Animal by Any Other Name?"

45. For a discussion of Heidegger and animality that also challenges Agamben's separation of *zoē* and *bios*, see Elden, "Heidegger's Animals."

46. Connolly, "The Complexities of Sovereignty," 29–30.

47. Mills, "Agamben's Messianic Politics"; for another detailed comparison of Agamben and Derrida, see Thurschwell, "Specters of Nietzsche."

48. Mills, "Agamben's Messianic Politics," 57.

49. Derrida, *Politics of Friendship*, 81.

50. I am indebted to Marie Suetsugu for drawing my attention to this point.

51. Derrida, *Politics of Friendship*, 80–81.

52. Nancy, *Being Singular Plural*, 3.

53. Ibid.

54. Ibid.

55. Ibid., 17.

56. Ibid., 99.

57. Nancy, *The Inoperative Community*, 35.

58. Ibid.

59. This is Žižekian terminology. Slavoj Žižek, *The Sublime Object of Ideology* (London: Verso, 1989).

60. Edkins, *Trauma and the Memory of Politics*, 214.

61. Edkins and Pin-Fat, "Through the Wire."

62. Jacques Derrida and Elisabeth Roudinesco, *For What Tomorrow . . . : A Dialogue*, translated by Jeff Fort (Stanford, CA: Stanford University Press, 2004), 65.

63. Jacques Derrida, "Remarks on Deconstruction and Pragmatism," 83.

64. Ibid.

65. Ibid., 83–84.

66. Ibid., 84.

FROM SOVEREIGN BAN TO BANNING SOVEREIGNTY

1. Alfred North Whitehead and Bertrand Russell, *Principia Mathematica*, 3 vols. (Cambridge: Cambridge University Press, 1910), 1: 40.

2. See Bertrand Russell, "Mathematical Logic as Based on the Theory of Types," *American Journal of Mathematics* 30 (1908): 222–62.

3. In his preface to the first American edition of his *Laws of Form*, George Spencer Brown claims the following: "Recalling Russell's connexion with the Theory of Types, it was with some trepidation that I approached him in 1967 with the proof that it was unnecessary. To my relief he was delighted. The Theory was, he said, the most arbitrary thing he and Whitehead had ever had to do, not really a theory but a stopgap, and he was glad to have lived long enough to see the matter resolved" (*Laws of Form* [New York: E. P. Dutton, 1979], xiii–xiv). For a résumé of his purported proof, see pages xiv–xv.

4. Ludwig Wittgenstein, *Tractatus Logico-Philosophicus*, translated by D. F. Pears and B. F. McGuinness (London: Routledge, 1961), 62–63.

5. James Brown Scott, *The Spanish Conception of International Law and of Sanctions*, Carnegie Endowment for International Peace, Division of International Law, pamphlet no. 54 (Washington, DC: Carnegie Endowment for International Peace, 1934), 1–2.

6. Jürgen Habermas, *The Inclusion of the Other: Studies in Political Theory*, edited by Ciaran Cronin and Pablo De Greiff (Cambridge, MA: MIT Press, 1998), 181.

7. John Rawls, *The Law of Peoples; with, The Idea of Public Reason Revisited* (Cambridge, MA: Harvard University Press, 2001), 81.

8. Carl Schmitt, *Political Theology: Four Chapters on the Concept of Sovereignty*, translated by George Schwab (Cambridge, MA: MIT Press, 1985), 5.

9. Ibid., 10.

10. Habermas, *The Inclusion of the Other*, 42.

11. Walter Benjamin, "Critique of Violence," in *Selected Writings*, edited by Marcus Bullock and Michael W. Jennings (Cambridge, MA: Harvard University Press, 1996), 1: 236–52.

12. Ibid., 199.

13. Ibid., 202.

14. Hannah Arendt, *On Revolution* (New York: Penguin Books, 1990), 22–24, 59–114.

15. Michel Foucault, *The History of Sexuality*, vol. 1, translated by Robert Hurley (New York: Viking Press, 1980), 142, 143.

16. Or, put the other way around, Hobbes historicizes the conditions that obtained in the New World following the Spanish, English, and French conquests. See, for example, Carl Schmitt, *The "Nomos" of the Earth in the International Law of the Jus Publicum Europaeum*, translated by G. L. Ulmen (New York: Telos, 2003), 95–97.

17. Richard Tuck, *Natural Rights Theories: Their Origin and Development* (Cambridge: Cambridge University Press, 1979), 22.

18. Linebaugh and Rediker chart the destruction of the commons and the rise of slavery in the seventeenth century, but also celebrate those pockets of resistance created by hybrid societies of sailors, ex-slaves, and others in the various nooks and crannies of the "revolutionary" Atlantic of the time. The memory of the various forms of the commons animate today's struggles, to which the closing lines of their study bear witness: "The globalizing powers have a long reach and endless patience. Yet the planetary wanderers do not forget, and they are ever ready from Africa to the Caribbean to Seattle to resist slavery and restore the commons" (Peter Linebaugh and Marcus Rediker, *The Many-Headed Hydra: Sailors, Slaves, Commoners and the Hidden History of the Revolutionary Atlantic* [Boston: Beacon Press, 2000], 353). For Hardt and Negri, the commons are not a space, but desire:

> It is sufficient to point to the generative determination of desire and thus its productivity. In effect, the complete commingling of the political, the social, and the economic in the constitution of the present reveals a biopolitical space that . . . explains the ability of desire to confront the crisis. The entire conceptual horizon is thus completely redefined. The biopolitical, seen from the standpoint of desire, is nothing other than concrete production, human collectivity in action. Desire appears here as productive space, as the actuality of human cooperation in the construction of history. This production is purely and simply human reproduction, the power of generation. Desiring production is generation, or rather the excess of labor and the accumulation of a power incorporated into the collective movement of singular essences, both its cause and its completion.

Michael Hardt and Antonio Negri, *Empire* (Cambridge, MA: Harvard University Press, 2000), 387–88.

THE DISCREET TASTE OF THE DIALECTIC

1. For the context of the Italian debate in the 1960 and 1970s, see Michael Hardt and Paolo Virno, eds., *Radical Thought in Italy: A Potential Politics* (Minneapolis: University of Minnesota Press, 1996).

2. One must bear in mind the dual meaning of the word *senso* that, like the French *sens*, comprises both "direction" and "meaning" (translator's note).

3. The reference is to *Altestes Systemprogramm des deutschen Idealismus*, by Hegel, Hölderlin, and Schelling (translator's note).

4. Negri makes a crucial distinction between *potere* and *potenza*, in his *The Savage Anomaly: The Power of Spinoza's Metaphysics and Politics*, translated by Michael

Hardt (Minneapolis: University of Minnesota Press, 1991), which he derives from Spinoza's distinction between *potestas* and *potentia* and that is missed in the English translations of Spinoza's works. I have followed Michael Hardt's rendering of these two terms as "Power" and "power," respectively. The distinction is both political and ontological, in that *potere* (Power) stands for a centralised transcendent force of command, while *potenza* (power) denotes rather immanent and local constitutive forces. For an excellent account of this distinction see the introduction to *The Savage Anomaly* (translator's note).

5. The reference is to the Bible: "But go thou thy way till the end be: for thou shalt rest, and stand in thy lot at the end of the days" (Dan. 12:13). In the Italian version of this passage, the reference to "time" is explicit. A literal translation from the Italian would be "to the end of times" (translator's note).

6. Deleuze had defined structuralism, *at one and the same time*, as the overcoming of the historical-dialectical relationship of the real and the imaginary, as the topological definition of conceptual space, as a place that can be recognised through the identification of a differential relation between symbolic elements, and, finally, as serial or multi-serial movement of the structure itself, that is, as internally self-regulating.

7. "Destining," "destinality," and "destinal" translate Heidegger's *Geschick*. See *The Question Concerning Technology and Other Essays*, edited and translated by W. Lovitt (New York: Harper and Row, 1977), 37, n. 3, in particular (translator's note).

8. For a detailed discussion of the concept of "constituent power," see Antonio Negri, *Insurgencies: Constituent Power and the Modern State*, translated by Maurizia Boscagli (Minneapolis: University of Minnesota Press, 1999) (translator's note).

9. Negri has said, in a private communication, that the image of the ferryman should bring to mind both Charon, who ferries the souls of the dead across the river Styx to Hades, as well as St. Christopher (the "Christ-carrier"), who dedicated his life to carrying people across a dangerous stream. (Translator's note.)

SITING AGAMBEN

1. See *Representing the Holocaust: History, Theory, Trauma* (Ithaca, NY: Cornell University Press, 1994); *History and Memory After Auschwitz* (Ithaca, NY: Cornell University Press, 1998); and *Writing History, Writing Trauma* (Baltimore: Johns Hopkins University Press, 2001).

2. Lucy Dawidowicz, ed., *A Holocaust Reader* (West Orange, NJ: Behrman House, 1976), 132–33.

3. See, especially, *The Differend: Phrases in Dispute*, translated by George Van Den Abbeele (1983; Minneapolis: University of Minnesota Press, 1988).

4. See, for example, *L'Entretien infini* (Paris: Gallimard, 1969), and *The Writing of the Disaster*, translated by Ann Smock (1980; Lincoln: University of Nebraska Press, 1986).

5. "The Force of Law: The 'Mystical' Foundation of Authority," *Cardozo Law Review* (July–August 1990): 920–1045, and my response to it in the same volume, *The Gift of Death*, translated by David Wells (1992; Chicago: University of Chicago Press, 1995).

6. *Specters of Marx*, translated by Peggy Kamuf (New York: Routledge, 1994).

7. "Heidegger's Silence," in *Martin Heidegger and National Socialism: Questions and Answers*, edited by Gunther Neske and Emil Kettering, translated by Lisa Harries, introduced by Karsten Harries (New York: Paragon House, 1990), 148.

8. For two important readings of Bataille, which were crucial in setting the tone of poststructural approaches to him, see Jacques Derrida, "From a Restricted to a General Economy," in *Writing and Difference*, translated, with an introduction and notes, by Alan Bass (1967; Chicago: University of Chicago Press, 1978), 251–77; and Michel Foucault, "A Preface to Transgression," in *Language, Counter-Memory, Practice*, edited and introduced by Donald F. Bouchard, translated by Donald F. Bouchard and Sherry Simon (1963; Ithaca, NY: Cornell University Press, 1973), 29–52.

9. *Remnants of Auschwitz: The Witness and the Archive*, translated by David Heller-Roazen (New York: Zone Books, 1999); hereafter cited parenthetically in the text. Any larger study of Agamben would have to include an extensive discussion at least of his *Homo Sacer* and *Means Without End*. Agamben conceives of these works, along with the more recent *Remnants of Auschwitz*, as composing a series. One may note that *la nuda vita* is translated as "bare life" by Heller-Roazen and as "naked life" by Binetti and Casarino. Moreover, the *Muselmann* in *Remnants of Auschwitz* is conceived as the extreme form or instance of the *homo sacer*, who is interpreted by Agamben as the bearer of *la nuda vita* and is reduced to this condition by sovereign power. It is open to debate whether and to what extent the notions of bare or naked life and *homo sacer* as, Agamben understands them, provide an adequate account of the sacred or even of the status of the Jew as victim under the Nazis. I would argue that this view accounts only for one dimension of the complex figure of the Jew for Nazis—the dimension related to the Jew figured as pest or vermin fit only for extermination. It does not, I think, account for the more ambiguous dimensions of the Jew (which Agamben rejects in the sacred itself at least as it is conceived in Roman law), whereby the Jew was also an object of quasi-ritual or phobic repulsion as well as invested with world-historical, conspiratorial powers of evil and made an object of quasi-sacrificial scapegoating and victimization. One of the difficulties in understanding Nazi ideology and practice involves the role of the shifting registers of pest control and quasi-sacrificial response with respect to the Jew. However, I shall later suggest a sense in which Agamben's view may itself be symptomatic of an exhaustion or depletion of the sacred and sacrificial in the recent past, which I would see as beneficial insofar as it counteracts victimization as a crucial dimension in the appeal of sacrifice. Agamben does not see how the banalized use of the term "Holocaust" may be in part

defended as itself symptom and performative force in the erosion or active depletion of the sacrificial and its attraction.

10. *The Drowned and the Saved*, translated by Raymond Rosenthal (1986; New
York: Random House, 1989).

11. Agamben does not comment critically but only in (dubious) etymological
respects on a term that is crucial to his account: *Muselmann*, or Muslim (44–45).
This prejudicial appellation was camp slang for the absolutely exhausted and beat-
en down who had given up hope in life and led a living death. The use of such a
term would seem to illustrate the tendency of the oppressed and abject to locate
invidiously a presumably even more abject group, and the history of strained relations between Jews and Arab Muslims renders particularly dubious the choice of
"Muselmann" as the term of distancing and denigration.

12. In *The Coming Community*, Agamben contrasts an ethics of pure possibility and openness (which in certain ways seems close to the early Sartre's notion of
pure, evacuated *disponibilité*) with a conception of morality. "Morality" is castigat-
ed and would seem to include any normativity, including repentance, responsibility, and guilt—perhaps any normativity at all. The correlate of Agamben's "ethics"
is an apocalyptic politics of the coming community of totally open and substitut-
able "whatever" singularities. The nature of this putative ethics is elaborated via an
analogy to the kabbalah in a fully apocalyptic-messianic manner reminiscent of
aspects of the thought of Walter Benjamin:

> In the society of the spectacle [that is, modern society], in fact, the isolation of the
> Shekinah [the word of God] reaches its final phase, where language is not only consti-
> tuted in an autonomous sphere, but also no longer even reveals anything—or better, it
> reveals the nothingness of all things. There is nothing of God, of the world, or of the
> revealed in language. In this extreme nullifying unveiling, however, language (the lin-
> guistic nature of humans) remains once again hidden and separated, and thus, one last
> time, in its unspoken power, it dooms humans to a historical era and a State: the era of
> the spectacle, or of accomplished nihilism. . . .
>
> The era in which we live is also that in which for the first time it is possible for
> humans to experience their own linguistic being not this or that content of language, but
> language itself, not this or that proposition, but the very fact that one speaks. Contempo-
> rary politics is this devastating *experimentum linguae* that all over the planet unhinges and
> empties traditions and beliefs, ideologies and religions, identities and communities.
>
> Only those who succeed in carrying it to completion—without allowing what
> reveals to remain veiled in the nothingness that reveals, but bringing language itself to
> language—will be the first citizens of a community with neither presuppositions nor a
> State, where the nullifying and determining power of what is common will be pacified
> and where the Shekinah will have stopped sucking the evil milk of its own separation.

Like Rabbi Akiba, they will enter into the paradise of language and leave
unharmed. (*CC*, 82–83)

13. For an account of the sacred that focuses on these features, see Julia Kristeva,
The Powers of Horror, translated by Leon S. Roudiez (1980; New York: Columbia

University Press, 1982). Kristeva does not apply her analysis of the sacred to the Nazi genocide, in part because, in her often apologetic understanding of Celine's anti-Semitism and sympathy for fascism, she focuses in an analytically isolating manner on aesthetic issues and even construes Celine's anti-Semitism in the narrowly biographical terms of a personal need for identity. And Kristeva is close to Agamben in bringing together the abject and the sublime (with the sublime functioning as a secular displacement of the sacred).

14. For an extensive, critical, yet sympathetic account of the postapocalyptic mode, see James Berger, *After the End: Representations of Post-Apocalypse* (Minneapolis: University of Minnesota Press, 1999). In certain important respects, Agamben's sensibility and approach to problems may be compared to that of Bill Readings in *The University in Ruins* (Cambridge, MA: Harvard University Press, 1997). See my discussion in "The University in Ruins?" *Critical Inquiry* 25 (1998): 32–55; as well as Nicolas Royle, "Yes, Yes, the University in Ruins," *Critical Inquiry* 26, no. 1 (1999): 147–53; and my rejoinder ("Yes, Yes, Yes, Yes . . . Well Maybe") in the same issue. See also Royle's ecstatically postapocalyptic *After Derrida* (Manchester: Manchester University Press, 1995).

15. See Carl Schmitt, *Political Theology: Four Chapters on the Concept of Sovereignty*, translated by George Schwab (1922, 1934; Cambridge, MA: MIT Press, 1985).

16. Compare the sober words of Levi, which, despite their own dubious aspects (for example, the facile invocation of pathology or the decisive opposition between humans and other animals with a limited idea of language serving as an invidiously differentiating criterion), may raise the question of the unexplored relations between certain forms of existentialism and of poststructuralism:

> According to a theory fashionable during those years [the 1970s], which to me seems frivolous and irritating, "incommunicability" supposedly was an inevitable ingredient, a life sentence inherent to the human condition, particularly the life style of industrial society: we are monads, incapable of reciprocal messages, or capable only of truncated messages, false at their departure, misunderstood on their arrival. Discourse is fictitious, pure noise, a painted veil that conceals existential silence; we are alone, even (or especially) if we live in pairs. It seems to me that this lament originates in a dangerous vicious circle. Except for cases of pathological incapacity, one can and must communicate, and thereby contribute in a useful and easy way to the peace of others and oneself, because silence, the absence of signals, is itself a signal, but an ambiguous one, and ambiguity generates anxiety and suspicion. To say that it is impossible to communicate is false; one always can. To refuse to communicate is a failing; we are biologically and socially predisposed to communication, and in particular to its highly evolved and noble form, which is language. All members of the human species speak, no nonhuman species knows how to speak. (*The Drowned and the Saved*, 88–89)

On Foucault, see my discussion in *History and Reading: Tocqueville, Foucault, French Studies* (Toronto: University of Toronto Press, 2000), chap. 3.

17. See Lawrence Langer, *Holocaust Testimonies: The Ruins of Memory* (New Haven, CT: Yale University Press, 1991), and my discussion of the book in *Representing the Holocaust*, 194–200.

18. For one chapter in the use of the term, see Gerd Korman, "The Holocaust in American Historical Writing" (first published in 1972), in *Perspectives on the Holocaust*, vol. 1 of the Nazi Holocaust series, edited by Michael Marrus (Westport, CT: Meckler, 1989), 284–303. For Korman, Wiesel did not coin the term *Holocaust* but with "other gifted writers and speakers" helped to make it "coin of the realm" (294).

19. See Shoshana Felman and Don Laub, *Testimony: Crises of Witnessing in Literature, Psychoanalysis, and History* (New York: Routledge, 1992). I comment extensively on Felman's contributions to this book in the three works mentioned in note 1.

20. I indicate ways Agamben himself seems to "unconsciously repeat the Nazis' gesture." This transferential repetition, which is often invoked dubiously as an ultimate "knock-down" argument, confronts all discourses on the topic, and the problem is not whether it threatens to occur but how one comes to terms with it in more or less explicit fashion—to what extent and how one acts it out and works it through.

21. Here, the reader may allow me a thought experiment concerning the response of an individual (or rather "singularity") who, after reading Agamben, is caught by a spouse or partner in bed with another "singularity": "The subject who made a commitment to you is a shifter, and the one you find in bed is a psychosomatic individual who is expropriated of all referential reality and is reduced to glossalalic potentiality that cannot speak." Does this scenario move too quickly from theory to practice for the sake of a joke?

22. The variant of existentialism to which I refer is pronounced in one important dimension of Sartre's *Being and Nothingness*, wherein the for-itself has a nihilating relation of disjunction and transcendence with respect to the in-itself, a relation that aligns the for-itself with pure possibility or *disponibilité* and with the imaginary. A variant of structuralism, while it may downplay or deny the freedom and agency of a "for-itself," it nonetheless stresses a relation of radical disjunction or epistemological break between structures.

23. For a different articulation of the relations between the transhistorical and the historical, one that does not collapse them or evacuate historical specificity by deriving the historical from the transhistorical, see my "Trauma, Absence, Loss," *Critical Inquiry* 25, no. 4 (1999): 696–727, a version of which is chapter 2 of *Writing History, Writing Trauma*.

24. The background noise in the following passage might seem to drown out any meaning, but the passage in its reference to the "non-coincidence of the whole and the part" might conceivably be read as countering a sacrificial logic:

In the concept of remnant, the aporia of testimony coincides with the aporia of messianism. Just as the remnant of Israel signifies neither the whole people nor a part of the people but, rather, the non-coincidence of the whole and the part, and just as messianic time is neither historical time nor eternity but, rather, the disjunction that divides them, so the remnants of Auschwitz—the witnesses—are neither the dead nor the survivors, neither the drowned nor the saved. They are what remains between them. (*RA*, 163–64) Is the philosopher, in Agamben's vision of him as one who sees the world from an extreme situation that has become the rule, one of these remnants?

25. Along with Lyotard's *The Differend,* see especially Friedlander, *Memory, History, and the Extermination of the Jews of Europe* (Bloomington: University of Indiana Press, 1993).

26. In *Homo Sacer,* Agamben explicitly links the state of exception and the threshold of indistinction: "The situation created in the exception has the peculiar characteristic that it cannot be denned either as a situation of fact or as a situation of right, but instead institutes a paradoxical threshold of indistinction between the two" (*HS*, 18). The question is whether the converse is also the case and whether the threshold of indistinction always creates a state of exception. The more important question is whether, in modernity and especially "after Auschwitz," the exception becomes increasingly the fundamental political structure and ultimately the rule.

27. For a careful, thought-provoking discussion of related issues, see Etienne Balibar, *Masses, Classes, Ideas: Studies on Politics and Philosophy Before and After Marx,* translated by James Swenson (New York: Routledge, 1994), especially part 3.

28. See also Slavoj Žižek, *Did Somebody Say Totalitarianism?* (London: Verso, 2001), chap. 2.

29. The Eichmann who is more like Himmler in his Posen speech is evoked by Saul Friedlander:

> Could one of the components of "Rausch" be the effect of a growing elation stemming from repetition, from the ever-larger numbers of killed others: "Most of you know what it means when 100 corpses are lying side by side, when 500 lie there or 1000." This repetition (and here indeed we are back, in part, at Freud's interpretation) adds to the sense of *Unheimlichkeit,* at least for the outside observer; there, the perpetrators do not appear anymore as bureaucratic automata, but rather as beings seized by a compelling lust for killing on an immense scale, driven by some kind of extraordinary elation in repeating the killing of ever-huger masses of people (notwithstanding Himmler's words about the difficulty of this duty). Suffice it to remember the pride of numbers sensed in the Einsatzgruppen reports, the pride of numbers in Rudolf Höss's autobiography; suffice it to remember Eichmann's interview with Sassen: he would jump with glee into his grave knowing that over five million Jews had been exterminated; elation created by the staggering dimension of the killing, by the endless rows of victims. The elation created by the staggering number of victims ties in with the mystical Führer-Bond: the greater the number of the Jews exterminated, the better the Führer's will has been fulfilled. (*Memory, History,* 110–11)

Friedlander also observes that "for further analysis, we would need a new category equivalent to Kant's category of the sublime, but specifically meant to capture inexpressible horror" (115). The question of course is precisely how one invokes this category, including the role of critical precautions concerning the possibility of transferential repetitions, particularly when an appeal to some aspect of the discourse of the sublime is undertaken in one's own "voice."

30. In his earlier discussion of Heidegger (*RA*, 73–75), Agamben does not quote the most notorious passage of the Bremen lecture of December 1949, which seems close to aspects of Agamben's own Auschwitz-now-everywhere perspective: "Agriculture is now a motorized food industry: in its essence it is the same thing as the manufacture of corpses in gas chambers, the same thing as blockades and the reduction of a region to hunger, the same as the manufacture of hydrogen bombs" (cited by Wolfgang Schirmacher, *Technik und Gelassenheit* [Freiburg: Alber, 1983], 25; author's trans.). Agamben goes on to argue that Auschwitz "calls into question the very possibility of authentic decision [particularly with respect to death] and thus threatens the very ground of Heidegger's ethics" (*RA*, 75). The apparent implication is that one must have an ethics that goes beyond even Heidegger in its fundamental radicality and break with the past—an ethics that Agamben seeks.

31. As Levi, in markedly nonsacrificial terms, puts it in *The Drowned and the Saved*, "one is never in another's place" (60).

32. *Did Somebody Say Totalitarianism?* 85.

33. See the discussion in Nancy Wood, *Vectors of Memory: Legacies of Trauma in Postwar Europe* (Oxford: Berg, 1999), chap. 3. See also the contributions to the special issue of *Cultural Critique* 46 (Fall 2000), *Trauma and Its Cultural Aftereffects*, edited by Karyn Ball.

34. Ernst Nolte, "Vergangenheit die nicht vergehen will," *Frankfurter Allgemeine Zeitung*, 6 June 1986; translated as "The Past That Will Not Pass," in *Forever in the Shadow of Hitler: Original Documents of the Historikerstreit, the Controversy Concerning the Singularity of the Holocaust*, edited by James Knowlton and Truett Gates (Atlantic Highlands, NJ: Humanities Press, 1993), 18–23. See also my discussions in *Representing the Holocaust*, chap. 2, and *History and Memory After Auschwitz*, chap. 2.

35. *The Drowned and the Saved*, 48, 49.

36. In *The Coming Community*, Agamben formulates what might be read as a view of the sacred as radically transcendent: "What is properly divine is that the world does not reveal God" (*CC*, 91). Paradoxically, he also has a notion of what could be termed transcendence from below: "The world insofar as it is absolutely, irreparably profane—is God" (*CC*, 90).

JAMMING THE ANTHROPOLOGICAL MACHINE

1. Judith Butler, Ernesto Laclau, and Slavoj Žižek, *Contingency, Hegemony, Universality: Contemporary Dialogues on the Left* (London: Verso, 2000), 321.

2. I am using the phrase "the question of the animal" in a manner similar to Jacques Derrida's use of the phrase. This question concerns the ethical and political

stakes of human relations with non-human animals, as well the very possibility of making and sustaining the human/animal distinction.

3. This question is a variation on a point made by Žižek in his dialogue with Butler and Laclau. See *Contingency, Hegemony, Universality*, 326.

4. Jacques Derrida and Elisabeth Roudinesco, *For What Tomorrow . . . : A Dialogue*, translated by Jeff Fort (Stanford, CA: Stanford University Press, 2004), 65.

5. The phrase "hyperbolic naïveté" is from Friedrich Nietzsche, *Will to Power*, translated by Walter Kaufmann (New York: Viking Press, 1968), section 12b.

BIOPOLITICS, LIBERAL EUGENICS, AND NIHILISM

1. Paolo Virno, *A Grammar of the Multitude* (New York: Semiotexte, 2004), 81–84; 83.

2. Mika Ojakangas, "Impossible Dialogue on Bio-power: Agamben and Foucault," *Foucault Studies*, no. 2 (2005): 5–28.

3. See Michael Dillon, "Cared to Death: The Biopoliticized Time of Your Life," *Foucault Studies*, no. 2 (2005): 37–46.

4. Michel Foucault, *The History of Sexuality*, vol. 1, translated by Robert Hurley (New York: Penguin Books, 1981). As this suggests, Foucault makes a distinction between *biopolitics* and *biopower*, wherein the former term refers to the constitution and incorporation of the population as a new subject of governance, whereas the latter is a broader term that encompasses both biopolitics and discipline. Even so, he does not rigorously maintain it, and because of the equivocation in his uses of the term *politics*, Jacques Rancière has accused Foucault of reducing politics to policing. Barry Hindess points out, though, that on occasion Foucault does use the term *politics* to refer to a more utopic or agonistic relation between techniques of power and its subjects or targets. This more agonistic conception of politics is intimated in the claim that life itself also provided the means of resistance to the techniques of power that emerged in the nineteenth century; thus, "life as a political object was . . . turned back against a system bent on controlling it. It was life more than the law that became the issue of political struggles, even if the latter were formulated through affirmations concerning rights" (*History of Sexuality*, 145). See Jacques Rancière, *Disagreement: Politics and Philosophy*, translated by Julie Rose (Minneapolis: University of Minnesota Press, 1999). Barry Hindess, "Politics and Governmentality," *Economy and Society* 26, no. 2 (1997), 257–72.

5. The phrase is Georges Canguilhem's, in "On *Histoire de la folie* as an Event," in *Foucault and His Interlocutors*, edited by Arnold I. Davidson (Chicago: University of Chicago Press, 1997), 28–32; 32.

6. Foucault's theoretical debt to Canguilhem has been well established, particularly in regard to the conception of normalization used in *Discipline and Punish*, as well as the early volume of *History of Sexuality*. See, in particular, Foucault's comments in *Abnormal: Lectures at the Collège de France, 1974–1975*, edited by

Valerio Marchetti and Antonella Salomoni, translated by Graham Burchell (New York: Picador, 2003), 49–50; Foucault, "Life: Experience and Science," in *Aesthetics, Method, and Epistemology*, edited by James D. Faubion, vol. 2 of *The Essential Works of Michel Foucault, 1954–1984*, translated by Robert Hurley et al. (London: Penguin Books, 1998), 465–78; Canguilhem's comments on the historical emergence of normalization is in Georges Canguilhem, *The Normal and the Pathological*, translated by Carolyn R. Fawcett, in collaboration with Robert S. Cohen (New York: Zone Books, 1991), 244–46. Also see Paul Rabinow, "French Enlightenment," *Economy and Society* 27, nos. 2–3 (1998); Rabinow, *Essays on the Anthropology of Reason* (Princeton, NJ: Princeton University Press, 1996); T. Osborne and N. Rose, eds., *Economy and Society*, 27, nos. 2 and 3 (1998), special issue on Canguilhem; Pierre Macherey, "From Canguilhem to Canguilhem by way of Foucault," in *In a Materialist Way: Selected Essays*, edited by Warren Montag, translated by Ted Stolze (London: Verso, 1998), 108–15; for a discussion of Canguilhem's influence on Foucault's epistemology and methodology, particularly in the "archaeological period," see Gary Gutting, *Michel Foucault's Archaeology of Scientific Reason* (Cambridge: Cambridge University Press, 1989), and Arnold I. Davidson, *The Emergence of Sexuality: Historical Epistemology and the Formation of Concepts* (Cambridge, MA: Harvard University Press, 2001).

7. Canguilhem, *Normal and Pathological*, 239.

8. Ibid.

9. Ibid., 239–40.

10. François Ewald, "Norms, Discipline, and the Law," *Representations* 30 (Spring 1990): 138–61; 157.

11. Rather, Canguilhem recognizes an important disjunction between an elaboration of biological norms and social norms, such that the former do not generate the latter, and nor in fact are the social and vital normative environments strictly analogous. Even so, Canguilhem is unable to explain this disruption or to fully reckon with its implications; the concept of power that Foucault develops may in part be seen as a response to this. See Canguilhem, *Normal and Pathological*, 250–56.

12. Michel Foucault, *"Society Must Be Defended": Lectures at the Collège de France, 1975–1976*, edited by Mauro Bertani and Alessandro Fontana, translated by D. Macey (London: Allen Lane, 2003), 39.

13. Ibid., 253.

14. Ibid., 38.

15. Ibid., 253.

16. Ewald, "Norms, Discipline, and the Law," 138.

17. Foucault, *History of Sexuality*, 139–40; Michel Foucault, "Governmentality," in *Power*, edited by James D. Faubion, vol. 3 of *The Essential Works of Michel Foucault, 1954–1984*, translated by Robert Hurley et al. (New York: New Press, 2000), 201–22.

18. See Thomas Lemke, "'The Birth of Bio-politics': Michel Foucault's Lecture at the Collège de France on Neo-liberal Governmentality," *Economy and Society* 30, no. 2 (2001): 190–207.

19. Foucault, *"Society Must Be Defended,"* 240.

20. Lemke, "'The Birth of Bio-politics,'" 248.

21. See Judith Butler, *Precarious Life: The Powers of Mourning and Violence* (London: Verso, 2004), and *Bodies That Matter: On the Discursive Limits of "Sex"* (New York: Routledge, 1993), for a further discussion of the notion of "unlivable lives."

22. Foucault, *"Society Must Be Defended,"* 248; my emphasis. Against this characterization, one might argue that Foucault's comments regarding the status of death within the operation of biopower can be understood as a transposition of the repressive hypothesis from sexuality to death. In suggesting that "death is power's limit, the moment that escapes it; death becomes the most secret aspect of existence, the most 'private'" (*History of Sexuality*, 138), Foucault echoes the theoretical fallacy that he accuses his opponents of with regard to sexuality. To posit death as the new limit of power, as that which escapes and undermines power's exercise over the unfolding of life, merely repeats, vis-à-vis death, the theoretical fallacy that sexuality opposes power in its privacy and secret force. Indeed, Foucault suggests exactly this interpretation in *"Society Must Be Defended,"* when he writes that "ultimately, it is now not so much sex as death that is the object of taboo" (247). But this demands the response that rather than being the limit of power, death is rather the means by which biopower functions—that is, it is precisely by recalling the risk of death, its immanence in life, that biopower operates, since it is the ever-present threat of death that justifies and rationalizes regulatory intervention in the life of populations and individuals. Therefore, rather than attempting to eliminate or privatize death, biopower presupposes it for its operation; death is not the limit of biopower but its precondition. Against Foucault, we might say that it is not so much that "a relative control over life averted some of the immanent risks of death" (*History of Sexuality*, 142), but that an increasing control over death averts the immanent risks of life and permits its administration. In this, Durkheim's study of suicide, which Foucault cites as evidence that death constitutes the limit of power, can be understood instead as an indication of the fact that within biopolitics "death becomes a social institution." See Herbert Marcuse, "The Ideology of Death," in *The Meaning of Death*, edited by Herman Feifel (New York: McGraw-Hill, 1959), 73. On the status of death within biopower, also see Dillon, "Cared to Death"; on racism, see Mitchell Dean, *Governmentality: Power and Rule in Modern Society* (London: Sage Publications, 1999), 138–48; and Ann Laura Stoler, *Race and the Education of Desire* (Durham, NC: Duke University Press, 1995).

23. Foucault, *"Society Must Be Defended,"* 254.

24. Ibid., 255–56.

25. Ibid., 256.

26. Ibid.

27. See Foucault's comment on the simultaneity of the individual's being an effect and vehicle of power, in Michel Foucault, "Two Lectures," in *Power/Knowledge: Selected Interviews and Other Writings, 1972–1977*, edited and translated by Colin Gordon (New York: Pantheon Press, 1980), 109–33; 78.

28. Canguilhem, *Normal and Pathological*, 242.

29. Jacques Derrida, *Limited Inc.*, translated by Samuel Weber (Evanston, IL: Northwestern University Press, 1988), 91–93.

30. See Ulrich Raulff, "Interview with Giorgio Agamben—Life, a Work of Art Without an Author: The State of Exception, the Administration of Disorder, and Private Life," *German Law Journal* 5, no. 5 (May 2004): 609–14, www.germanlawjournal.com/article.php?id=437# ednref8 (accessed 12 October 2006).

31. Because the exception is here taken as synonymous with the anomic or, broadly speaking, the lawless, the crucial questions for Western political and juridical thought concern the nature and role of the anomie. This is worth noting because it already indicates the distance between Agamben and Foucault, for, as Canguilhem suggests, it is only by virtue of semantic and etymological confusion that the "anomic," the "anomalous," and the "abnormal" can be seen as co-extensive. Canguilhem, *Normal and Pathological*, 131–33.

32. See Jean-Luc Nancy, "Abandoned Being," in *The Birth to Presence*, translated by Brian Holmes et al. (Stanford, CA: Stanford University Press, 1993), 36–47.

33. Canguilhem, *Normal and Pathological*, 239.

34. Giorgio Agamben, "The Messiah and the Sovereign: The Problem of Law in Walter Benjamin," in *P*, 160–74; 169–71.

35. Hannah Arendt, *The Human Condition*, 2nd ed. (Chicago: University of Chicago Press, 1998), 63.

36. Agamben, "The Messiah and the Sovereign," in *P*, 171.

37. Cited in ibid., 171.

38. Pre-implantation genetic diagnosis, or PGD, is a procedure used in IVF (in vitro fertilization) treatment, which allows screening of the genetic profile of an embryo before it is implanted in the mother's uterus, and involves isolating a single cell from the early pre-embryo. To date, it has primarily been used to detect whether hereditary genetic conditions have been passed to the embryo, but has recently been more controversial for its use in sex selection and in conjunction with human leukocyte antigen (HLA) tissue typing in the so-called savior-sibling controversies.

39. For authoritative accounts of the history of eugenics, see, in particular, Daniel Kevles, *In the Name of Eugenics: Genetics and the uses of Human Heredity* (Cambridge, MA: Harvard University Press, 1995); and Dian B. Paul, *Controlling Human Heredity, 1865 to the Present* (Atlantic Highlands, NJ: Humanities Press, 1995).

40. See Nicholas Agar, "Liberal Eugenics," *Public Affairs Quarterly* 12, no. 2

(April 1998): 137–56, for an overview of these positions. Also see Nicholas Agar, *Liberal Eugenics: In Defence of Human Enhancement* (Oxford: Basil Blackwell, 2004).

41. The right to found a family is particularly important in defenses of reproductive cloning, such as John Harris, *On Cloning* (London: Routledge, 2004).

42. Agar, "Liberal Eugenics"; Allen E. Buchanan et al., *From Chance to Choice: Genetics and Justice* (Cambridge: Cambridge University Press, 2000), 104–55.

43. Buchanan et al., *Chance to Choice*, 82, *passim*.

44. Jürgen Habermas, *The Future of Human Nature* (Cambridge: Polity Press, 2003); also see Francis Fukuyama, *Our Posthuman Future: Consequences of the Biotechnology Revolution* (London: Profile Books, 2003).

45. Habermas, *The Future of Human Nature*, 50–51.

46. Ibid., 65.

47. Ibid.

48. Agar, *Liberal Eugenics*, 135.

49. John Harris, "'Goodbye Dolly'? The Ethics of Human Cloning," *Journal of Medical Ethics* 23, no. 6 (1997): 353–60; Harris, *On Cloning*.

50. Agar, "Liberal Eugenics," 139–40.

51. Foucault, *Abnormal*, 317.

52. Foucault, *Society Must Be Defended*, 248.

53. One key question to arise from this, then, is the philosophical and political difference made by the exposure to death at a earlier stage of empirical life. Of central concern in this would be issues about rights, the attribution of which to prenatal life is increasingly contentious. There is no need to enter into this debate here, but it would require careful thought in analysis of the biopolitics of genetic technologies.

54. Michel Foucault, "On the Genealogy of Ethics: An Overview of Work in Progress," in *Ethics: Subjectivity and Truth*, edited by Paul Rabinow, vol. 1 of *Essential Works of Michel Foucault, 1954–1984*, translated by Robert Hurley et al. (London: Penguin Books, 1997), 253–80.

55. See *RA*.

AGAMBEN AND FOUCAULT ON BIOPOWER AND BIOPOLITICS

1. Michel Foucault, *"Society Must Be Defended": Lectures at the Collège de France, 1975–1976*, edited by Mauro Bertani and Alessandro Fontana, translated by D. Macey (London: Allen Lane, 2003); *Sécurité, Territoire, Population: Cours au Collège de France, 1977–1978* (Paris: Gallimard/Seuil, 2004); *Naissance de la biopolitique: Cours au Collège de France, 1978–1979* (Paris: Gallimard/Seuil, 2004).

2. "J'avais pensé pouvoir vous faire cette année un cours sur la biopolitique. J'essaierai de vous montrer comment tous les problèmes que j'essaie de repérer là actuellement, comment tous ces problèmes ont pour noyau central, bien sûr, ce quelque chose que l'on appelle la population. Par consequent, c'est bien à partir de là

que quelque chose comme une biopolitique pourra se former. Mais il me semble que l'analyse de la biopolitique ne peut se faire que lorsque l'on a compris le régime general de cette raison gouvernementale dont je vous parle, ce régime général que l'on peut appeler la question de vérité, premièrement de la vérité économique à l'intérieur de la raison gouvernementale, et par conséquent si on comprend bien de quoi il s'agit dans ce régime qui est le libéralisme . . . c'est une fois qu'on aura su ce que c'était que ce régime gouvernmentale appelé libéralisme qu'on pourra, me semble-t-il, saisir ce qu'est la biopolitique" (Foucault, *Naissance de la biopolitique*, 23–24).

3. Foucault, *"Society Must Be Defended,"* 254.

4. Ibid., 240.

5. Ibid., 245.

6. Ibid.

7. Ibid., 246.

8. Ibid.

9. Ibid. By "security" here Foucault does not mean the life or personal safety of individuals but the achievement and maintenance of overall equilibrium or regularity in a population.

10. Ibid., 247.

11. Ibid., 240.

12. Ibid.

13. Ibid.

14. Ibid.

15. Ernst Kantorowicz, *The King's Two Bodies: A Study in Medieval Political Theology* (Princeton, NJ: Princeton University Press, 1957).

16. Foucault refers to Kantorowicz's study in *Discipline and Punish* in order to propose a parallel status of the condemned individual subject to the sovereign power to punish: just as the surplus power of the king underwrites a duplication of his physical body so the punitive power exercised on the condemned man gives rise to a non-corporeal double, namely, the "soul" that is the correlate and object of a certain technology of power over the body (Foucault, *Discipline and Punish: The Birth of the Prison*, translated by Alan Sheridan [London: Penguin Books, 1977], 28–29). Agamben also devotes a chapter to Kantorowicz, arguing against his interpretation of the incorporeal body of the king as representation of the continuity of sovereign power. Rather, it represents the sacred life of the sovereign, "the absolute and inhuman character of sovereign power" (*HS*, 101).

17. Foucault, *Society Must Be Defended*, 240.

18. If this is a correct understanding of the argument, Foucault overstates his case in suggesting that "the very essence of the right of life and death is actually the right to kill," or that the right of the classical sovereign is "essentially the right of the sword" and that "there is no real symmetry in the right over life and death" (*Society Must Be Defended*, 240). The dissymmetry arises at the level of exercise of sovereign right. It does not necessarily affect the character of the right itself.

19. Foucault, *Society Must Be Defended,* 241.

20. Ibid.

21. Thomas Hobbes, *Leviathan,* edited by Richard Tuck (Cambridge: Cambridge University Press, 1991), 153.

22. Foucault, *Naissance de la biopolitique,* 39–40.

23. Ibid., 40–48.

24. Michel Foucault, *Power,* edited by James D. Faubion, vol. 3 of *The Essential Works of Foucault, 1954–1984,* translated by Robert Hurley et al. (New York: New Press, 2000), 474–75; see also Patton "Power and Right in Nietzsche and Foucault," *International Studies in Philosophy* 36, no. 3 (2004): 43–61.

THE ONTOLOGY AND POLITICS OF EXCEPTION

1. To be consistent with Agamben's thought, we must make sure we understand the phrase "one's own incapacity" as "one's own capacity not to." In Sartre, the category of lack has to do mainly with one's capacity, which of course includes the fundamental capacity of saying "no," the capacity not to, as is particularly evident in some of his plays, notably *Dirty Hands.*

2. John Duns Scotus, *Philosophical Writings,* translated by Allan Wolter (Indianapolis: Hackett Publishing, 1987), 55; first emphasis added.

3. Ibid., 54.

4. Ibid., 55.

5. Ibid.; emphasis added.

6. Ernst Bloch, *Natural Law and Human Dignity,* translated by Dennis J. Schmidt (Cambridge, MA: MIT Press, 1987), 47; cf. John Duns Scotus, *On the Will and Morality,* translated by Allan Wolter (Washington, DC: Catholic University of America Press, 1986), 198–207.

7. Aristotle, *Nicomachean Ethics,* translated by Terence Irwin, 2nd ed. (Indianapolis: Hackett Publishing, 1999).

8. Agamben's book on Paul, *Il tempo che resta,* is the result of a series of lectures that Agamben gave at different universities, from the Collège International de Philosophie in Paris in October 1998 to the University of California (Berkeley) in October 1999. I attended the first series of lectures in Paris. Translations from this text are by the author of this chapter.

9. The Revised Standard Version of the Bible reads: "Every one should remain in the state in which he was called."

10. I am using the Revised Standard Version of the Bible. Brackets have been added to approximate more closely Agamben's original Italian text.

11. Walter Benjamin, "Critique of Violence," in *Reflections,* translated by Edmund Jephcott (New York: Schocken Books, 1978), 287. The whole passage reads:

> Unlike law, which acknowledges in the "decision" determined by place and time a metaphysical category that gives it a claim to critical evaluation, a consideration of the police

institution encounters nothing essential at all. Its power is formless, like its nowhere tangible, all-pervasive, ghostly presence in the life of civilized states. And though the police may, in particulars, everywhere appear the same, it cannot finally be denied that their spirit is less devastating where they represent, in absolute monarchy, the power of a ruler in which legislative and executive supremacy are united, than in democracies where their existence, elevated by no such relation, bears witness to the greatest conceivable degeneration of violence. (287)

We live today through this degeneration of violence, the age of the police, when the law (especially international law) is reduced to nothing. The contrast between sovereign power and naked life is inscribed in the very logic of the suspension of the law represented by the institution of the police, which becomes a global institution.

    12. Ibid., 295.

    13. "Red Cross Suspects U.S. Hides Detainees," Associated Press, 7 July 2004.

    14. Walter Benjamin, "Theses on the Philosophy of History," in *Illuminations*, translated by Harry Zohn (New York: Schocken Books, 1968), 257. The two occurrences of the phrase "state of emergency" in the English translation of Benjamin's "Theses on the Philosophy of History" are rendered with the phrase "state of exception" in Agamben (*HS*, 55). Both are common translations.

    15. Ibid.

    16. In this sense, see our discussion of potentiality, as well as of the concept of time with respect to Agamben's comment on Paul, above. We have seen that the structure of potentiality/impotentiality is the most fundamental ontological figure in the constitution of the state of exception—and yet, it is only when the full power of this ontology invests the political that we have the "effective" or "real" situation called forth by Benjamin, that is, a situation in which the law is brought to completion. With respect to Paul's concept of the time that remains, we have seen that what appears between time and its end is really a higher order, not simply of time, but of the law and of the world. As for time in particular, the contraction of messianic time cannot be other than the contraction of all time, that is, time in its most fundamental and substantial form—ontological time.

    17. Etienne Balibar, *The Philosophy of Marx*, translated by Chris Turner (London: Verso, 1995), 41.

    18. Speaking of some tendencies within medieval philosophy, in *The Coming Community* Agamben says, quite correctly in my view, that the contraction of the common into the singularity of its expression "is not an event accomplished once and for all, but an infinite series of modal oscillations" (*CC*, 19).

Index